NOTES ON AN UNDIRECTED LIFE:

AS ONE ANTHROPOLOGIST TELLS IT

ESTHER S. GOLDFRANK

For Leonard
stimulating scholar & good friend
6/6/80
Esther

Queens College Publications in Anthropology
Queens College Press, Flushing, N.Y. 11367
Number 3   1978

Cover Design: Rhoda Cohen. Isleta Painting #102:
    drawing after "Sweeping the Racetrack to the Sun"

ISBN O-930146-11-5

Price: $10.00

CONTENTS

Part I

Part II

Like many others, big and little, this book has taken an unbelievably long time to complete. In extenuation I may say there were months and even years when I didn't work on it at all. And I spent considerable time in rewriting and research beyond the call of duty—which enriched my understanding of past events but had little relevance for the story I was trying to tell.

Particularly important for these *Notes* was access to Professor Boas' correspondence which was deposited with the American Philosophical Society and was made available to me on tapes at Columbia University. I thank both Institutions and Franziska Boas for permission to cite from them without restriction. My gratitude also goes to the American Anthropological Association, the American Ethnological Society, the American Folklore Society, the *Southwestern Journal of Anthropology*, the American Museum of Natural History, the University of New Mexico, the University of Chicago, the University of Southern Illinois, and the Smithsonian Institution for the valuable assistance provided by their publications. I also wish to express my thanks for permission to cite from Margaret Mead's 1959 book *An Anthropologist at Work; The Writings of Ruth Benedict,* and also to Houghton-Mifflin for granting their permission for the same citations. Ruth Benedict's manuscripts and other materials are at Vassar. Thanks also to International University Press for permission to quote from George Devereux's 1951 publication: "Reality and Dream," and the University of New Mexico, publisher of the *Southwestern Journal of Anthropology,* for use of material written by John Bennett. I also wish to express my gratitude to Rhoda Cohen for her ability to bring photographs over fifty years old to life, and for her careful reinterpretation of my favorite picture from Isleta Paintings, which appears on the cover of this book.

I would also like to thank my close friend and Barnard classmate, Edna L. Coplan, for her unfailing willingness to assist me in innumerable ways in the early phases of this book, and Susan Schimer and Monica Singer for their help in the later phases. I am grateful too to the numerous friends who read parts of my manuscript at various stages of its development and made helpful suggestions. My husband, Karl August Wittfogel, was ever ready to listen to my plaints and allay them by his cheerful certainty that all would go well.

And indeed this was the case from the moment Gloria Levitas, editor of Queens College Publications in Anthropology, read my manuscript. I myself have been an editor and at numerous times have dealt with others so designated, but I have marveled at and been endlessly grateful for her proficiency, exceptional concern, and optimism at all points in the preparation of these *Notes* for publication. Here I can only say: "Thank you, Gloria."

Esther S. Goldfrank

New York, 1978

ABBREVIATIONS:

AA   *American Anthropologist*
AAA   American Anthropological Association
AES.   American Ethnological Society
AMNH American Museum of Natural History
APS   American Philosophical Society
BAE   Bureau of American Ethnology
JAFL   *Journal of American Folklore*

These *Notes* are my answer to the question posed so often by my young friends: "What was anthropology like then?" Of course, *then* was that long-ago time before my questioners were born. Here I have done both less and more than they may have expected. Less, since this was inevitable given the nature of things and persons and the exceptionality and limitations of my own experience. And more, since I have gone beyond the *then* of my questioners, in fact, within a few short years of the *now* which, predictably, will be a *then* for future generations of anthropologists—and others.

PART ONE

1. Introduction to Anthropology and Franz Boas

As I begin to write on this night of January 19, 1968, I am 71 years old, going, as the songster would say, on 72. What I want to recall are events and impressions, many of which go back nearly 50 years. This will be a "my-eye" view, with all the limitations anthropologists are so correct in noting—"no one knows his whole culture"—to which should be added the truism that even what we know will be distorted by pre- and post-experiences. At a later time I may record memories of my childhood, particularly those moments that years afterward thrust themselves persistently and meaningfully into consciousness. Here I shall start by saying that I graduated from Barnard College in 1918—a fortunate time when the student was not overly constrained by directives, and seeking out the "stars"—and reaching them—was still possible. My major was economics. I do not remember my minor—perhaps because it was so minor—but I do remember the stars: Robinson and Beard (their jointly authored book created an impression of a single identity—a notion soon dispelled by even a most superficial acquaintance with them and clearly to the benefit of Beard), Shotwell, Carlton Hayes, David Muzzey, Raymond Mussey, Seager, Seligman, Baldwin, who looked like Shakespeare and had little respect for my daily themes—and Franz Boas.[1]

I had taken Dr. Boas' introductory course in anthropology in my last term at Barnard. Most of the class found him difficult to understand because of his German accent and the speech impediments resulting from an operation for cancer that had partially paralyzed the left side of his face. But we knew we were listening to America's outstanding anthropologist, and listen we did.

Dr. Boas made no concessions to beginners. In his lectures he moved quickly from place to place, from group to group, from detail to detail. It was no easy task to determine the major lines of his thinking. There were questions, not many to be sure, and although he did not resent them, his answers were invariably short, and he would quickly

1

return to the point he had been making. Yet even when we did not understand fully, we began to sense the range of human relationships, their similarities and differences, and to comprehend the weaknesses in nineteenth-century theories of evolution and the strengths of Boas' cultural-environmental approach for the understanding of man and his works.

I got a B in anthropology, and in the late fall of 1919 a note from Professor Boas asking if I would be interested in becoming his secretary at $25 a week and a month's vacation annually. A Wall Street dropout, my answer was an immediate "yes."

In the spring of 1918, the United States, together with its allies, England and France, was still at war with Germany (Russia had made a separate peace after the October Revolution). To my memory, Dr. Boas only rarely injected his personal philosophy into the anthropological lectures I attended, and then without elaboration. But he had behaved very differently in April of the previous year when, upon learning that Columbia's "trustees wished to investigate the loyalty of the faculty," it seemed "best" to him to present his "point of view to the students."[2] And his behavior was very different in November 1917 when, in his Barnard class, he expressed his skepticism regarding "the absolute value of so-called national ideals," stated his view that "history is never rational," and that among other "segregated classes," the intellectuals, steeped as they are in history, "are little able to think clearly." And he urged the examination, from the standpoint of "human ethics," of "some of the passionate convictions that determine our conduct in times of war."[3]

Dr. Boas' reticence on these subjects in our classroom in 1918 may well have been a response to trustee and faculty reactions, but I have no specific knowledge of what these may have been. However, during and after 1917, he continued to use public platforms to expound his ideas on the war and social problems just as he had been doing since 1914.[4] His communications appeared in *The New York Times*, German-language papers, *The Nation, The Atlantic Monthly, The Dial, School and Society,* and in Socialist Party organs—*The New York Call* and a leaflet circulated by the Socialist Party of Bergen County, N. J. (the state in which Dr. Boas was then residing). In December 1914, the Socialist Party had issued an antiwar manifesto which, according to Professor Daniel Bell, was particularly congenial to its supporting "German, Jewish and foreign-language elements" (Bell, 1952: 313) whose memories of the European scene inclined them to join "radical movements" (309). And the opening lines of Dr. Boas' *An Anthropologist's Credo* lend substance to this statement. "The back ground of my early thinking," he wrote there, "was a German home in which the ideals of the revolution of 1848 were a living force" (Boas, 1938: 201). Further insights regarding his political development and motivations can be gleaned from his letter to *The New York Times* dated January 7, 1916. In it he indicated the reasons for his disillusionment with the United States. "At the time of my arrival here, more than 30 years ago," he wrote, "I was filled with admiration of American political ideas. . . . I thought of it as a country that would not tolerate interference with its own interests, but that it would also refrain from active interference in the affairs of others, and would never become guilty of the oppression of unwilling subjects." In this letter he also told of his "rude awakening" in 1898 when "the aggressive imperialism of that period showed that the ideal had been a dream." He added, "Well I remember the heated discussions which I had that year with my German friends when I maintained that the control of the colonies was opposed to the fundamental ideas of right held by the American people, and the profound disappointment I felt when at the end of the Spanish War these ideals lay shattered" (Stocking, 1974: 331-35).

No doubt Dr. Boas did have heated discussions with German friends in 1898, but it was well over a decade before he felt impelled to make his private views public. And then the U.S. was at war, not with Spain, but with Germany.

As a Barnard student, I was no avid reader of *The New York Times* or other newspapers and journals in which Dr. Boas had been and was publishing his views. But it was no secret, when I was taking his introductory course early in 1918, that our professor stood four-square behind Germany. True, he had resided for decades in America, had married and raised a family of five here. But his roots were in Germany, the land of his birth and, understandably, much of his heart. He had family and close friends there and many and long-time contacts with German scholars. And, as I learned soon after I became his secretary, he liked to speak German—in his home it was still a major language—and, after dinner, he liked to sit at the piano and play Bach, Mozart, Beethoven, and particularly German folk-tunes, his children around him, lustily singing the words they knew so well.

Of course, during these years, Dr. Boas published many scholarly articles—on race, on differences in physical growth and development, on linguistics, religion, art, and mythology—and this could certainly be expected from the man who, for more than two decades, had dominated the anthropological scene on virtually every level. But the road he traveled was often a rough one. In 1894, and after an association of two years, he had severed his official connection with the Columbian Field Museum in Chicago—according to Alfred L. Kroeber, because of tensions (1943a: 13ff.). Tensions also led to his separation from the American Museum of Natural History in New York in 1905. And when I joined him in December 1919, tensions were clearly present between him and Columbia University.

2. A SECRETARY AMONG ANTHROPOLIGISTS

The quarters of the Department of Anthropology comprised three rooms, all of them modest in size and furnishings, on the seventh floor of Journalism: Dr. Boas in 703, his secretary (now me) in 704, and, since the previous April when the instructorship of A. J. Goldenweiser, Dr. Boas' sole assistant, was cancelled without explanation, no one in 705.

Saying "yes" was all I had to do to become Dr. Boas' secretary. No one else was considered, there was no formal interview, no test of my technical efficiency, no inquiry into my attitudes (Dr. Boas' memory of me as an average student in his Barnard class apparently sufficed), and no effort to bring me up to date on his. When I arrived on December 8, Dr. Boas was "The Department" and I, "The Staff."

It was immediately clear that, in largest part, I would learn about Department affairs, and the many unrelated matters in which Dr. Boas was deeply and actively involved, from his dictation. And in my first days, I learned much in this way. Indications of the scope of his interests—and his industry—are apparent in the letters I typed at this time. Fortunately for my present task, all of them bore the initials FB/S—FB for Franz Boas, S for Schiff, my maiden name.

On December 8, I wrote a letter to Dr. Elsie Clews Parsons enclosing a bill for her to pay. A short time later I discovered that she was the Department's "angel," financing A. M. Espinosa's trip to Spain (to hunt up parallels to Pueblo myths), as she had Dr. Boas' trip to the Southwest the previous summer. As associate editor of the *Journal of American Folklore*, a position she held from 1918 until her death in 1941, Dr. Parsons was making good its all-too-regular deficits. It was not long before I also learned that she, and not Columbia, was paying my salary.

On this same day I typed a letter to George Hunt, Dr. Boas' long-time Indian informant on the ethnology of the Kwakiutl (Dr. Boas began working with him in 1893). The first volume resulting from their collaboration was published in 1921 as the 35th Annual Report of the Bureau of American Ethnology, seven years after the manuscript had been initially submitted. No wonder Dr. Boas was impatient with the slow arrival of the proofs. I must have shared in reading and correcting them, for when this volume finally appeared, he gave me a copy inscribed: "To Esther Schiff with thanks for her help in the preparation of this work."

Then there was a letter to James Teit, who had been studying Indians on the Northwest Coast since 1896 in association with Dr. Boas, as editor of the publications of the Jesup Expedition to the North Pacific Coast, sponsored by the American Museum of Natural History (AMNH). Actually Dr. Boas was much more than his title implied. He had formulated much of the Expedition's program and found suitable personnel to implement it in Russia, Germany, and America. Another letter was written to Raymond Pearl, well known in the field of genetics. At this time, Dr. Boas was also engaged in an extensive study of physical measurements and growth patterns.

On December 9, I typed a letter to Dr. Pliny E. Goddard and another to Dr. Robert H. Lowie, both at the American Museum of Natural History, asking each of them to give a graduate extension course at Columbia two hours a week—the emolument: $200 per 15-week term. Both arranged to do so.

On December 10, Dr. Boas wrote Professor Buck at the University of Chicago about the review of a paper by Paul Radin, a Boas student who had received his Ph.D. from Columbia in 1911. On this day a letter also went to Clark Wissler at the American Museum of Natural History, the President of the Council of the American Anthropological Association, about a manuscript from Wallis (most probably Wilson D. Wallis, who, later and for many years, headed the Department of Anthropology at the University of Minnesota).

On the same day, Dr. Boas wrote a letter to Manuel Gamio, with whom he had been associated in founding the International School of American Archaeology and Ethnology, with headquarters in Mexico City. As a visiting fellow and resident director, Dr. Boas had spent the year 1911-12 at the School, giving some lectures, but concerning himself primarily with archaeological matters. Under his guidance Gamio had made important stratigraphic discoveries at Azcapotzalco. But revolution in Mexico and difficulties with the U.S. government had seriously hampered the work of the School, and the outbreak of war in 1914 had put an end to this scholarly venture. In this December 10 letter, Dr. Boas remarked, "I feel very badly on account of the constant attempts that are being made here to embroil Mexico and the United States. I think you know my position and my opinion that it is absolutely wrong for one nation to try to impose its opinion on another one." Indeed, the possibility of reactivating the International School along the lines set at its establishment seemed dim.

In the same letter, Dr. Boas, somewhat elliptically, referred to his intention to print "something" which he felt would be of interest to Gamio, but "owing to a long continued printers strike," this "something" had not yet appeared, and there was no assurance that it ever would.

Also on December 10, a letter was dispatched to Dean Hawkes of Columbia University asking that an assistant (no doubt a partial replacement for Goldenweiser) be appointed to introduce students in Dr. Boas' introductory course in anthropology to relevant exhibits in the American Museum of Natural History. This request was summarily refused.

And on December 10, Dr. Boas wrote to Morris Hillquit, a leader of the Socialist Party in New York City, asking for an appointment to discuss his (Boas') last article on international work that had appeared in *The New York Call*. Presumably, this was his "Program for Equal Educational Opportunity," published on December 7.

On December 11, Dr. Boas wrote Natalie Curtis Burlin regarding funds for C. K. Simango, a Bantu-speaking Xandau tribesman who, for some time, had been in the U.S. working with him on African languages. On May 5, 1920, Dr. Boas wrote Mr. George Foster Peabody, who was also a Simango sponsor: "My present plan is to get from him whatever he knows, to write it out and then give to him this material when he goes back to Africa, with specific questions in regard to doubtful points and in regard to points that he does not know, so that he may have a complete guide for his work. He is very intelligent and deeply interested." This was exactly Dr. Boas' *modus operandi* with his Kwakiutl informant, George Hunt.

Also on December 11, Dr. Boas wrote a U.S. official asking his help in getting a U.S. visa for the father of Herman K. Haeberlin, the talented Boas student who had died in 1918. His Ph.D. thesis, "The Idea of Fertilization in the Culture of the Pueblo Indians" was published in 1916 as an *AAA Memoir*. This same day Dr. Boas wrote to Haeberlin's father, telling him how difficult it was to secure permission for a German citizen to enter the United States, and he also wrote to Harry Williams in the Philippines regarding tales he had been collecting, and to Dr. Leo J. Frachtenberg, another of his students, regarding publication of a manuscript.

On December 12, a letter to Mr. G. M. Heckscher, prominent in German-American circles, asked that he call a meeting "soon" of the Board of Directors of the Germanistic Society, an old and honored organization, which Dr. Boas hoped would coordinate the activities of similarly oriented groups to re-establish relations and accelerate the exchange of publications between German scientists and their counterparts elsewhere, particularly in the United States. This is the project he later said was "nearest" to his heart, and not many months later it became known as "The Emergency Society for German and Austrian Science."

The week-end probably intervened, for the next letters I typed were dated December 15. Among them were two short notes, one to a member of the U.S. Bureau of Geological Survey, one to a member of a U.S. Bureau (which one is not clear) concerning charges being brought by the Department of Justice against a Professor Moens (his full name is not given). The wording is vague in both letters, and I have no memory of ever having been told what was involved. Stocking (1968: 274, 356, n. 8) cites a letter written by Dr. Boas on October 24, 1919—more than a month before my arrival at Columbia—to T. H. Cremer, Minister of the Netherlands, stating that Professor Moens, whom he had known for some years, had been accused by the U.S. Department of Justice of being a German spy. As Stocking reports it, "In defending himself, Moens gave government agents access to his personal papers in which they found unretouched nude photographs which were then used first for an attempt at what was apparently official blackmail, and then for an obscenity prosecution." Adds Stocking, "Actually the photographs involved were simply anthropological studies of mixed races, but two Washington anthropologists nonetheless testified against Moens when the case came to court" (Stocking: 1968: 274f). And Dr. Boas' concern did not stop there. The day following his two notes to Washington, he wrote to someone connected with the Smithsonian Institution (name indistinct) regarding Moens.

Also on December 15 Dr. Boas wrote to J. Walter Fewkes of the Bureau of American Ethnology (BAE) about galleys, and to Marius Ransome, Bureau of Education, Hydaburg, Alabama, about Indian tales. He wrote his good friend Dr. Henry Donaldson, Wistar Institute for Anatomy and Biology in Philadelphia, enclosing a letter from Paul Rivet, a prominent French anthropologist, "which will show you that there are few people who keep their sense even in France" —that is, few who as yet were willing to cooperate with Austrian and German scientists. And on December 15, Dr. Boas also wrote to Dr. Dobrowschki, advising him to remain in Germany and continue his work there.

On December 16 there was a letter to Martha W. Beckwith (she had received her Ph.D. degree from Columbia in 1918 and was now at Vassar), asking what numbers of the *Journal of American Folklore* she needed for her work, and another to John R. Swanton, with the BAE in Washington, discussing linguistic data.

On December 18, in a letter addressed to the Germanistic Society, Dr. Boas asked to be "authorized" to propose certain policies at the next meeting of the Society. He particularly stressed his desire to contact German departments in universities and improve the exchange of publications. Dr. Boas wrote to Dean Gildersleeve acknowledging receipt of $200 (apparently for himself) and $100 for an assistant to instruct Barnard students at the AMNH (a position that would be filled by Erna Gunther); to Edward Grant, acting supervisor of examinations at Columbia, asking that a date be set for examining the "over twenty undergraduates" in his introductory course; to Robert Lowie asking him to send Paul Radin's paper to Professor Buck at the University of Chicago, and to Alfred M. Tozzer, Harvard professor, regarding problems connected with the *Journal of American Folklore* and manuscripts to be published in it.

The bond between Tozzer and Dr. Boas was a warm one, inspired by a shared interest in Mexican anthropology. At this time Tozzer was writing his Maya grammar and kept Dr. Boas regularly informed on his progress. But they were also in close touch on questions in many other areas of anthropological activity. Enough here to mention their sizable correspondence in the months just preceding my arrival concerning nominations of AAA members for service on the Council of the Division of Anthropology and Psychology, newly established by the National Research Council. Tozzer had refused the chairmanship, which then fell to Clark Wissler. Dr. Boas, after considerable urging, had consented to serve as a member.

Also on December 18 there was a letter to Professor Max Walter, Real Schule Director in Frankfort, enclosing a "clipping" regarding conditions in Germany and particularly regarding the problem of school maintenance. With respect to this last, Dr. Boas suggested that with the abolition of obligatory military service, the question might well become

> whether an obligatory economic service for both men and women would not be of greatest educational advantage for the purpose of educating the young people to the recognition of the value of serious steady work, and further, for the purpose of raising the consciousness of social obligation. [This point was also made in Dr. Boas' December article in the *Call*.] Secondarily, economic service of this kind might be so organized that it would make possible a highly developed educational system without over-burdening the State and the community with a tremendous financial outlay. It might make the school in the future self-supporting.

Today few would reject Dr. Boas' ends, but, in the light of what we have learned in the last decades, many would reject his means. He added:

> The questions which trouble German educational institutions at the present time are exactly the same as those that are troubling us here. It seems to my mind that at the present time when the whole industrial development is clearly in the direction of a strong

8

reduction in the time of labor, it becomes more and more the duty of the school to prepare the students not only for effective, productive work, but to teach them also to utilize the time for recreation advantageously. In other words, the general cultural studies instead of becoming less important ought to become more important.

On December 19, Dr. Boas wrote a letter to President Butler thanking him "for the increase granted me in the middle of the year"; and he added, "I beg to assure you that this is a relief in a very difficult situation." He ended it "Yours very respectfully." On the 18th, President Butler had written Dr. Boas that his annual salary would be raised to $6,000 and ended his communication "With best wishes for a Merry Christmas and a Happy New Year, I am faithfully yours." No hint here, nor in Dr. Boas' response, of the strained relations between them, but I do not remember a single University function that Dr. Boas attended during my years as his secretary, not even a Commencement ceremony.

And on December 19, Dr. Boas wrote again to Martha Beckwith, this time specifically about riddles. He also wrote again to Haeberlin's father, regretting his failure to get him into America.

Also on this day, Dr. Boas again wrote Manuel Gamio, telling him that he had just received a letter from Dr. S. V. Hartman, Director of the Ethnological Museum in Stockholm, asking for assistance in smoothing the way for Prince Wilhelm, the youngest son of the King of Sweden, "to carry on archaeological explorations in Yucatan." Dr. Boas also expressed his fear that Gamio's "wish for hearty cooperation between Mexico and the United States will be very slow of realization, because our public press is driving all the time towards misunderstandings between Mexico and the United States. Unfortunately, Mexico has too much silver and oil." And on the next page he commented, "You will remember that a few years ago we had at heart the problem of assisting in early educational attempts of Mexico. I have entirely withdrawn from this movement, because it [there?] is too much of a tendency to impose American methods upon the educational institutions and a disregard of the individuality of their own country." He also assured Gamio that his "only wish is to promote friendly relations between the two nations." But Gamio "would have to recognize," as did he, "that there is a powerful party which, as people put it here, wants to clean up Mexico, forgetting entirely that we have enough to do to clean up our own country." In his opening paragraph Dr. Boas had informed Gamio that he was sending him "a copy of *The Nation* of the 20th of December which contains in the Department of Correspondence a letter written by me." This letter was manifestly the "something" he was referring to when he wrote Gamio on December 10. It was addressed to the Editor of *The Nation* and entitled "Scientists as Spies." It read:

> In his war address to Congress, President Wilson dwelt at great length on the theory that only autocracies maintain spies; that these are not needed in democracies. At the time that the President made this statement, the Government of the United States had in its employ spies of unknown number. I am not concerned here with the familiar discrepancies between the President's words and the actual facts, although we may perhaps have to accept his statement as meaning correctly that we live under an autocracy; that our democracy is a fiction. The point against which I wish to enter a vigorous protest is that a number of men who follow science as their profession, men whom I refuse to designate any longer as scientists, have prostituted science by using it as a cover for their activities as spies.
>
> A soldier whose business is murder as a fine art, a diplomat whose calling is based on deception and secretiveness, a politician whose very life consists in compromises with his conscience, a business man whose aim is personal profit within the limits allowed by lenient law—such may be excused if they set patriotic devotion above common everyday decency and perform services as spies. They merely accept the code of morality to which modern society still conforms. Not so the scientist. The very essence of his life is the service of truth. We all know scientists who in private life do not come up to the standard of truthfulness, but who, nevertheless, would not consciously falsify the results of their researches.
>
> It is bad enough if we have to put up with them, because they reveal a lack of strength of character that is liable to distort the results of their work. A person, however, who uses science as a cover for political spying, who demeans himself to pose before a foreign government as an investigator and asks for assistance in his alleged researches in order to carry on, under his cloak, his political machinations, prostitutes science in an unpardonable way and forfeits the right to be classed as a scientist.
>
> By accident, incontrovertible proof has come to my hands that at least four men who carry on anthropological work, while employed as government agents, introduced themselves to foreign governments as representatives of scientific institutions in the United States, and as sent out for the purpose of carrying on scientific researches. They have not only shaken the belief in the truthfulness of science, but they have also done the greatest

10

possible disservice to scientific inquiry. In consequence of their acts every nation will look with distrust upon the visiting foreign investigator who wants to do honest work, suspecting sinister designs. Such action has raised a new barrier against the development of international friendly cooperation.

Franz Boas

October 16, 1919

Insofar as I have been able to determine, it was only in writing to Manuel Gamio that Dr. Boas referred to this *Nation* letter—on December 10, without indicating its intent or content, and on December 19, to announce that a copy was on its way to him. Almost surely Gamio would be especially interested, since some, if not all four, of the anthropologists involved had done scientific work in Mexico, and Gamio himself had cooperated closely with Dr. Boas in 1911-12 and later. And almost surely, since in one case there had been an arrest, Gamio would be familiar with the extra-scientific activities Dr. Boas was now exposing. But it is of interest that, when he first learned of the spying, Dr. Boas chose to say nothing about it and to hold his fire "until the close of the war" (on January 15, 1920, he wrote a friend in Washington that he had arrived at this decision because he was then "very actively interested in a committee which intended to promote Mexican education" and he had his "hands full" seeking to prevent "the use of this movement to impose upon Mexican schools types of American teachers whom the Mexicans did not want." Which types these were he did not explain.) Whatever his reasons, Dr. Boas did not reveal his information at the end of the war either. But his decision to tell his story late in 1919 in *The Nation*, when anti-German feeling was unabated, was quite probably triggered by the Palmer raids and the Moens charges (cf. Stocking, 1968: 274f).

In reviewing the letters I typed for Dr. Boas on December 19, the day he sent the copy of *The Nation* to Manuel Gamio, and on December 20, 22, and 23 (there were no letters on December 21, presumably a Sunday), I find no reference to what would become an anthropological bombshell. Two letters were written on December 20 to Felix Von Luschan at the Volkekunde Museum in Berlin, one just before his letter arrived and one immediately afterward. In the first, Dr. Boas discussed his difficulties with the mails, his desire to hear from his German friends, his willingness to raise funds to publish the work on the Negroes done by Von Luschan during his stay in America, the possibility of publishing the *International Journal of Linguistics* abroad. One paragraph reviewed the situations of his five children. Helene, his eldest daughter, is married and she and her husband "are intending to sail to Switzerland on Saturday of next week"; his son Ernst is a "practitioner" and is also married; Gertrud "is through with college and is trying her hand at child welfare work"; Henry "is studying agriculture"; and "the baby is in college now." Dr. Boas then gives what, for him, is an unusually detailed description of the operation on his face some years previously and the ulcer of the duodenum which was still plaguing him. (I remember him often sitting alone at his desk slowly eating his uninviting lunch of milk and cold porridge, both brought from home.) And then immediately after writing about his health and before mentioning his "very interesting" work on Jewish children ("the differences due to different economic conditions are almost incredible"), Dr. Boas wrote, "Naturally the general political conditions have oppressed me very much and the only relief I had was to explode periodically in print." And he added, "After that I would feel a little better for this." In his second letter, he further discussed the pro- and anti-German attitudes of his colleagues in the U.S. and abroad. But there was no reference to the Moens case, to his *Nation* letter, or to the relief he experienced when he exploded in print.

On December 22, Dr. Boas wrote Alfred Tozzer at Harvard, Berthold Laufer at the Field Museum of Natural History in Chicago, and Alfred Kroeber at the University of California, his major concern in each case being the choice of AAA members to serve on the Council of the NRC's Division of Anthropology and Psychology. To Kroeber he commented, "Helene and her husband are going to leave for Switzerland on Saturday." Also on this day he wrote to Mr. Pagenstecher about Germanistic Society matters, to T. T. Waterman, then in the Far West, about the publication of Haeberlin's material, and to J. Walter Fewkes of the BAE about the publication of Kwakiutl material and certain of Frachtenberg's data. To this last he added, "I hope we may have the pleasure of seeing you here [in New York for the NRC meeting] next Saturday, and I trust you will be able to be at the [AAA] meeting at Cambridge." No reference in any of these communications to his *Nation* letter. On December 23, and at considerable length, he wrote Carl Von den Steinen regarding his efforts to get support for German scientific societies, and again no reference to his *Nation* letter.

Strange as it may seem in view of my secretarial duties, Dr. Boas felt no more impelled to discuss with me the situation and issues raised in "Scientists as Spies" than he had with those to whom he wrote in these first days after his *Nation* letter was published. Being a storm center was no new experience for him, nor would the certainty of such an eventuality have changed his plan of action. Robert Lowie has written that Franz Boas was not one "to remain in the ivory tower of scholarship." He added, "When his feelings were deeply stirred—and for a man of his intellect he was singularly emotional—he would plunge into the hurly-burly of the workaday world, heedless of the consequences" (JAFL, 1944, 57: 59).

But if Dr. Boas avoided reference to his *Nation* letter, his colleagues did not. The quickest official response came on December 26 in the form of a resolution submitted by the Anthropological Society of Washington for consideration at the AAA meeting in Cambridge "with a request for suitable action" to indicate its members' "emphatic disapproval" of Dr. Boas' behavior (a considerable number of them had long been at odds with Dr. Boas and not a few had worked in Mexico). And Dr. Boas' *Nation* letter did become a major battleground at the Council meeting of the AAA.

The annual meeting of the American Anthropological Association was held at the Peabody Museum, Harvard University, beginning on December 27, just a week after Dr. Boas' letter appeared in *The Nation*. The *American Anthropologist*, under the aegis of his good friend Pliny E. Goddard as editor, and his erstwhile student, Robert H. Lowie, and his close collaborator, John R. Swanton, as co-editors, reported that at the Council meeting on December 30 (which was open to all Fellows of the Association) Dr. Neil M. Judd moved the following:

> *Resolved*: That the expression of opinion by Dr. Franz Boas contained in an open letter to the editor of *The Nation* under date of October 16, 1919, and published in the issue of that weekly for December 20, 1919, is unjustified and does not represent the opinion of the American Anthropological Association.
> Be it further resolved:
> That a copy of this resolution be forwarded to the Executive Board of the National Research Council and such other scientific associations as may have taken action on this matter.
> Yes: Judd, Hyde, Hooton, Kidder, Wilder, Farabee, Spinden, Hager, Wardle, Lothrop, Saville, Fewkes, MacCurdy, Gates, Guernsey, Guthe, Gordon, Dixon, Hodge, Morley.
> No: Speck, Spier, Kroeber, Peabody, Lowie, Nelson, Parsons, Tozzer, Goddard.
> Not voting: Willoughby, Wissler (presiding). (*AA*, 1920: 93f).

On December 29 and while he and Mrs. Boas were staying with Professor Tozzer in Cambridge, Dr. Boas had written the Chairman of the Nominating Committee of the American Anthropological Association, "I understand that a number of members of the Council of the Anthropological Association do not wish me to represent them on the Research Council on the ground that they take exception to my letter 'Scientists as Spies' published in *The Nation* of December 20th. Since considerable feeling seems to be manifested on account of this matter and, since I care infinitely more for the well-being of the Anthropological Association than for my own membership in the Research Council, I request my name not be considered." After giving the reasons for his action and reviewing the principles involved, he stated, "I hold with this position uncompromisingly." And he added: "Since it does not seem to agree with the concept of professional ethics of many members of the Council I consider this disagreement a recall." In closing, he asked that "this letter be read at the meeting and be made part of the minutes."

Whether this letter was read at the Council meeting of the AAA or made a part of its minutes, as Dr. Boas wished, I do not know. But in the report of the Proceedings given in the *American Anthropologist,* there is no reference to either request. However, the *Anthropologist* did carry the following resolution, which was adopted unanimously:

> That the Chairman be instructed to transmit to the Executive Board of the National Research Council the resignation of Professor Boas, with regret that the division must lose the services of the most eminent anthropologist in America and a man of unimpeachable devotion to his ideals with the recommendation that Professor Boas' resignation be accepted. (*AA,* 1920: 94)

To my knowledge the first notice in print that further punitive action had been taken against Dr. Boas at this Cambridge meeting (and again, strange as it may seem, this was the first time I learned of it) was almost twenty-five years later when it appeared in Kroeber's lead article in *Franz Boas 1858-1942*. Here Kroeber stated, "The printed record of the Proceedings omits mention of the most stinging action voted by the association" (Kroeber, 1943a: 20). That this referred to the fact that Professor Boas had been removed from the Council of the American Anthropological Association at the December meeting is clear from his subsequent remark, "Within a few years Boas was back, not only on the Research Council but on the Council of his own Association."

In the list of Council members given in the 1921 January-March number of *American Anthropologist,* Dr. Boas was indeed "back on the Council of his own Association," and his was the lead-off name in the list of its members—which did not follow alphabetical order (*AA,* 1921: 103).

I do not know when Dr. Boas returned from Cambridge, but the first letter I typed for him was dated January 15. It was his answer to a letter from a Washington friend written two days previously which reviewed the background of the Washington Society's resolution and noted that this friend had "refused to support it"—not, he explained, because he agreed with Dr. Boas, but because he "did not think we ought to take action as a scientific body," and because he "did not agree with the terms of the resolution either."

In his reply, Dr. Boas explained, as indicated above, why he had delayed publicizing his discoveries, and he "confessed" his "loss to understand why there should be so few people who had understood my position." And while he also noted that "more or less definite information of various sorts has, of course, poured in, telling me that British scientists did the same thing in Spain and that the Red Cross people did the same wherever they went," he concluded, "But it seems to my mind that it draws the issue only more clearly and makes it incumbent upon those who believe in the fundamental principles of truthfulness to stand by their colors."

This exchange of letters continued for some weeks without either correspondent altering his position. There was also an equally friendly exchange between Dr. Boas and one of the four unnamed anthropologists he had attacked in his *Nation* letter. And despite the information that had "poured in"—and I never saw any part of it—both Dr. Boas' friends and his enemies, while staunchly standing by their colors, seemed ready, for different reasons, to ring down the curtain on what his Washington correspondent on January 13 had characterized as "the late unpleasantness" (the quotation marks are his). In fact, all that I learned at this time about this "late unpleasantness" I learned from the letters I typed, and Dr. Boas was not inclined to go beyond the dictated word. I saw no copy of the *American Anthropologist* in which the report of the Cambridge meeting appeared. Neither Dr. Goddard nor Dr. Lowie, on their short tours of duty at Columbia, was disposed to discuss with me, the newly installed secretary, what had happened during these historic days. Gladys Reichard and Erna Gunther, both first-year graduate students in anthropology at Columbia, had gone to Cambridge, but since they were not yet Fellows of the Association, they had been excluded from the December 30 Council meeting. And it was only in 1968, when I was writing these *Notes* and before I saw Stocking's detailed report (1968: 270-93), that I was given any personal recollections of what had transpired there—and this by Erna, a "nonparticipant" observer.

Erna and I were then both attending the Annual Meeting of the AAA in Seattle, where she had resided for years, during many of which she had been head of the Department of Anthropology at the University of Washington. And since I had spent considerable time in Seattle in the fifties and sixties, we had seen a good deal of each other. But we had never discussed the 1919 AAA meeting.

When I asked her at long last what she knew about this meeting, she immediately reminded me that she had not been a Fellow, and therefore had not been present at the crucial session. But at its conclusion, she told me, a "tremendously agitated" Kroeber emerged. As soon as he saw her he said, "I can't stand it here. Will you go for a ride with me if I can get Dixon's car?" Erna readily agreed to accompany him, and for well over an hour they drove around Cambridge, and unlike his usual self, Kroeber "talked a blue streak." But he told her nothing about what had occurred behind the closed door. Only much later—presumably after she married Leslie Spier, who had voted against censure at the 1919 meeting—did she learn that Dr. Boas had been dropped from the Council of the Association.

On March 1, 1920, Dr. Boas wrote Kroeber, "That my relations with the Bureau have been severed you know." Boas had been given an honorary position in the Bureau of American Ethnology in 1902 and from then on had worked on a massive compilation of Indian languages, which was enthusiastically acclaimed by Major J. W. Powell, the Director.[5] The first *Part* (*Part* being the not too appropriate term for this sizable volume) appeared in 1911, the second in 1922, and although there were two more (the last in 1941, the year before Boas died), this 1922 *Part* was the last to be government-sponsored.

Dr. Boas' laconic reference to his severance from the Bureau gives no indication of how deeply hurt he must have been by the Bureau's "stinging action" after so many years of constructive cooperation. But for Boas what mattered most was not the glorious or inglorious past, but the immediate present. Quite in character, the opening sentence in this letter reads, "Nothing in particular has happened here, since you left." And in large part this was so. To be sure, he was feeling "the usual pressure being put upon my time" by the "special courses" he had to give during "the second term."

But the pressure on his time was also, and notably, greatly intensified due to his efforts in behalf of scientists abroad. In April 1920, a circular financed by him was sent out to many institutions and private persons in the hope of increasing and accelerating the exchange of American and European scientific literature and information. Interestingly, the word "German," so prominent in Dr. Boas' earlier appeals, does not appear in this one, which was signed by him and 22 others, including ex-President William H. Taft, Harlan F. Stone—a Columbia professor of law who would become Chief Justice of the U.S. Supreme Court—two university presidents, a Cardinal, and representatives of the arts, sciences, and business.

At this time Dr. Boas was collaborating with Elsie Clews Parsons on Spanish tales from Laguna and Zuni, with José Maria Arreola on tales of the Mexican *Milpa Alta,* and continuing his work on the Kwakiutl, the influence of environment upon social development, the classification of Indian languages, the methods of ethnology, and the fallacy of the racial myth (cf. his Bibliography for 1920). But there was one noteworthy change from his previous practice. In his Bibliography there is no record for 1920 of the publication of any speech or article on a political subject.

And there was still another change—no doubt a minor one in Dr. Boas' book, but a major one in mine. Not long after he returned to Columbia he asked me—and I will not guess at his motives, which almost surely were mixed—to join the Tuesday "lunchers" who met each week at the Hotel Endicott on Columbus Avenue and 81 St., a location convenient to the American Museum of Natural History, to which the "regulars"—Pliny Goddard, Robert Lowie, Nils Nelson, and Leslie Spier—were attached. (Clark Wissler, for his own reasons, had never been among them.) Elsie Clews Parsons came whenever she could get her "mother's car" (she lived most of the year in Harrison, N.Y., and did not drive or have a chauffeur at her disposal, although, as the daughter of a prominent banker, the wife of a prominent Republican, and the mother of several teenagers, she surely had access to one "family car," and probably more, for suburban living), and now the students, Erna Gunther and Gladys Reichard, and I, the lone secretary, also joined the "regulars." But since Erna and Gladys worked at the Museum a good deal of the time, I was usually Dr. Boas' only traveling companion in our weekly trek. Of course, when they were in town, Kroeber, now well-established at Berkeley, and Edward Sapir, less-contentedly established in Canada, were "regular irregulars." In large part, the luncheon talk concerned field-work, past and projected, and publication problems. Departmental problems were discussed rarely, and what had happened at Cambridge at the end of December, never.

3. THE STUDENTS

On December 18, 1919, Dr. Boas, it will be remembered, had written Columbia's Acting Supervisor of Examinations that "over twenty undergraduates" were registered in his introductory course. How many "over" he did not state. Nor in this letter did he mention any others, although in writing Kroeber on March 1, 1920, he did mention the "usual pressure" on his time, owing to "the special courses" he had to give in the second term. However many undergraduates there may have been at this time at Columbia, I can recall meeting none of them. There was no regular time for student consultation and apparently none was requested. At Barnard, Dr. Boas' parallel course was surely as well attended, and Kroeber (1943a: 15) remarked that "contrary" to his Columbia experience it "afforded him gratification." This was spelled out again by Gladys Reichard, who, in 1923 and on Dr. Boas' recommendation, became Instructor of Anthropology at Barnard College and, after the Department of Anthropology was established there, its guiding spirit. In her review of Dr. Boas' contribution to the study of folklore (ibid., p. 55) she wrote: "He once told me that if he should stop teaching all classes but one, that was the one he would prefer to keep."

In seeking a reason for Dr. Boas' clearly felt "gratification," Kroeber suggested that "he may have been less uncompromising toward the girls" who "sensed more quickly than their brothers the genius which underlay his unpalatable presentation." But whether or not this was so, there can be no doubt that the war had significantly affected college attendance. Young men had been conscripted and young women had become career-minded. Jobs were plentiful but a college education gave promise of a better one—in fact, this last point was being regularly stressed during my years at Barnard—and with its many inviting areas for field-work and many problems still unresolved, anthropology may well have attracted more qualified women students during these years.

In his July 23, 1920 letter to Berthold Laufer, Dr. Boas wrote, "I have had a curious experience in graduate work during the last few years. All my best students are women." In this connection it is of interest that, beginning in 1901 and until 1916, his Ph.Ds, some eleven of them, had with one exception been men: Alfred L. Kroeber in 1901, William Jones in 1904, Albert B. Lewis in 1907, Robert H. Lowie in 1908, Edward Sapir in 1909, Alexander Goldenweiser in 1910, Paul Radin in 1911, Thomas Waterman in 1914, Fay Cooper Cole and Herman K. Haeberlin in 1915. The sole woman, Laura E. W. Bennett, whom I have been unable to identify further, received her degree in 1914. In 1916, 1917, 1918, and 1919 no man was given a Ph.D. in anthropology at Columbia. Martha W. Beckwith in 1918 was the sole woman who achieved this honor during these years.

In 1920, the pattern changed again. In that year, Leslie Spier was awarded his doctorate, and including him and through 1940, both sexes were equally represented—20 men and 20 women earned their Ph.D. in the Department of Anthropology during this period. After 1941 and through 1972, the end-point of *Graduate Study in Anthropology* issued by Columbia University, the pattern changed again. A count, perhaps not completely accurate due to the difficulty of identifying in a number of cases the sex of the individuals, indicates that, during these years, 193 men and 111 women received their Ph.D. Without doubt this altered ratio reflected a number of factors, among them a greater desire on the part of young women to raise a family, to stop working for a Ph.D. even after considerable study, in order to accompany a husband into the field, to turn to another discipline, or to enter the world of commerce.

In December of 1919 I can remember only two graduate students—Erna Gunther and Gladys Reichard, both of whom, as already noted, spent a great deal of their time at the AMNH. Also, in his July 1920 letter to Laufer, Boas, obviously stressing the unusual, wrote, "I have a student now who I think may do good work on Africa, but it will take a couple of years until he is ready." This student was Melville J. Herskovits, and he did do good work on Africa, and much much more. But in those early weeks of 1920 I remember most clearly his friendly smile and his eagerness to discuss his violin playing.

Margaret Mead, in 1923 and still in her senior year at Barnard, became "so enthusiastic" about her introductory course in anthropology that she "began to attend all the graduate courses, little groups of five or six students under a professor who had no time for administrative red tape and who was perfectly willing to let an undergraduate go where an undergraduate wished" (Mead, 1959a: 5). Thus, and despite the intrusion of Barnard students, graduate classes in anthropology were still small in the spring of 1923—indeed almost as small as I remember them to have been in the early months of 1920. And it may just be coincidence that the only male student Mead mentioned is Melville Herskovits, who, as she put it, "chose" to investigate "the cattle culture of East Africa" (Mead, 1959a: 11), a topic Boas some three years earlier had hoped he would become interested in (see Boas' letter to Laufer, July 23, 1920).

Just one male student of promise. But Mel's entry into the anthropological family at Columbia was a first signal that a change was again in the making. To be sure, women students continued to be attracted to anthropology, to be inspired by Boas, the man and the teacher (Ruth Benedict arrived in 1921 and Margaret Mead in 1923). But once again male students were registering for graduate study in anthropology, although from 1920 to 1930 more women than men were still being awarded their Ph.D.

Margaret Mead also wrote, "The Columbia University Department of Anthropology was in the early 1920s a small embattled group" (1959a:9). The fact of the matter is that the early 1920s were the calm after the storm—the storm that had been brewing for years, that had become increasingly threatening after 1914, that had reached its peak in December 1919 (see Kroeber, 1943a: 19). And the Boas of the early twenties, who was intensely immersed in his scholarly tasks and his efforts to reconsolidate U.S. and European science, who was avoiding public actions of the kind that had been condemned even by his friends, was a much less austere presence than, in their student days, he had appeared to be to Kroeber, Lowie, and Sapir.

Let me quote briefly from some later works, to indicate how those "early students" viewed their famous professor. In "Franz Boas, The Man," Kroeber, the first to receive his Ph.D. at Columbia with Dr. Boas participating in his examination, wrote:

> As a teacher, Boas was decidedly one-sided. . . . Essentially, he would teach nothing but principles, methods, and problems, fortified by only such concrete data as were sure for his rapid mind to understand the situation. The load was wholly on the student; if he assumed it, Boas was ready to give him intellectual guidance. (Kroeber, 1943a: 15)

In "Franz Boas 1858-1942," which appeared in the *Journal of American Folklore* in 1944, Lowie wrote, "The immediate effect Boas produced in my Columbia years (1904-1907) was awe of his omniscience, and his critical judgment" (99). Lowie also stated: "He was not mellow . . . not a uniformly easy person to cooperate with, as he himself confessed on a memorable occasion" (64) — the formal presentation of the *Boas Anniversary Volume* at a meeting of the University Council on April 16, 1907. And on October 19, 1925, Sapir wrote Ruth Benedict, "Zuni myths are important toys, of course, but your verse, even when you're not pleased with it, is a holier toy. You may quote this to Boas if you like. I have strayed from the paternal roof and no longer fear the Sire's displeasure" (Mead, 1959a: 181). The capital S tells a good deal about Sapir's early attitude toward Dr. Boas.

But whatever criticisms these "early students" expressed in their later writings, they all recognized their teacher's great scholarly contribution and deep humanity. In "Franz Boas, The Man," Kroeber wrote, "He was of the Titans—a self-disciplined Titan; a Prometheus rather than an Apollo or Hermes. In many ways the epithet of greatness describes him better than that of genius" (24). In "Franz Boas 1858-1942 " Lowie wrote, "There was in him no petty vanity, no messianic strutting; only the Work was sacred as it was to a Michael Angelo and a Beethoven." On January 26, 1925, in answer to a letter from Ruth Benedict, Sapir wrote, "I was awfully sorry to hear of Dr. Boas' illness. It is with regret that one is reminded that this beloved hero is subject to the frailties of death" (Mead, 1959a: 170).

An orthodox Freudian would probably say that Boas' relation to his early students manifests a love-hate relationship typical for father and son. Would that all fathers had as much insight and gave as much scope to their sons as Boas did to his male students. To judge from the record, his toughness and teaching generated no tribe of submissive disciples as psychoanalysis would lead us to expect—but a group of innovative, dedicated, and influential scholars who themselves came to dominate departments of anthropology in our land. In conclusion, let me cite Robert Lowie once again. "To me," he wrote, "his less is more." And these six words those of us who knew Boas well would readily echo.

4. PIONEERS— SECOND WAVE

ELSIE CLEWS PARSONS

In a formal sense, Elsie Clews Parsons cannot be considered a Boas student. I do not remember her ever attending a class or a graduate seminar in the Department of Anthropology, but once she came to know Dr. Boas—after her visit as a tourist to the Southwest in 1915 she was introduced to him by Dr. Pliny E. Goddard—they met frequently to discuss her anthropological benefactions and her researches, particularly those concerned with her new interest. In the bibliography given in *Pueblo Indian Religion,* published two years before her death, she lists under her name more than sixty titles dealing exclusively with the Pueblos, several more exploring relations to such nearby complexes as the Pima and Kiowa, and more distant ones in Mesoamerica, where the implications for Pueblo development and practice were becoming increasingly evident. But long as this list is, it gives little indication of the breadth and depth of her interest in many other geographical areas and in problems of everyday life.

Elsie Clews Parsons was the first graduate of Barnard College to get a Ph.D. in sociology at Columbia. She was also a woman of great independence. Her books *The Family* (1906) and *The Old-Fashioned Woman* (1913) dealt so frankly with sex ethics that she was dropped from the Social Register, a decision that certainly did not disturb her and may, in fact, have strengthened her determination to continue her campaign to alter what she considered traditionally unacceptable attitudes. In 1915, she published a small volume, *Social Freedom,* which not only reflected her familiarity with a broad spectrum of nineteenth-century writings but also evidenced her concern with aspects of American society she felt needed to be changed.

Handsome as a finely bred filly, she hovered over the anthropological scene like a queen. And though personally reserved, she readily discussed her scientific views and listened attentively to opinions that differed from her own, even when they were advanced by a neophyte.

By 1919, she and Dr. Boas were close friends and cooperators; and she had come to rely, in large part, on his recommendations. This was certainly so when he consulted her with regard to my joining him in the summer of 1920 on his follow-up stay in Laguna, where Dr. Parsons also intended to spend some days, accompanied by Grant LaFarge, the father of Oliver LaFarge, as court photographer. In her answer she made it clear that the decision to include me would be entirely his, but if he accepted full responsibility for me, she would pay my board and the costs of my informants should there be any.[6] (I would pay my rail fare, as I had already planned to go West during the summer.) In my case Dr. Parsons was certainly not "outraged" at "sending an untrained person into the field and to a Pueblo at that!" as Ruth Bunzel claims she was in her case in 1924 (see Goldschmidt, 1959: 34). Writing in 1959, Bunzel seems to have forgotten what she certainly knew after she had replaced me as Dr. Boas' secretary—that I was as untrained in 1920 when I went on my first field trip, and to a pueblo at that, as she was a few years later.

In this 1959 account, Bunzel also commented that Dr. Parsons "threatened to withdraw her support of the mythology project" were she "permitted to go." The mythology project here referred to was surely Ruth Benedict's southwest mythology project, and it was not impossible that Bunzel's desire to join Benedict in the field, as she had suggested doing, caused Dr. Parsons to hesitate when Dr. Boas solicited her aid. As Margaret Mead noted in *An Anthropologist at Work*, "Ruth Benedict's relations with Dr. Parsons were never easy and usually were mediated through Boas" (Mead, 1959a: 342). On February 12, 1923, Benedict had written in her diary, "Dr. Boas talked to me about a fellowship in SW folklore. He'd had a letter from Mrs. Parsons falling in with his suggestion" (65). On February 15, she wrote, "Said nothing to Mrs. Parsons at lunch—nor she to me. Dr. Boas said I was to approach her. Oh well—Discussed it with M.I.A. p.m.—it seemed more possible" (65). On February 16 she noted,

"~~Couldn't.~~

~~Wrote Mrs. Parsons I'd take the job~~. Wrote Mrs. Parsons I was interested" (65).

(Here I have reproduced the sentence placements as given by Mead. The crossouts speak for themselves.) On February 19, she noted, "Found a letter from Mrs. Parsons with details—$1000 and a study of SW mythology" (66). On February 20 came the last entry on this subject: "Wrote Mrs. Parsons I'd take the job" (66).

As Bunzel put it in her 1959 statement, "Elsie Parsons capitulated: I was permitted to go" (Goldschmidt, ed., 1959: 34). For years Dr. Parsons supported Bunzel's work in the Southwest. And in her short Foreword to *Zuni Mythology* (1935) Benedict wrote, "The first summer was sponsored by the Southwest Society"—specifically Elsie Clews Parsons, who increasingly preferred this title to the use of her name.

Other anthropologists saw Dr. Parsons very differently. After her death, Gladys Reichard wrote that Dr. Parsons never "cut off funds because of youthful mistakes," nor did she "exert pressure on a worker or his theories. . . . If one trait of her character were to be stressed more than another, it must be her absolute regard for truth. She had her own ethical ideals, other people had theirs" (JAFL, 1943: 48).

In his Foreword to the *The Pueblo of San Felipe*, Leslie White, after thanking his Pueblo "friends," wrote:

> My greatest debt, though, is to Dr. Elsie Clews Parsons. Not only has she made my several field trips possible, but she has advised and encouraged me at every step, from the gathering of the data to the reading of the manuscripts. I have had the benefit of her wide and detailed knowledge of the Pueblo area for comparative purposes, and her understanding of general features of Pueblo culture as well. But most of all, I think, I value the inspiration which the example of her indefatigable labors and devotion to science has given me. I can only express my deep gratitude to her; my obligation will always remain. (White, 1922: no page)

Leslie Spier, a "regular" at our luncheon meetings in 1920 and later professor of anthropology at the University of New Mexico and for many years editor of the *Southwestern Journal of Anthropology*, wrote after her death:

> Her attitudes were grounded in intensity of feeling but were dispassionate in expression. She was wise, tolerant, and reticent; she never forced her views on anyone; it took much to provoke her into an expression of opinion of persons. Her friendship and encouragement were the signs by which she acknowledged integrity; sham, personal and intellectual, were recognized and ignored. (Spier, 1943: 243)

In the same volume, Alfred Kroeber wrote:

> Intellectually, her outstanding quality was perhaps the faculty of making up her mind. She forged her own convictions, often slowly, sometimes painfully; put them to the test; and did not lightly discard them. She did reforge them, to the end, as might seem needful. But their temper represented self-trial, experience, resolution, and tenacity against which contrary views were likely to shatter, especially if based on shallow enthusiasm or alloyed with facile dexterity or any ingredient of pretense. In this quality she was spiritually kin to Boas. (Kroeber, 1943b: 255)

And in 1928 Boas himself wrote on the first page of his *Keresan Texts:*

Dear Elsie,

I dedicate this book to you in sincere friendship and in remembrance of the weeks of joint labors. Accept it as a slight expression of gratitude for your energetic and unselfish labors that have brought about a revival of interest in Southwestern ethnology.... Those who have had the good fortune to be associated with you owe much to the stimulus that your thoughtful investigations have given to them.

Yours faithfully,

Franz Boas

Mead has commented, "With Dr. Parsons his relationship was always a little formal" (1959a: 346), but the passage she cites from Dr. Parsons' answer to these lines strongly belies this judgment. "Dear Dr. Boas," Parsons wrote, "I am delighted with your wish to dedicate to me the Keres texts—who would not be?—and with the expression you give it." (A little formal, one might say.) But she then continued: "As I used to tell you I *do* like compliments from friends and from boys, and I don't worry over whether or not I deserve them." (A little coy, one might say, but hardly a little formal.)

My own relation to Dr. Parsons fits well with the image evoked by Reichard, White, Spier, Kroeber, and Boas. She contributed to the costs of my first trip and financed my three subsequent trips to the Southwest completely, the last apparently without any suggestion from Dr. Boas and when she had already indicated that my tentative schematization of the structure of Cochiti was not at all to her liking—and she said so as late as 1939.[7]

Letters written to me from 1921 to 1927, which I reproduce in full, will do more than any words of mine to indicate Dr. Parsons' attitudes, scientific dedication, and methods of work.

The earliest letter I have (no year is given, but it was surely 1921) was sent from Gallup, N.M. in September, reaching me at Laguna, N.M., where Dr. Boas and I were still working. (After some weeks there we went on to Cochiti to break ground for an intensive study of that pueblo, which we carried further in the following June.) Her letter reads:

A full account of hunt practices would be of value, I think. My accounts have been fragmentary only, got from women or non-hunting men. As for the K'atsena accounts, if you could see the Yakohano [Laguna Corn Dance, called Darawee there] this coming Sunday and then get information on that—it would be of value. Without having seen any K'atsena dances at Laguna or elsewhere, I doubt if you could make much of the information; but why not try it?

Did the Cushing and Rychkberg reach you?

I'm on my way back to Jemez from the three days I allowed myself at Zuni. I saw the last night of the culminating day of the scalp dance, with a subsequent day for information on it. We thought it extinct. Had I known what it was to be—Mrs. Lewis'[8] telegram was garbled into "Stack dance," I would have strongly urged you and Dr. Boas to come on. It is probably unique, among the Pueblos, and although not as showy as the masked dances extremely interesting for its Plains Indian character.

E.C.P.

About all in tonight an attack of sinus, menstruating and three hours on a terrific road; but I got some good food at Zuni and the last two nights some unbroken sleep. The first night I spent, after arriving at 10:30, with the others around the pole. Brown hair, and Nick thinks it came from a barber shop.

Apparently Dr. Boas or I had written Dr. Parsons that I was getting data on hunting practices, and in December 1921 (under name of Esther Schiff), I gave my first paper at an annual meeting of the American Anthropological Association in a joint session with the American Folklore Society (the grand total of papers given in all sessions that year was 28). My paper was entitled "The Deer Hunt in the Southwest." (It was more than thirty years later, in 1954, that, stimulated by Charles H. Lange's account of hunting practices in Cochiti, I published my "Notes on Deer-Hunting Practices at Laguna Pueblo, New Mexico.") And Dr. Boas and I did see the Yakohano, and not only in Laguna, but the following week also in nearby Pohuati.

Dr. Parsons' next letter, dated June 15, 1922, and sent from Stonover Farms, Lenox, Mass., no doubt reached me at Cochiti before Dr. Boas and I joined Mrs. Boas and went on to Berkeley, where Dr. Boas was to lecture during the summer session. Her letter reads:

Dear Esther:

Your letter is very interesting and promising. Except as to dance patterns. Without seeing the dances or Kachina dances elsewhere I don't see how you can do much with that topic. Don't overlook these women's societies, and all data on the moiety organization of the Kwirana and Koshare.

As for disintegration in application of kinship terms it is loose among all the Pueblos. It will be a nice question for you to distinguish between that characteristic looseness and disintegration.

Too bad about your nice room and Mrs. Ripley [a pseudonym]. Why don't you explain to Dr. Boas?

Did you succeed in getting a census of society memberships?

The use of prayer-feathers by the layman and confining prayer-sticks to society members is interesting. That is the Jemez system, their term for society being "tie feathers."

Are there any Tewa or Taos visitors in Cochiti, or Felipe or San Domingo? Anything you could pick up from these sources would be of value.

E.C.P.

Find out definitely if no prayer-sticks are made by laymen, notably at the solstices.

Dr. Parsons' next letter, which was also sent from Stonover Farms, was written during the summer or early fall of 1924, that is, not long after she allegedly was "outraged" by the thought that Ruth Bunzel, without training, should go to Zuni. (In December 1922, I had married Walter S. Goldfrank, who had three sons — 6, 9, and 12 — by a previous marriage; our daughter was born in May 1924.)

Her letter reads:

Dear Esther:

My idea was to invite you to make a field trip for the Southwest society to [study] the Laguna split to Isleta. We think it is important to have that group studied to see what variations have occurred. The idea came to me in connection with you this month while I was making some very interesting comparisons between the Northern Tewa and their split off two hundred years ago to First Mesa. In the Laguna case we have another fixed date. From your Laguna knowledge you would be well qualified, also if the town prove difficult you would be good at working into it.

I have almost decided to go down for a month, Nov.-Dec. to the Northern Tewa. I do not propose that we go together, but at our mutual convenience, then after hearing from you I would go on to Albuquerque for a few days to consult with you, also to look up some points about Isleta.

How about it? But even if I didn't go, why not you? Leave behind a good nurse, and everybody will profit.

Sincerely,

Elsie Clews Parsons

Dr. Parsons also had four children—three sons and a daughter—and perhaps it was this similarity in our situations that led her at this

26

time to "invite" me to make a field trip for the Southwest Society. Ruth Benedict's reaction to my "acquired" family was quite different and, for someone who bewailed her own lack of children as she did, quite surprising. In her diary for January 15, 1923—just two weeks after I returned from my honeymoon—she wrote, "Call on Esther Goldfrank: I don't envy her" (Mead, 1959a: 60).

Dr. Parsons' suggestion fell on fertile soil. Despite a full and satisfying domestic life, my early feminist involvements (among other things, I had paraded up Fifth Avenue with a sizable Barnard contingent as part of the campaign of Votes for Women) encouraged me to think that, like Dr. Parsons, I might also mix marriage and anthropology. I had a "good nurse" for my infant daughter, a sympathetic husband, and a maiden aunt (by affinity) who was ready and happy to take over the reins of our household during my short absence. I left for Isleta early in November.

During my first nine days there I suffered many frustrations, and I must have told Dr. Parsons about them. On November 25, 1924 she wrote me from San Gabriel Ranch, Alcalde, New Mexico:

> Don't be discouraged. That you got somebody to take you in at once was an achievement. Story tellers will turn up. I suggest that you take down stories from Isletans. We have no accurate ones. I suppose you will be paying visits over to the Laguna settlement. Get an informant over there, if possible, and keep him or her secret from your host family. Look for old José's daughter around the likely places of the Laguna set. Look out for prayer-sticks. The Isletans use them too, planted in the middle of fields, where else I don't know.
>
> I have had contretemps too. My Taos man has not turned up yet—a broken buggy! So I did some work with a poorish Tesuque man. I have heard from my Hopi-Tewa man who will come. Please buy me a ticket from Winslow, Arizona, to Albuquerque or vice versa, if they will sell that way, explaining to the agent it is to send to someone at Winslow, who can't buy it there himself, and mail it to:
>> George Cochise
>> Polacca
>> Arizona

> If they won't sell you the ticket, send a postal money-order to G.C. Sorry to trouble you, but the time connection is difficult. I ought to be in Albuquerque and out to Isleta some time later next week, if only my Taos man turns up today or tomorrow. Good luck.
>
>> E.C.P.

Although Dr. Parsons and I were in the Southwest at the same time, we did not meet. Before I returned East, I was convinced that accomplishing anything worthwhile in Isleta would entail a much longer stay. I was also convinced that I could not leave my family whenever an opportunity for research offered, no matter how attractive it might be.

I gave a copy of my typed-up notes to Dr. Parsons (all of them virtually from a single informant), and during the winter of 1924-25 we met several times at her Harrison home to discuss problems they raised. Both of us recognized their fragmentary character and that they were completely unchecked. Dr. Parsons thought she had found a partial solution when she wrote me on August 5, 1925, again from Stonover Farm:

Dear Esther:

What would you say to inviting your Isleta man on East this late autumn, say from November 15 to Dec. 15? He could stay at my house or at yours, as much or as little as you wish. I would like to pay his traveling expenses and $5 a day. I would like to do some comparative Taos work with him and you could work on with your Isleta memoir. Do I recall rightly that he did not know folk tales? If so, it might be well to write to him now, if you think well of the plan, about it, suggesting that meanwhile he acquire from others what folk tales he can, at this untimely season.

Sincerely,

Elsie Clews Parsons

I could not, in my complicated household, board and work with Juan Abeita,[9] and in fact I did not think well of uprooting him so radically from his home environment. It was one thing to work with an informant 13 miles from his village unhampered by domestic responsibilities (see below), and quite another to bring him into an utterly strange setting without family, friends, or the festivals that were so much part of Pueblo life.

Dr. Parsons' offer was a generous one. She knew I did not want to go to the Southwest at this time—and she thought this would give me a chance to check my notes. In the end she herself went to Isleta in November 1925, found Juan Abeita and, as I had done, she worked with him outside his native village. She wrote me on November 27:

Dear Esther:

I stepped off at Albuquerque and motored to Isleta and within ten minutes had kidnapped Abeita ... *without* his daughter who had to stay to care for the grandfather. After two weeks of work here I took Abeita up to Taos, leaving him for a week's visit to relatives and detective work, I hope. This Sunday I expect him back. Meanwhile let me make some sort of a report to you. A word about Abeita as informant. He is frank enough, but of accuracy he has no sense whatever. He will string together ritual patterns in describing a ceremony in the way he thinks they should be, which is probably at times the way they are.

He has a very striking imaginative turn of mind, something I have never seen before in a Pueblo Indian. Of course how much is cultural and how much personal it is difficult to decide—when he is talking of bringing down the sun, moon, stars, or bringing in a living deer or the horned serpent, living, not an image. The Taos people have made reference to the *power* of the sacerdotalist in somewhat similar Plains Indian vein. And it is tempting to think that we have here a blend of Plains and Pueblo. In view of Abeita's psychological makeup our joint notes are bound to show many discrepancies. I will try to outline only what I am so far pretty sure of, thereby answering several of your queries. Within a week I will send you a more detailed report.[10]

E.C.P.

Following her return she sent me a copy of her notes. I have no memory of seeing her in 1926 (I had an operation in January and a complicated recovery), nor do I have any letter from her until June 17, 1927 when she wrote me from North Haven, Maine:

Dear Esther:

Will you please mail my Isleta duplicate ms. to Miss. M. J. Roderick, 217 Spring St., Newport, R.I. I am incorporating more material which I got last December from two Isleta women. Did you make a report on your Isleta notes at the annual A.A.A. meeting? And have you any plan for publishing them? If not and if you would care to intrust the editing to me, and if after looking them over again, I decide that they can be combined with my notes in one publication, I suggest that we publish a joint memoir. If this plan appeals to you I would like to do the editing this summer, soon in fact. My address will be North Haven, Maine.

I was very sorry not to get to your picnic party, which everybody said was most enjoyable. I came back from the West Indies field trip this year considerably below par and with no energy to spare for anything, except necessary chores, and that day I was especially low.

Sincerely yours,
Elsie Clews Parsons

My undated reply demonstrates the genuine give-and-take in our relation—despite my being 20 years her junior.

My Dear Dr. Parsons:

I am sorry you are not just as well as you could wish and trust you will soon feel yourself again. I had hoped you would come to the picnic as I should have liked to talk things over somewhat.

I have made no report of any kind on the Isleta material, but have written a short paper for the J.A.F.L., copy of which I enclose and which I would like to have returned when you have read it as it is my sole one.

I am very glad that you feel our material should be included in a joint publication, particularly as the bulk of it was obtained from the same informant, and I wonder whether you have any suggestion as to the form you would like it to take. Your material is so much fuller, it would seem wise to present it in the form indicated in your manuscript, while the duplication in our respective accounts would make it unnecessary to publish mine complete. However, the fact and character of the variations are in themselves interesting and warrant discussion. Don't you think this might appear in the form of a concluding chapter or appendix, incorporating the new material in my notes and worked out along the general lines of the paper I am enclosing. I think the elasticity evidenced in the two studies is characteristic of Pueblo attitudes and that this interesting point would be obscured if the material were presented piece-meal.

If you would like to have me work the material out along these lines, I should be glad to do so this summer, but it would be necessary for me to have your manuscript which I have already returned to your secretary as you requested.

Sincerely,
[Esther]

On July 1, 1927, she wrote me again from North Haven, Maine:

This is an interesting paper. The tales should be in print for the reader to refer to; but so tardy are the returns from the JAFL that they probably will be before the paper is published. The tales should be published together, of course, as intact variants and as part of the monograph. I think, as for your other material, some of it should also be edited in the same way, i.e., where you have an account of a ceremony that I have not, your account should be given whole. Where we both have accounts they should be combined in various ways depending on the data; but indicating the source, yours or mine. Commentary on the discrepancies might go into a special section, or you might write a paper on them similar to this one on the tales, for another publication. I would have to use my discretion as editor on these points, my primary object in the monograph being a clear and orderly presentation of the facts. To this end I should wish to have your notes written out merely as descriptive data, without comparison with mine or with other material. After that I could send you the duplicate ms. for your comparative discussion. You see I don't care to have description and discussion combined. Our methods of approach differ; that is why we cannot edit this material together. I cannot make this too clear at the start, because if I did not we would be sure to be involved in controversy later.

This Maine life has set me up wonderfully, as Westchester country never could.

As ever
E.C.P.

Abeita's variations from the wall of the Laguna Fathers are about the same as in his tales—animals placed differently, four anthropomorphic figures as against two, three stars as against one, you get a duck, I get a possible badger! But the patterns are there, O.K.

Dr. Parsons was entirely right—our approaches did differ. To be sure, we were both eager to establish patterns, but I was more concerned than she with larger structures and economic problems than with a mere juxtaposition of "descriptive data" (it may be of interest that 15 years before I heard the name Karl August Wittfogel, my notes on irrigation in Isleta went beyond what Dr. Parsons reported later in her monograph). Moreover, since we used the same informant, she had been able to go over my notes with him, elaborate and correct them. But their greatest value appeared to me to be their use in indicating what an informant questioned by one anthropologist might learn about his own society before being interviewed by another anthropologist. (The advantage to an anthropologist of having access to notes made previously needs no underlining. My later work with the Blood Indians of Alberta, Canada, benefited greatly from Clark Wissler's comprehensive studies on the U.S. Blackfoot. And Dr. Parsons would be the first to acknowledge that my small beginnings were a useful starting point for her fuller study.)

I must have sent Ruth Benedict a copy of Dr. Parsons' July 1 letter. On July 9 she wrote me from West Alton, New Hampshire:

31

Dear Esther:

Elsie goes up three points in my ranking. I never thought, last winter, that she would be as sensible. It would seem to me that your article for the AA discussing the points involved might be just your chance, and besides the material will all see the light of day and be paid for. You'd publish it differently, but I don't see any reason why this shouldn't come out all right. Yes, I will see that a note will accompany your article in the JAFL. Didn't you think the article sounded well? It's a good paper. I told them to put it first in the issue, but they'd already paged others articles first and it did not seem worth changing them. Position does not make much difference.

I'm starting Friday. My address will be Sacaton, Arizona. I feel somewhat "like the galley slave at night"—it's so nice up here I hate to go, and it seems ridiculous to leave Stanley.

Affectionately,
Ruth

Despite Benedict's optimism, Dr. Parsons and I were unable to cooperate on a joint monograph. To publish separately raised other problems. I would have had to wait until her material was in print before using it for comparison. Had my preliminary data been inserted at relevant places in a joint publication, it would have been easier to use. To reprint lengthy passages from a published and much more advanced monograph seemed an unnecessarily cumbersome and costly way of making my scientific points, although I did not consider them at all unimportant. Rightly or wrongly, I decided to rest on my paper, "Isleta Variants: A Study in Flexibility," which appeared in volume 39 of the *Journal of American Folklore*. The publication year is given as 1926, but on July 1, 1927, the number containing my article had not yet been distributed.

In her introduction to *Isleta, New Mexico* in the 47th Annual Report of the Bureau of American Ethnology for the year 1929-1930 (which appeared only in 1932), Dr. Parsons wrote:

Isleta has been a baffling place to the student of the Pueblos. Isletans are particularly secretive, and what information was obtained from them contained contradictions. The only student who ever lived in the Pueblo was Charles F. Lummis, and his interest in the life of the town has expressed itself scientifically only in a collection of folk tales rendered in a more or less literary form. So that when in 1924 Esther Schiff Goldfrank undertook a study of the Pueblo, and after much difficulty succeeded in securing an informant, there was matter for congratulation. Mrs.

Goldfrank has published an analysis of the folk tales she and I recorded, in the Journal of American Folklore.

In 1925, thanks to Mrs. Goldfrank's introduction, I was able to work with her informant where he and I were not subject to Pueblo inquisitorial pursuit. It was soon apparent that our fluent informant was of a type unusual among the Pueblos. Shrewd as he could be at times, he was exceedingly credulous. . . .

That a man of this mentality should not be accurate in description at large is not surprising. And Juan Abeita would be, in fact, quite as glib about ceremonial he had not seen as about what he had seen. . . . But in all his descriptions he does not depart, I think, from the pattern, i.e., he may improvise the combination of patterns, but not the patterns themselves. His very credulity is quite according to the pattern. . . . However, it is obvious enough that the outcome of work with such an informant by two students must vary. This fact, the emotional irresponsibility of our informant, as well as differences in our own methods of study, have led Mrs. Goldfrank and me to keep our observations in separate forms." (201 f.)

My own feeling is that it was neither the variations in our accounts nor the emotional irresponsibility of our informant, but the differences in our methods of study—more precisely in our "methods of approach," as she herself had written on July 1, 1927—that led us to reject joint publication.

But this was not to be the end of the matter, although after the publication of my monograph on Cochiti in 1927 I pretty much dropped out of anthropology. To be sure, I still read the journals, but I took no courses, did no writing, and cannot remember meeting with anthropologists, not even with Dr. Boas, until I returned to New York almost a decade later. And it was 1940, shortly after I married Karl August Wittfogel, before Dr. Parsons, at dinner in her New York City apartment (besides us, only Duncan Strong and her daughter were present) referred again to our Isleta experience. Said she, "Esther, you were certainly a good sport to turn over your Isleta notes to me." I answered that at the time I was sure I would not soon be able to go back into the field—in fact, it was 1939 before I did—and that I was then convinced, and indeed am still convinced, that it is deplorable to sit on untouched notes for decades (as many anthropologists do) when these notes can be useful to others. Dr. Parsons smiled "her slow direct smile," as Kroeber described it in 1943, and said nothing further.

I cannot help thinking she was trying to say, without putting it into words, that she recognized certain deficiencies in her treatment of my data; she had neither cited them specifically in her Isleta

33

monograph nor dealt in any substantial way with the theoretical points I had raised, not even with those developed in my "Isleta Variants."

Dr. Parsons died December 19, 1941. Gladys Reichard, her literary executor, phoned me shortly afterward to say that she had dedicated a still unpublished volume of paintings by an Isletan Indian to me. Said Reichard, "I have never known Elsie to dedicate anything to anyone before." Actually the dedication was to me and Julian H. Steward and it read, "To whom I owe the opening of Isleta." Years later Steward assured me he had never worked in Isleta; in fact, the only contribution he might have made was in forwarding to Dr. Parsons the letter the artist had addressed to the BAE. Years later I also learned that the covering letter had been written by Dr. Matthew W. Stirling, the then director of the BAE (see Goldfrank, 1967: 5). But whatever Steward's role may have been, I did indeed open up Isleta for Dr. Parsons. And when Kroeber wrote that she could "reforge" her convictions "as might seem needful," he was speaking truly. In her encyclopedic *Pueblo Indian Religion*, which had appeared in 1939, a year or so before our dinner meeting, she had mastered and marshalled, as Spier has pointed out, an enormous amount of data, and in her three terminal chapters she dealt with "variation, borrowing and other processes of change"— topics that manifestly went beyond her "primary object" in 1927: "a clear and orderly presentation of the facts."

And now let Elsie Clews Parsons speak for herself. In her brief conclusion to *Social Freedom* she wrote what may well be considered her credo:

> Each [social] category more or less strives to impose its character upon what lies without its natural boundaries. Between them the categories divide up phenomena much as the Chinese divide up nature into the elements of water, fire, wood, metal, and earth, or as we classified in our childhood in a game called "Twenty Questions," its first question always, "animal, vegetable or mineral?" From such a rigid classification the mind as it matures seeks escape. So a maturing culture struggles against its categories. At first it aims for mobility within them and then, as in these latter days, for freedom away from them. Ultimately, the "fetishistic influence" of the categories of age and sex, kinship, occupation, neighbourhood will count merely like other facts in life. As factors in personality they will have to be reckoned with, but as social barriers they will be negligible. The freest possible contact between personalities will be recognized as the *raison d'être* for society, and to the developing of personal relationships will be turned the energies spent in the past upon blocking and hindering them. No more segregated groups, no more covetous claims

through false analogy, no more spheres of influence, for the social categories. And then the categories having no assurances to give to those unafraid of change and tolerant of unlikeness, to those of the veritable new freedom, to the whole-hearted lovers of personality, then the archaic categories will seem but the dreams of a confused and uneasy sleep, nightmares to be forgotten with a new day.

And this in 1915. It remained as vital for Dr. Parsons until her death as it is for us today.

RUTH BENEDICT

When Ruth Benedict came to Columbia in 1921, she was 33 years old, a Phi Beta Kappa graduate of Vassar College. She had been a social worker, a teacher in a girls' school in California, a serious though still unpublished writer of prose and poetry, the prose strongly feminist, the poetry turbulent, passionate, and searching. She had been married to Stanley Benedict, a biochemist of parts, for seven years, and from 1919 to 1921 she had been a student at the New School for Social Research in New York City, where she took courses given by Elsie Clews Parsons and Alexander Goldenweiser. Her diary for 1923 clearly shows that it was Goldenweiser who had been her major interest there and, inferably, the person who in 1921 induced her to go to Columbia—and Boas. She rented a room near the University, where she stayed weekdays. Weekends she usually spent at Bedford Hills with her husband, who had no stomach for anthropologists. During a day-long picnic at their charming old white frame house, to which I, along with Boas and several others, had been invited, Stanley Benedict remained barricaded in his darkroom, ostensibly developing pictures he had taken.

Relations between Ruth and Stanley Benedict were already strained when she registered as a graduate student in anthropology at Columbia. Even before they married he had written her on January 14, 1913, ". . . Ruth—the question is *whether we'd be happier together* or apart . . . your mask is getting thicker and thicker. . . . You shouldn't *have* to wear it at all, for it's certain to grow to be a part of you if you do—and then you'll be altogether alone" (Mead, 1959a: 540). She herself in her Journal for "Oct. 1912, Sunday" had referred to the mask she wore to conceal "my real *me*" (119).[11] In an undated manuscript written seemingly around 1909 she already speaks of "the charm of concealment" (116).[12]

Ruth Fulton and Stanley Benedict were married in the summer of 1914. In October 1916 Ruth wrote in her journal, "Again another winter. It is hard for me to look with any satisfaction on the two winters that are passed" (135). Winters manifestly, of domesticity, good works, and some writing. "Mary Wollstonecraft," she continued, "I do believe in—but will she ever be published? I doubt it, and more and more I know that I want publication" (135). On Christmas 1916, she again notes in her journal, "I've pledged my word to a 'business in life' now. Last night Stanley and I talked. We hurt each other badly . . . he is inexorable. . . . I said that for the sake of our love—our friendship rather—I must pay my way in a job of my own. . . . He said that whatever the job, it would not hold me; nothing ever had, social work or teaching. Children might for a year or two, no more (138). . . . I told him he should see. My past list of jobs proved nothing. . . . Now I understood. I cared and cared deeply, and for what I wanted I was willing to pay high. I should prove that I could do better than to drift into a meaningless routine. . . . I have committed myself to the endeavor for *success—success* in writing . . ." (139). In October 1920 she wrote in her journal, "There is good in me, and Oh! there is great good in Stanley. . . . Why must we go on hurting each other so cruelly. . . . So we grow more and more strangers to the other . . ." (143). On January 1, 1923 she wrote in her diary, "The New Year in with sheets of rain, and a southeast wind. . . . Toward sunset, cleared under gale from northwest—Walked in its teeth as far as sleeting roads allowed, past farm house and to Switz House and played Go Bang![13] —A good day" (56). The following Saturday, again at Bedford Hills she wrote, "Go bang till 11 p.m.!! I beat two to one" (57).[14] A week later she wrote "Go bang till ten" (59); on January 21, "Played Go-bang with S——. A good day" (61); on the next Saturday, "met S——. Evening played Go Bang" (62); and on the next day, "More Go Bang" (62); on February 3, she wrote, "Go bang with S—— night" (64); on February 25, "It's as if we inhabited opposing poles" (66); and on March 8, "I dread intense awareness. . . . And oh, I am lonely—" (67). The last words of her poem "Preference," which seems to have been written in 1925, but which certainly expresses thoughts harbored much earlier, reads, " 'Twere best we kissed before the wind and went as smokeclouds do" (178).

The mask Stanley Benedict had wanted her to remove in 1913 was still on in 1921; and the depth of the chasm that separated her from her husband during these years was barely sensed at Columbia. When we first met, she had told me, "I don't have children, so I might as well have Hottentots." And when she and I lunched together the day after I had decided to marry Walter Goldfrank—and his three boys—and indicated that in the bright light of morning I was beginning to recognize

36

the responsibility I had so complacently assumed the previous night, she asked, "When will you see him again?" "Tonight," I answered. And then she said, "If you have fun, it will be all right." Had I known then what I know now, I would have found her simple solution more than suspect. I would have guessed that she probably already felt, as she wrote in her journal in June 1934, that "the great reward" her temperament had given her was "detachment and unconcern" (155). But I wanted to believe—and that night Walter and I did "have fun"—and that and a great deal more during our years together.

As a student, Ruth Benedict was friendly but aloof, nodding assent or smiling quizzically at some passing remark, unaggressive in manner, a person of few words. Contrasting her own and her husband's way of dealing with situations, she had written in her journal in October 1920—that is, shortly before she came to Columbia, "It is my necessary breath of life to understand and expression is the only justification of life that I can feel without prodding. The greatest relief I know is to have something in words . . ." (143). But it was through the written and not the spoken word that she found relief, and it is her poems that particularly reveal her deepest passions and frustrations. That she found equal relief in her studies may well be doubted. On March 8, 1923, she had written in her diary, "It seems to me terrible that life is passing, that my program is to fill the twenty-four hours each day with obliviousness, with work" (67)—and this just as she was about to get her Ph.D. degree. But however uncongenial her routine, she labored with utmost concentration, and in December 1921 she read her first important anthropological paper, "The Vision in Plains Culture," at the same joint session of the AAA and AFLS at which I read my report of deer-hunting practices in Laguna. Benedict's paper clearly showed her broad knowledge of Plains literature (to which Goldenweiser had probably introduced her) and the ability that later became her trademark—to distinguish patterns of culture. But her basic method of analysis was still the diffusionist method that Boas had utilized so exactingly in his Tsimshiam Mythology (1909-10) that his students had employed and were employing in their various studies, particularly in their studies of Plains society—Kroeber for the Arapaho, Lowie for the Crow, Spier for the Sun Dance. However, her last paragraphs show that she was already concerned with configurations as well as patterns of culture, and that, for her, recognition of the psychological set of given societies was indispensable for understanding their similarities and dissimilarities.

Having discussed various Plains tribes and noted the uneven distribution of traits customarily linked to the vision quest, she compared the Crow and the Pawnee. "Any survey of Pawnee vision complex must be inadequate," she wrote, "unless we take also into account a difference in psychological attitude which places them at the opposite pole, for instance from the Crow." She then gave the following Crow text as typical: "Medicine Crow fasted and prayed for four days. He cut off a finger joint and offered it to the Sun. 'Sun, look at me. I am poor. I wish to own horses. Make me wealthy. That is why I give you my little finger'." The Pawnee, on the other hand, "made the transition from this view of the vision as a mechanistic means of controlling forces and events, to a view of it as a means of spiritual contact. That is, a certain transfer of emphasis has taken place from material to spiritual values" (34). After listing numerous diversities present, "even in one culture area such as the Plains," she noted that "correlated" with them "are and must be psychological attitudes." And in conclusion she asked, "Is it not our first task to inquire as carefully as may be in definite areas to what things the religious experience attaches itself, and to estimate their heterogeneity and their infinite multiplicity?" (35).

At this time Benedict may not have been familiar with Haeberlin's "The Idea of Fertilization in the Culture of the Pueblo Indians" which was published as an *AAA Memoir* in 1916 and which did for Pueblo and Navajo society almost exactly what she was doing for the Crow and Pawnee.[15] But Haeberlin's conclusions were amazingly similar. "Every cultural phenomenon," he had written, "involves some psychic process, which determines the singularity of its significance. Thus every individual case of diffusion, for example, is not a mechanical phenomenon of historical contact and therefore not automatic, but is rather a phenomenon with a specific psychological content and is therefore of singular nature." Diffusion, psychic process, singularity—the Haeberlin-Benedict triad!

For some time before I joined Dr. Boas, the Southwest had been a major field of interest, and this continued to be so during my years at Columbia, and indeed for many afterward. Kroeber had written on the Zuni; Lowie on the Hopi; Parsons had done ethnological work in several pueblos; Nelson, Spier, and Alfred Kidder had done archaeological work in New Mexico; Goddard had been among the Apache; and, as already noted, Dr. Boas, in the late spring and early summer of 1919, had accompanied Dr Parsons to Laguna, and would accompany him to Laguna in the summer of 1920.

Benedict entered upon her study of Zuni mythology in 1923; and in 1928 at the 23rd International Congress of Americanists held in New York City, she read her paper "Psychological Types in the Cultures of the Southwest." Her inspiration stemmed from Nietzsche and it was in this paper that she first developed her Apollonian and Dionysian classification of cultures. "The Southwest Pueblos," she stated, "are, of course, Apollonian, and in the consistency with which they pursue the proper valuations of the Apollonian they contrast with nearly the whole of aboriginal America" (Proceedings, 1950:573).

I do not think I am exaggerating when I say that her "of course" is convincingly refuted by the writings in the late nineteenth century of Voth (*The Oraibi Powamu Ceremony*), Cushing (*My Adventures in Zuni*), and Stevenson (*The Zuni Indians*), and in the twentieth by those of Elsie Clews Parsons ("The Zuni A'doshlĕ and Suukĕ"), Lee W. Simmons (ed., *Sun Chief*), Julian H. Steward ("Notes on Hopi Ceremonials in their Initiatory Form in 1927-1928"), Dorothy Eggan ("The General Problem of Hopi Adjustment"), Wittfogel and Goldfrank ("Some Aspects of Pueblo Mythology and Society"), Goldfrank ("Socialization, Personality, and the Structure of Pueblo Society"), Edward P. Dozier ("The Rio Grande Pueblos," in Edward H. Spicer, ed. *Perspectives in American Indian Culture Change*, and *The Pueblo Indians of North America*)—and, ironically and devastatingly, in the *Zuni Texts* assembled by Bunzel, who was Benedict's major source of information for her famous, stimulating, and highly problematical *Patterns of Culture*, which appeared in 1934 and upheld, without change or reservation, the Apollonian character of Zuni society that she had first presented to a professional international audience six years earlier. In fact, she told me that in its first year the paperback *Patterns of Culture* had sold 10,000 copies, compared to the 5,000 in hard cover in the preceding ten years. When I asked her whether, in view of the new material and new concepts being presented, she had included a new introduction, she was surprised at the question, and answered, without hesitation or excuse, "No, it has been published just as it was printed originally."

Writing of a time shortly before and immediately after Benedict's arrival at Columbia, Mead notes that "the atmosphere of the department was being humanized as first one of [Boas'] Barnard graduate secretaries, Esther Schiff Goldfrank, and then a second, Ruth Bunzel, moved from the close relationship of a secretary to that of a student." She adds that within "the German Jewish ethos which they shared, the remote, frightening Herr Professor became 'Papa Franz' to all of us" (Mead, 1959a: 345).

Actually the onset and development of this humanizing process was quite otherwise. It will be remembered that, after the disturbing events of December 30, 1919, Dr. Boas seemed less austere and, perhaps as a corollary, more accessible to his students, and particularly to his women students. He had always been more than tolerant toward me, but it was only after the weeks we spent together during June and July 1920 in Laguna, where he shed his role of employer to become, in effect, my "father-protector," that I began speaking of him—and to him—as "Papa Franz." And it was not long before he and I began speaking of "Mama Franz,"—a mode of identification Mrs. Boas also soon adopted when referring to herself.[16]

It should be clear that the origin of the address "Papa Franz" had no more to do with "the German Jewish ethos" I shared with Ruth Bunzel, who replaced me in the fall of 1922—a full two years after my first field trip with Dr. Boas—than it had to do with the German Jewish ethos I shared with him. But there is no doubt that this mode of address pleased Dr. Boas when I first used it and that, in later years, as Mead says, he became " 'Papa Franz' to all of us" (345).

One last point. In *An Anthropologist at Work*, Mead has a chapter headed "The Years as Boas' Left Hand." In it she records Ruth Benedict's involvement with Columbia's Department of Anthropology and shows how slowly official recognition was given this unusually talented and, in many ways, unusually strange woman and scholar. In 1930, after carrying a substantial teaching load for years, she was still only Lecturer. The following year she became Assistant Professor, but even this title did not adequately reflect the responsibilities thrust upon her in 1931 and 1932, when Dr. Boas was seriously ill. Writes Mead, "Then almost the whole conduct of the department fell to Ruth Benedict" (347). When Dr. Boas returned to his desk, and even after he became Emeritus, he still depended on her.

And Benedict depended on him no less. In a letter sent from Pasadena, California on December 26, 1939, she wrote, "Your physical weakness distresses me daily . . . there has never been a time since I've known you that I have not thanked God all the time that you existed and that I know you. I can't tell you what a place you fill in my life" (417).

In view of what Mead has written about the Benedict-Boas relation, her chapter heading, "The Years as Boas' Left Hand" implies something less than the reality. If she was saying that for Benedict, Boas was God on earth (see Mark 16: 19, 14: 62, King James Bible), this surely implies something more than the reality. To my mind, to invoke a favorite Boas phrase, "The Years as Boas' Right Hand" would more accurately have introduced the story Mead was about to tell. But this is a small criticism. Mead once said to me that, despite years of close friendship and scholarly exchange with Ruth Benedict, there was much she learned about her only after her death. For myself, I can say it was only after reading Mead's 1959 book that my own experiences with Ruth Benedict became wholly meaningful.

5. I BECOME A FIELD-WORKER

In the spring of 1920, I had already made plans to join three of my New York friends on my first trip West. We expected to leave sometime in July. Late in April I learned that Dr. Boas was returning to Laguna in June to continue his study of the Keresan language. I then started coaxing, and those who know me well will testify that I don't give up easily. "Why," I asked him, "since I am also going West, shouldn't I leave before my friends, stop off at Laguna and be some sort of help to you?" Once he had mastered his surprise at my ingenüousness, he replied, "What in the world would I do with you in the field?" Actually, there wasn't much I could do for him—but time in the field, however short, could do a lot for me. Eventually Dr. Boas weakened. He would talk it over with Dr. Parsons who, with Grant Lafarge, also expected to spend some time in Laguna in June.

Presumably, Dr. Boas wrote her by hand. There is no typed copy in the APS files of any letter on this matter. In any event, on April 24, 1920, and without mincing words, Dr. Parsons wrote him by hand from Harrison.

> Dear Dr. Boas:
>
> Taking Miss Schiff or not is really up to you. As I am going to take in Zuni, Hopi, and a pueblo near Albuquerque there will be a considerable amount of time when I won't be with you and she would be on your hands for I would not ask her to go along with me. On our journey or settled at Laguna or the other Keresan pueblo (how about San Felipe?) that we may select, with you as a buffer to my prejudices against my own sex, I wouldn't object in the least to her company. And if she gets to work, I'd be glad to contribute the expenses of informants, and if she is of service to you in any way, her boarding expenses. So you see it is entirely up to you. I write all this as I doubt if I [will] come in to lunch on Tuesday—the motor trip is so tedious and takes so much time. I find I don't have to be back before the middle of July, so let's consider again not starting until June (or perhaps May 25).

And then on to really important matters:

> I enclose a copy of the Anwik [?] paper which I think I'll send to the Journal of the Anthropological Institute, since so much of the other material was published there. I'd be grateful if you'd read it and point out N.W. coast resemblances.
>
> Yours,
E.C.P.

Dr. Boas must have been a good pleader. I was elated. Some of my aunts and uncles thought it dangerous for a young woman to live in an Indian village and even more dangerous to live there with a male companion, even if he was Professor Franz Boas and almost forty years my senior. I had no such concerns.

The Southwest had been a frequent topic of conversation at the Tuesday lunches, and it was not long before I came to understand how intriguing—and how frustrating—research could be in this area, with striking similarities between villages and tantalizing differences in historical experience, structure, and language. Even today the strands of knowledge remain tangled. Despite a more refined methodology and the great increase in information, reconstructions are still little more than sophisticated guesses (cf. Fox, 1967).

Dr. Boas and I left New York separately—I on June 10, with a stop-over in Colorado Springs, where I stayed for a couple of days. There I joined a group of local tourists on a jaunt up to Pike's Peak. I had had no previous experience with high altitudes and after a cocky farewell to our automobile, which had gone as far as was feasible, I struck out, without pause, for the summit. I never reached it. Gasping and groggy, I staggered back to the car. It was not to be my last defeat by a mountain.

In Colorado Springs I learned that no "good" train stopped at Laguna (actually, at New Laguna, an off-shoot of the old village three miles away). I settled for the only alternative—an upper berth on a "tourist" train that could be flagged to a stop. I boarded late in the day. Like all uppers, my berth had no window—nor did it have a light or bell to summon assistance. In the morning, I dressed as best I could, opened the curtains, and wig-wagged until the porter came and helped me down.

The lower berth was occupied by a plump elderly mother and her plump elderly daughter. The car was already suffused with cooking odors; and passengers were already boiling coffee and frying eggs in a recess for this purpose at one end of the car. Women in mother-hubbards or kimonos were awaiting their turn. My two section companions munched oranges and bread and butter. I had brought no food and was delighted when the train stopped at a station that boasted a Harvey House where one could choose between quick (and cheap) service at a counter and a leisurely (and more expensive) meal in the dining room. I chose the counter. When I returned to my seat, my two ladies had finished breakfast. The porter had righted our section and I spent the morning listening to the never-married daughter's woeful tales of life in Colorado.

All this has nothing to do with field work in an Indian Pueblo, and there have surely been more bizarre ways of approaching an anthropological site. But for me it was a first, and I tell about it since this "homey" mode of travel is no longer possible in our country—in fact, it was eliminated during World War II. And for what it is worth, I report on the rest of "my day" on my way to Laguna, N.M.

Shortly before lunchtime I went to the platform to smoke—there was no club car on this train. I was joined by a man of middle years, apparently moved by the same desire. We exchanged the usual commonplaces—the peculiarities of our train (he was obviously an Easterner too), the passengers, and the weather; and when the train stopped—again at a Harvey House station—he and I made our way to the counter and found two seats side by side. After lunch, he invited me to join him in his otherwise unoccupied section. Then we went beyond the commonplaces. He told me he was on his way to the Republican convention in San Francisco, and from there to the Philippines on an official mission. I told him I was getting off at Laguna, sometime after eleven. He looked at me in amazement, and asked, "What do you expect to do in Laguna in the middle of the night?" I answered, "I am meeting Professor Boas of Columbia University." Before I could tell him why, he exclaimed, "I know Boas. We have offices in the same building. I'm Walter Pitkin of the School of Journalism." I knew of his book, *Life Begins at Forty*, which was extremely popular, although at this time it had little allure for me. At 11:30 he handed me over to a surprised Professor Boas and after a quick exchange of "hellos" we waved him on his way.

LAGUNA, N.M., JUNE 17-30, 1920

Dr. Boas and I lugged my bulky carryall across the tracks to the "hotel" where he was staying—Dr. Parsons, who had stopped there on her way to and from Zuni "in the years 1917-1918" called it a "house" (cf. Parsons, 1920b). I was quickly settled in my simply furnished room on the second floor. Besides an iron bed, small pine bureau, and straight chair, it contained those necessary adjuncts of semi-civilized life—a wash bowl, pitcher, slop pail, and chamber pot. I fell asleep quickly.

The next morning I made a short tour of inspection. Our hotel was a moderate-sized structure of weathered wood. As I remember it, there was a combination living-dining room, the most prominent object in it being, quite understandably, a large dining table. Beyond it loomed the sizable kitchen, ruled over by Margaret Eckerman,[17] the proprietor's wife. Outside and to the left a covered walk led to the privy. The land roundabout was flat, sandy and empty, except for a few small cedar trees—a marked contrast, as I would soon learn, to Old Laguna with its closely placed adobe houses set on a rocky hillside and its fine view of Mt. Taylor, the most sacred shrine of the Laguna villagers, over which the cloud spirits hovered to predict "the outlook for good crops and success in hunting" (Parsons, 1918: 184f.; Boas, 1928: 38, 194).

43

Besides being our host, Mr. Eckerman drove us mornings, if his car and health permitted, to Old Laguna where Dr. Boas and I, and later Dr. Parsons, worked with our several informants until he came for us in mid- or late-afternoon. He was White and in his forties, his face furrowed and tanned, his hands horny, his manner gruff. However hard he may have worked in his early years, his chief occupation now was the hardly onerous task of driving drummers and tourists to their desired destinations. His wife (Dr. Parsons speaks of her as Mrs. E. F. Eckerman, but in my diary I refer to her husband as "Robert") was a mixed blood—her father was W. G. Marmon, the brother of Robert W. Marmon, who had come to Laguna as a government school teacher in 1862 and had been governor of the village at the time of the great split off to Isleta around 1880. Both Marmon brothers married Laguna townswomen. Margaret's mother and her mother's sister and brother, Giwire, a *Kurena Shikani* medicine man, had been, along with a close friend and helper of the latter, Dr. Parsons' major informants. Margaret's mother died in 1918, Giwire in June 1919. Margaret had interpreted for the four of them.

Margaret Eckerman was soft-spoken, patient, and hard-working. Usually she was clothed in that symbol of acculturation, the mother-hubbard. (I never saw her in the traditional handwoven black wool manta, skin mocassins, and leggings still being worn by many women in Old Laguna.) She kept the house neat with the help of her two oldest though still small daughters (there were six Eckerman children, ranging from babyhood to 8 or 10 years of age)—but she was an atrocious cook. After joining us, Mr. Lafarge, who was quite a gourmet and fancied himself as a chef, took over whenever he could. Once, as the *pièce de resistance* he served up a cheese omelet with jelly. Dr. Boas strongly disliked melted cheese. He looked at me across the table, took one mouthful and quit. Nothing was said, but Mr. Lafarge was obviously dismayed. I cheered him by eating with gusto. Mrs. Parsons just ate. Food meant little to her—good or bad—and she was quite content to eat an apple at midday and call it lunch. Not I. I carried a sandwich with me every morning—and was often impatient for the session to end so I could devour it.

In 1920, Dr. Boas and I worked entirely in Old Laguna. Having been there the previous year, he had his contacts. In his Keresan Texts he names his informants: Ko'ᵗ\ʸe, from whom he obtained "the bulk" of his material, Pedro Martin, Gʸ i̱'mi, Robert Marmon, Solomon Day and "a woman called Tsai'tʸ'i." Of Robert Marmon, Dr. Parsons wrote, "To native ceremonial he is indifferent, not having attended the solstice ceremonies" (Parsons, 1920: 109, n.4). Ko'ᵗʸe's "American name" was Robert Brown. It is almost certain that Margaret Eckerman was the original go-between for Dr. Parsons in 1917-18. In her introduction to her *Laguna Genealogies* (1923), Dr. Parsons names Margaret Marmon, surely Margaret Marmon Eckerman, as her English-speaking informant. Moreover, at this time it was almost impossible to go beyond an initial contact—and this was also the situation in Cochiti in 1921 and 1922. Thirty years later Charles H. Lange was able to do so. But when Dr. Boas and I worked there we were still compelled to rely on the same little company of progressives who were tolerant of the White man and the U.S. government and were usually kin or friends.

Some time after breakfast on that first morning in the Southwest, Mr. Eckerman drove Dr. Boas and me to Old Laguna. Dr. Boas took me first to the house of Jennie Day (as I call her in my diary), with whom he and Dr. Parsons had lived in 1919. In her *Laguna Genealogies*, Dr. Parsons refers to her as Jennie Johnson, using her husband's patronymic, and in my 1921 deer-hunting paper I do also. ("Day" was in all probability Jennie's maiden name.) Her mother was the then Mrs. Brown, the wife of Robert Brown. And it seemed altogether likely that it was through Jennie's initiative that Dr. Boas met that other "Day"— Solomon Day—who, along with his wife, Katie, and their almost constant associate, Carl Leon, became my major informants in Laguna in 1921—and my best friends there (see correspondence on pp. 62-67).

Jennie was expecting me. She was, I judged, in her forties, and like most Pueblo women, short and thick-set. She gave an impression of self-confidence and capability, perhaps reflecting the fact that descent in Laguna was still counted through the maternal line.

Jennie's house was very neat and comfortably appointed. I remember being particularly struck by her sewing machine. Laguna was a comparatively new settlement—not much more than 300 years old, (Parsons, 1939: 888), and the Pueblo had been strongly exposed to outside influences. It was near the Atchison, Topeka, and Santa Fe Railroad, and many Laguna men found working for this company a lucrative way of life (see letters of Carl Leon and Solomon Day below). In my diary I wrote, "At first the village struck me as very *nouveau*. A lot of Albuquerque furniture, cheap prints, tin roofs, and ruffled petticoats ripped up for bed sheets."

Apparently I didn't start working immediately. My diary continues: "Took a long walk in the sun over the sand dunes with Dr. B. and came back pretty well petered out. Then started with Mrs. Brown (Jennie's mother) and Alice Marmon as interpreter." Dr. Boas had gone on his way to work elsewhere in the village.

Dr. Parsons, in her *Laguna Genealogies*, has this to say about Jennie Johnson, whose Indian name is Dzaid'yuwi´. Jennie, she notes, was "communicative," but also "an extremely restless informant" who "much preferred housework to systematic presentation and discussion of kinship terms. It is likely also that she was 'talked to' either by her husband [no. 17 in Genealogy IV] (Parsons, 1923a) or others about the danger her relatives ran from giving me their names." In a footnote, Dr. Parsons writes, "Within the year one brother-in-law did meet with an untimely fate, death from lightning—but this peculiarly supernaturalistic accident was never thrown up against me" (Introduction, 139). Apparently, "after living for a few years in the rather large household of Dzaid'uywai's mother," Jennie and her husband "decided to move out. I'g'ugai never got on with his stepfather-in-law [Robert Brown] whom both . . . condemned as lazy."

> Dzaid'uywi's maternal grandfather Si·'rowaisiwa (Gen. II, 14) who lived in the household and who as a weaver and sheep owner was well off, bought for Dzaid'uywi the rear room of her present house. In the course of time the couple bought, with money from sheep given Dzaid'uywi by the same grandfather and from I'g'ugai's daily wages [he worked for Whites in the Irrigation Service], the two front rooms of the house. The rear room and one of the front rooms belong to Dzaid'uywi, the other front room to I'g'ugai. It was Dzaid'yuwi's two rooms we [Dr. Parsons and Dr. Boas in 1919] occupied, and she asserted quite emphatically that she did not have to consult her husband about renting, for the rooms were hers. (Spellings as in Parsons, 1923a: 177)

Dr. Parsons also notes on the same page that in Laguna "male ownership in houses is a familiar idea." But she adds that while "in practice there is conjugal pooling of property . . . there is no pooling in the theory of ownership"—that is, property is still held to descend matrilineally.

On that first afternoon, Jennie and I went over to her mother's house to work. In my diary I wrote: "Mrs. Brown's house was not as clean as Jennie's and lots more children, most with whooping cough. The older people have trachoma. Mrs. B. practically blind. A new baby sans papa, but with a cousin's husband suspected."

For me, it was an exciting first session. The recording of cooking recipes and methods of cooking was continually punctuated by crying and whooping children and uninvited callers, no doubt eager to check on what was happening. When they learned what we were doing, they proved eager to show their knowledge of the culinary arts. The end result: "general confusion."

During the next days I concentrated on cooking and allied matters, and it wasn't long before I found the interruptions quite bearable—in fact, an important part of the Laguna ethos. When Dr. Parsons arrived we joined forces and continued an investigation of the medicinal uses of plants that she had begun the previous year. My memory is that several women brought us specimens that were later identified, sometimes after considerable argument.

In my diary I note that one afternoon an old Indian woman, a shiwana cheani, was our informant—I don't give her name. At the start she was much more concerned that someone might learn she was divulging secret medical knowledge than with the money she would receive for it—but in the end, and probably because the damage was done, she demanded double pay since Dr. Parsons and I were both taking notes. Dr. Parsons was treasurer, and she paid our informant the amount that had been agreed on when the session began. That put Dr. Parsons in the clear, but our medicine "man" refused ever again to work with me alone or with both of us together. I was able to continue my inquiry into medicinal uses with another old woman who had lived with Whites in Gallup. My only comment on her was, "Interesting to see how she uses her Indian secrets and civilized methods."

Before Dr. Parsons' arrival, Dr. Boas and I, after lunching, would walk out over the dunes. Whenever we could, without arousing suspicion, we peered beneath the cedar trees hoping to find prayer-sticks. Dr. Parsons had "collected" some previously and, as can be seen from her letter to me on June 15, 1922, she continued to be interested in their identification. In *Pueblo Indian Religion* and speaking generally, she wrote,

> Indeed it can be said that Pueblo ceremonial consists of prayer-stick-making and offering together with prayer and other ritual. Buried in field or riverbank or riverbed; cast under shrub or tree or into pits; sunk in water, in springs, pools, lakes, river or irrigation ditch; carried long distances to mountain tops; immured in house or kiva wall or closed-up niche; set under the floor or in the rafters, in cave or boulder or rock-built shrine; placed on altar or around image or corn fetish . . . held in hand during ceremonials or cherished at home for a stated period or for life, prayer-sticks are used by members of all ceremonial groups, and in the West by "poor persons" [read: persons not belonging to a society], even by children. (Parsons, 1939: 270)

According to my diary, the prayer-sticks of the ordinary man or woman (i.e., persons not affiliated with any society) were some 6 or 7 inches long and about as wide as a thumb. Black paint covered all but two or three inches near the pointed top end, which was scooped out and painted green for the man to recall the valued turquoise, symbolic of strength and winter, or yellow for the woman to recall ripe corn, symbolic of fertility and summer. Black lines indicated eyes, nose, and mouth, and feathers were tied to the rounded bottom.

The prayer-stick of the cheani or medicine men differed from these and also differed from society to society. The prayer-stick of the shiwana (thundercloud) cheani, I noted, was carved in a zig-zag to represent lightning. On one side it was painted yellow, on the other green. Since I never saw this shiwana cheani prayer-stick, my notes were probably based on a description given me by Dr. Parsons, who had gotten it from José, the shiwana cheani with whom she had worked previously (Parsons, 1920b:87).

These noon-time hunts were not very rewarding—and perhaps this was what we deserved for daring to come between the people of Laguna and the spirits whose help they were seeking for their own or the community's benefit. I can only hope that those we filched had already satisfied their offerants' wishes.

Once we came upon a small stone figurine, quite primitive and set in a niche in a rocky hillside. Our guess was that it was a female deity—perhaps Old Stone Woman (Parsons, 1962, 290-91)—but Dr. Boas felt that in this instance ignorance would serve us best. We wanted to continue our noonday excursions and, more particularly, our work in the village. Any imprudent act could have closed all doors to us; and nothing could have set tongues wagging faster than the knowledge that we were bent on ferreting out secret and sacred places.

We did learn about a rocky slope not far from the village where youths would go and, holding a pebble between their toes, slide from top to bottom. If they held on to the pebble throughout the descent they would be lucky at games; if they dropped it, all might not be well. Sick people used the slide to determine whether or not they would recover. We were shown the rock—there was nothing sacred about it— and from the deep ridges we could tell that many had sought an answer to their problems by this means. (For an excellent picture, see Parsons, 1923a: 291).

Cross-fertilization between cultures is endlessly intriguing, at least to the ethnologist, and it certainly was to me on this first visit to the Southwest. In Laguna its most spectacular manifestation—one that was continually visible—was the Catholic Church, a small, almost jewel-like, adobe building. Dirt floor, no pews, with a picture of Christ dominating the altar panels. The ceiling and walls were given over to Indian elements of worship: on the ceiling were portrayed sun, moon, stars, rainbow, and lightning; on the walls, animals, clouds, mountains. The cornices and beam supports, obviously inspired by the Spanish spiral so familiar in Colonial churches in Mexico, appeared here in the step design common in Indian dwellings and kivas. Mr. Lafarge took many photographs of its details inside and out, and of other features of village life and the surrounding landscape. I shall never forget him returning to the village in the late afternoon, staggering under the merciless sun and the weight of his heavy Graflex (one of the first of the color cameras), his tall tripod and cumbersome glass plates. Although we commiserated with his fatigue, we knew his agony was self-imposed, and we expected a great pictorial record from his labors. Imagine my dismay—I cannot bear to think of his—when months later I learned that something had gone wrong with his camera, making many of his pictures unusable. So, in the end, a few of my quickly taken shots also appeared in Dr. Parsons' *Laguna Genealogies.*

In Zuni it was possible for outsiders to see the masked Kachina dances; the public parts of the Shalako, the great ceremony that began in late November or early December to signal the turning south of the sun and the beginning of a new year; the house visits of the Kachina bogeys—the old man, holding "a large knife, the old woman, a basket to carry off a child to devour" if the child had proven excessively recalcitrant (Parsons, 1939:518n).)

All this an outsider could see in Zuni. In Laguna—and in other "Eastern" Pueblos—the situation was and is quite different. A non-Indian can witness only unmasked dances and such activities as occur on a Saint's Day. Dr. Parsons tells how in Laguna in 1919, when that part of a ceremony open only to Indians was about to start, she and Dr. Boas were locked in their house by the head war captain, who also "borrowed" their lamp, to rule out even the least glimpse of what was going on (Parsons, 1939:536; cf. Parsons, 1923a:140, n.5).

The only celebration I witnessed in 1920 was given on San Juan's Day, June 24. In my diary, which was written up considerably later, I speak of San Pedro's Day and not of San Juan's Day. This was, I believe, an error on my part. I distinctly remember observing the celebration with Dr. Parsons and Mr. Lafarge, who left Laguna before San Pedro's Day. And I remember observing only one Saint's Day. Moreover, my account and Dr. Parsons' in her *Laguna Genealogies* (p. 279) are virtually identical.

On this Saint's Day, all Juans and Juanas in the village—of course, each of them also had an Indian name—were on notice that their houses would be visited by the townsfolk and whoever else wanted to join them. According to my diary, at about four in the afternoon a great crowd—men, women and children, each armed with a large sack in which to carry off the loot—gathered before the house of a Juan. If he had not been on the roof, raucous cries would soon have brought him there. However, the first Juan was already up, surrounded by the gifts he intended to throw to those below. He could give what he wanted and as much or as little as he wanted. To me it seemed that all the Juans and Juanas gave most generously, even prodigally. No doubt they hoped on another Saint's Day to recover a good part of what they were now throwing away.

Flung down from the roofs that June afternoon I saw loaves of bread—some store-bought, some baked at home—candy, bottled drinks, quarters of lamb, money, jewelry, household furnishings, and live animals. There was plenty of good-natured pushing and tugging. When the giver's supplies were exhausted, a bucket of water—symbol of the rainfall so necessary for fertility—was emptied on the assemblage below (for a picture taken on St. Lorenzo's Day, 1947, see Lange, 1959: pl. 21). Clothes might be dampened, but spirits not at all. Gaily everyone moved on to the next Juan or Juana, and the fun started all over again.

Somewhere along the line a live rooster, as was expected, was thrown down, and after all the Juan and Juana houses had been visited there was a rooster pull. One young man, mounted on a horse, the rooster in one outstretched hand, led off. Whoever had a horse and wanted to, gave chase and tried to grab the rooster. Certainly it was not a good time for the bird.

The race continued for about an hour. In the end a Navajo had the rooster. Then the unprecedented happened. Flouting tradition, he tried to make off with it, going beyond the village limits. Angry Laguna youths rode after him, retrieved the rooster, stripped the Navajo, and ran him out of town. Later Jennie told me that everyone was worried, that now something dreadful might happen to the people of Laguna, that the old hostility between the Pueblo people and the Navajo was still a living thing and that the Navajo nursed their grievances for a long time. As far as I know there was no ugly aftermath, neither that year nor the year after. At the Laguna harvest festival that Dr. Boas and I attended in September 1921 there were many Navajo—but no fights between them and their hosts.

Two other experiences on this first field trip led to my better understanding of certain facts of Indian life in the Southwest. The first, a day's visit to Acoma, provided a picturesque reminder of the difficulties encountered long ago by cliff-dwelling Pueblo Indians; the second, besides its immediate impact, brought a quite unexpected reality to a study I made of the relation of flood-water farming to Navajo leadership more than 20 years later (see Goldfrank, 1945a).

Dr. Boas and I, along with Robert Eckerman's young son and "a man from Pennsylvania," not otherwise described in my diary, were driven to Acoma by Mr. Eckerman sometime after our first week in Laguna. Other than my train ride from Colorado Springs this afforded my first wide view of the New Mexican landscape—its sandy stretches, sparse plant cover except along running streams or well-watered mountain slopes, its mesas—the Spanish word for "table" describes, probably as well as any, these flattened eminences. Some of them, like Mesa Verde, Puyi, etc. had, in times long past, supported sizable populations who preferred the security of these table fortresses to the dangers of the open plain below; but they grew the bulk of their crops on the plain where springs and run-offs made cultivation feasible. The choice required frequent climbs up the mesa's steep slope, the men laden with produce, the women balancing on their heads jars filled with water from springs, was no small price to pay for peace—and this long before the Spaniards took over the area.

On our way we passed the Enchanted Mesa, an austere rock that to our untutored eyes seemed impossible to ascend, not only then but ever. Yet legend has it that in olden times the Indians did make it to the top by climbing a stone ladder hewn for them by the elements. Then an earthquake—some say a cloudburst—shook the land. The ladder was destroyed and, lacking a means of descent, the whole population perished.

Centuries passed before Professor Libby of Princeton and an assistant climbed to the top, and then a few weeks later Frederick W. Hodge of the BAE and his party did likewise. The Hodge party found an arrow point, two or three pieces of shell ornament, pieces of broken pottery—enough to establish the validity of Acoma claims that the mesa had been inhabited, although no remains of dwellings were found. Strong winds and rains had apparently destroyed them.

Acoma, too, is perched on a high mesa, as anyone who has read Willa Cather's *Death Comes to the Archbishop* will know; and although there was now a graded path by which to reach the village, we chose the ancient way still used, and apparently preferred, by many of the natives. Small nicks in the rock served as toe-holds and narrower and deeper slots accommodated our hands. We made our way slowly to the top. The Indians who preceded us seemed to fly by comparison.

In 1920 the village of Acoma consisted of three "streets" of multi-storied houses. The first also served as a plaza or "dance place." Dome-shaped Spanish ovens where the bread for everyday use was baked stood outside some of the houses. But here as in Laguna, wafer bread, the batter made of finely ground blue corn-meal and spread quickly on a flat stone griddle, was still prescribed for ceremonial occasions. Behind the "last" street, there was what seemed to be a natural depression. Today I am sure that, like the cenotes in Yucatan, it was largely man-made. As I remember it, this waterhole was about 20 feet deep, but it was only about a quarter full. We climbed down a stone ladder, very much like the one we used to get to the top of the mesa. The rocky surface above the water's edge was covered with tiny toads, gray with green spots, their bodies protectively echoing the colors of their immediate surroundings. Further back stood the church and cloister, whose sleeping quarters were windowless and worse, I thought, than many a dungeon. Besides coping with native hostility, former occupants could hardly have found life pleasant there. Now no one was in residence.

We soon were followed by young children, curious about us but also hoping for some small gift—candy especially. The village was almost empty of men (they had gone early to their fields). But several enterprising women, having quickly recognized us as prospective buyers of pots, invited us into their houses. The making of pots—here, as everywhere in the Americas, without the use of the wheel— was still flourishing, and sales to tourists provided a welcome source of income. I bought two—a water jar, its outer surface nicely painted, and an old mixing-bowl which I was particularly pleased with. Both pots reached the East safely; but three years later in White Plains a gusty wind blew the mixing bowl off our porch table, smashing it beyond repair. Some months later, the water jar met a similar fate. But while these material reminders disappeared long ago, memories of my day in Acoma, so removed from the usual manifestations of modernity, so alone above the desert sand, are still vivid. More than any other "living" pueblo that I have seen, it has given me a sense of what life must have been like many centuries ago in this strikingly beautiful—but often harsh— environment.

The second experience had, as I have already said, an important if belated impact on my understanding of Navajo economy and society.

Dr. Parsons and Mr. Lafarge had left us and gone to San Felipe to explore the possibilities for field work there (we were to meet them shortly at nearby Algadones). Immediately after their departure, Mr. Eckerman came down with a severe tonsilitis. For three days Dr. Boas and I were forced to hoof it to Old Laguna and back. The summer rains had started; and our short-cut along a small river, which was fed by several small arroyos, was already soft with mud. In the winter, the river was a dry bed, but now it was enjoying a constant, though not heavy, flow. On each of our trips we had to cross it twice, stepping carefully on a number of widely spaced and slippery stones—once near Old Laguna and once near our "hotel"—and without mishap on the first two days.

But things were to be different on the afternoon of the third. Just as we were about to leave Old Laguna, the sky darkened ominously. The rains came—torrential rains accompanied by jagged streaks of lightning from three directions and thunder so crashing that the older of the twin war heroes, Masewi, must have been especially angry and determined to show his might. An hour passed as we sat in Jennie's house waiting for the storm to abate. It was an uneasy hour for me. I do not like storms, and, quite irrationally, it is the thunder that upsets me more than the lightning. Dr. Boas remained unperturbed, reviewing what he had recorded during the day. As soon as the sky cleared, we started for home.

The stepping stones at our first crossing were still visible, although the water in the river had risen considerably. We made our way gingerly to our footpath, now heavy with mud that clung tenaciously to our shoes, adding its unwelcome weight to that of our many notebooks, which, filled or partially filled, we never left unattended. With three miles behind us and our "hotel" in sight, we reached our second crossing. Here, to our dismay, our stepping stones were gone. The empty arroyos of the morning were now turbulent streams pouring their waters rapidly into the usually tame river. One glance was enough. We turned back to Old Laguna. We had to get there before the stepping stones at that end were submerged by this unexpected rush of water. If not, we would be stranded, probably for hours and without cover. We just made it. Seconds after we crossed, our stony escape disappeared. Without a moment's respite—I wanted to rest a while at Jennie's—Dr. Boas insisted that we go right home, this time by way of the longer automobile road, which was now also a sea of mud.

It was well over an hour before we saw our "hotel" again. Mud-caked and weary, we went immediately to our rooms, to emerge the following day, just before we were scheduled to leave Laguna and our friends there for untried and—as it turned out—unrewarding fields.

I had learned from this last afternoon in Laguna that time and tide—in our case, rushing waters—wait for no one, not for Dr. Boas, nor for me, nor—and this I realized fully only years later—for the small flood-water farmers of the Southwest who, if they don't want to go hungry, have to work fast and furiously to bring the unpredictable summer rains to their maturing crops.

ON THE ROAD TO ALBUQUERQUE

We left Laguna on June 30, spent the night at the Alvarado Hotel, a comfortable Harvey House that adjoined the Albuquerque station of the ATSF Railway. The next day we went on to Algadones, four miles from San Felipe, where we were met by Dr. Parsons and Mr. Lafarge. They led us to the low building where they were staying. The front yard was white with the fluff of a spreading cottonwood tree, and a fence kept a gaggle of geese from wandering into the road. A sign told us that this dwelling place also served as the headquarters of a mining company and a chicken farm—both of which were owned and managed by our host, Mr. Balcomb, who had left Salem, Mass. in 1868 and never gone back, and his two sons, who were off prospecting.

Before the arrival of Dr. Parsons and Mr. Lafarge, Mr. Balcomb had been alone for well over a week. He had been cooking for himself and he had fed the geese (I can't remember any chickens). But he had not bothered to clean. Dr. Parsons said that Mr. Lafarge, who was most fastidious, had removed buckets of dirt from the small room she and I were to share. Despite his efforts, there was plenty left and the two of us spent a good part of the afternoon finishing the job.

Another major problem was a kitchen sink full of unwashed dishes, pots, and pans. Mr. Balcomb's system was a simple one. He used clean dishes as long as they lasted. Now the cupboard was bare. Mr. Lafarge, who was the cook as usual, and I, who was his chief helper—Dr. Parsons never participated in these homely chores—did what we could to get rid of the mess. Mr. Balcomb was well pleased with our efforts. His contribution was standing by and regaling us with tales about New Mexico and Indians.

Dr. Parsons and I made one serious mistake. After our labors we rested in the shade of a cottonwood tree, unaware that we were sharing it with a crowd of vigorous ants. That night we didn't sleep very well.

San Felipe had not been kind to Dr. Parsons or Mr. Lafarge. He had been run out of town for photographing the church! And she had been able to persuade only a single man to cooperate in her research. A frightened soul, despite his daring decision, he was brought to Dr. Boas, who was trying to establish dialectical deviations between Laguna and other Keresan pueblos. Also among my extra-anthropological duties that first afternoon was standing guard, not unlike a pueblo war captain at ceremonial times. The moment a stranger hove into sight I was to rush indoors to see to it that Dr. Boas and his San Felipan were concealed behind closed doors.

Dr. Parsons, Mr. Lafarge and I left Algadones the next morning. Our car, piled high with luggage and photographic equipment, bumped uncomfortably along the road to Albuquerque. (Dr. Boas was staying one more day in Algadones to continue working with his San Felipe man.) On our way we stopped at Santa Ana, where Dr. Parsons had previously found a family willing to work with her, and we went directly to their home. Seated at a table on the porch, an unusual adjunct to an Indian dwelling, were three persons, obviously awaiting our arrival—an old mother, her married daughter, and her young granddaughter, I learned. Dr. Parsons began immediately to interview the married daughter.

I wandered off alone. Dr. Parsons' informant may have given me a hint about where to go; but in my diary I merely stated I "found" a family whose female members, with one elderly exception, spoke English. I told them what I had been doing in Laguna and mentioned Jennie Johnson. Then they really became interested. Yes, they knew the Johnsons well, and particularly Mr. Johnson, who had been away from Laguna the whole time I had been there. It seemed a small sin to imply that he too was my friend. In any event, I had no difficulty in eliciting cooking recipes.

Our car had remained parked in front of the house where Dr. Parsons was working, Mr. Lafarge in it. But apparently not for long. Restless by nature and hoping to escape notice, he had set up his camera just back of the car. And there it was when I returned, Mr. Lafarge beside it, focussing on the group on the porch. Then it happened. The old woman suddenly got up from her chair, grabbed a sizable piece of pottery and shook it menacingly at Mr. Lafarge. Her voice rose angrily, her outstretched hand emphasizing her demand for payment. Mr. Lafarge, speaking in Spanish, still the second language of older puebloans, assured her that as yet he had taken no picture. She remained unconvinced. Reluctantly he gave her a silver dollar. This satisfied her, but Mr. Lafarge wanted his picture all the more since he had paid for it. Again he took his stand behind his camera. Again she protested angrily. Unwilling to fork over another dollar, he surrendered, put his camera in the car and sat down beside it. Dr. Parsons did not intercede; and I, understandably, also remained a silent witness. We left shortly afterward. Goodbyes on both sides were most friendly. No one would have guessed that minutes before we had been embroiled in a small war with Santa Ana.

ALBUQUERQUE, JULY 2-6, 1920

In San Felipe I had been bothered by my appendix, and when we reached Albuquerque I decided to consult a doctor. We found one at the hotel who advised an ice-bag and rest and assured me there was nothing urgent about my condition. By late afternoon I felt well enough to visit the famous Harvey Museum next door to the hotel and to enjoy examining the fine old blankets, jewelry, basketry, and ceremonial objects, mostly from tribes of the greater Southwest.

As train time approached Indians seemed to pour in from everywhere. They arranged themselves along the platform, the women squatting behind their pots; the men, standing, exhibiting their bows and arrows, belts, jewelry and small rugs—all hoping to make quick sales while the train was in the station. It seemed a good time to scout for informants. We found an Isleta woman and a Santo Domingo man who said they would work with us. Both proved costly and not very helpful.

The Isleta woman brought her aunt along the next day, doubling the expense and adding little to our knowledge. Both morning and afternoon sessions were held in my room while I lay on my bed amid notebooks and plants, the two Isleta women with Dr. Parsons alongside near enough to identify them. It was hot, and a weak electric fan gave little relief. But that was the least of our troubles. We soon discovered that the name our informants assigned a plant in the afternoon was often entirely different from the one they had given it in the morning. A gray stemmed specimen with a yellow flower might be called "gray stem," then "yellow flower." We were soon convinced they were making up names as they went along, and after two sessions we dismissed them.

The man from Santo Domingo presented different problems. By arrangement I went out again to the station platform around 8 o'clock to meet him—he said he would work with Dr. Boas after the train expected at that time had pulled out. I found him set to sell his bows and arrows and surrounded by four of his townsmen obviously bent on learning what was up. No doubt they had seen us talking to him a few hours earlier. (Among the pueblos, Santo Domingo was considered the most hostile to Whites, virtually hounding them from the village. It was said that trains had been kept from passing nearby while a masked dance was being given there. Although the pueblo is still "conservative," all visitors are welcome today at the Corn Dance, which here as elsewhere in the pueblos is an unmasked dance.)

Our Domingan saw me approaching, but he gave only the barest sign of recognition. After the train left he packed up what he had not sold and joined me. His "friends" melted away, but as we walked down the platform, I noticed that one of them was following us. I asked him to come along with us and meet Dr. Boas, who was waiting in the hotel lobby. He did, and after some general talk he left, his curiosity apparently satisfied. Dr. Boas and his informant then went up to Dr. Boas' room. In less than five minutes they were back again. The Santa Domingan was dissatisfied with the amount to be paid him. Dr. Boas had already raised our standard rate of a dollar a session (usually three hours) to a dollar an hour. But the Domingan also wanted to share Dr. Boas' bed! He addressed his complaints to me, probably because he had met me first. Not quite comfortable in the hotel lobby, he suggested that the three of us return to Dr. Boas' room. When I thought everything was under control (the Domingan finally understood that he would not share Dr. Boas' bed), I rose to go, but our Indian insisted that the "muchacho" stay. My presence did not induce him to work any more seriously. First he examined Dr. Boas' notebook, but this he quickly put aside—the linguistic symbols had no meaning for him. After considerable prodding he did translate a few words, but, for the better part of the two hours he spent with us, he argued about his pay. However unmaterialistic pueblo villagers may be within their own society, in their dealings with the world outside they are no less materialistic than their countrymen, the White Americans.

After our day with the Isleta women, we held a "family" council.

My appendix was still bothering me. Two alternatives were considered. I could abandon all my fine summer plans, return to New York and be operated on there, or I could go to Los Angeles, be operated on there, and after a term of convalescence, join my friends for the remainder of the trip. I had no difficulty coming to a decision. I would go to Los Angeles—and neither Dr. Boas nor Dr. Parsons tried to persuade me otherwise. I left Albuquerque on July 6. So ended my first field trip.

AN ASSESSMENT

An exceptional experience? In certain ways, yes. But in one way it fitted into a pattern already established by Dr. Parsons. Whatever her reasons—attachment to her husband, her children (the youngest of whom was still, I believe, in his early teens)—she never discussed them with me, but her visits to the Southwest had been little more than a month in duration and usually they encompassed several villages. When she invited Dr. Boas to join her in 1919, he followed her pattern. Leaving New York "late in May or early in June," Leslie A. White notes, "Boas was in Laguna by June 16, and had returned to New York by July 10" (White, 1963:9f). In 1920, he was in Laguna a few days prior to my arrival on June 17, and we left together on July 1, he spending two more days in San Felipe before joining Dr. Parsons, Mr. Lafarge, and me in Albuquerque, where he remained a few days after my departure.

This routine must have appealed to him too. At the time the whole responsibility for the department at Columbia rested on his shoulders and, in addition to his work on the mountains of Kwakiutl data he had been assembling since 1887, he was involved as already noted in an almost unbelievable number of projects—in physical anthropology, linguistics, and ethnology, not to mention his "Emergency Society." Only during the summer months at Lake George was he assured of uninterrupted time for writing. The brief trips to the Southwest in 1919 and 1920, and also in 1921 and 1922, provided a congenial solution for a busy scholar who, despite his 60-plus years, still had the zest to enter new areas and tackle new problems.

In 1920 I too could fit into this pattern. Only the accident of a planned trip to the West had led me to suggest that Dr. Boas take me with him. I had no other asset to recommend me—no systematic training in anthropology, no familiarity with the varieties and complexities of Pueblo society or with "field techniques." I am endlessly grateful for the happenstance that took me West that June and that Dr. Boas and Dr. Parsons were flexible and generous enough to endure my ignorance—and, without condescension, to help me overcome it.

But the company and mode of operation did make this trip

exceptional. For many years it has been customary to set up anthropological field laboratories during the summer months. For the most part, they included several graduate students under the leadership of an experienced professor (the Viru Valley Project under W. Duncan Strong and others, the Puerto Rican Project under Julian H. Steward, the Hopi Project under Leslie A. White, the Pomo Project under the Aginskys, and the Apache and Blackfoot Projects under Ruth Benedict). In most cases, although not all, there was frequent stock-taking, comparisons of work done by participants, and suggestions by them and the group leader for improving techniques.

During this first field trip of mine, there was nothing of the sort. Conversations, whether with Dr. Boas or Dr. Parsons, were completely informal. To be sure, there was some exchange of information, but I can remember no time when either of them systematically discussed with me the data they had obtained in 1919 in Laguna or its relevance for Southwest society in general, or suggested how I should proceed.

Regarding informants I had no problem. Dr. Parsons had made congenial and capable contacts in previous years, and in 1920 they accepted me as the "friend of their friend." Besides, there was nothing esoteric about cooking recipes, and when I began to work with plants (whose medicinal properties were less readily reported), Dr. Parsons almost always carried the ball.

At the start, then, I was very much on my own, but I was spared the worry of securing adequate informants (I learned how difficult this could be four years later). And as befitted my training—or more precisely, my lack of training—I was assigned a simple and, from my standpoint, a very dull topic.[18] When the information I sought touched on more sensitive areas, I had in Dr. Parsons a ready, experienced, and unassuming tutor. Surely an exceptional setting for a first field trip and, surely, an exceptional company for an "accidental" anthropologist.

6. AGAIN A SECRETARY

Back at Columbia at the end of September and back at the old routine. My three weeks in the Southwest had not notably altered my perspectives. I was still Dr. Boas' secretary, still a Tuesday luncher. But I did begin to attend some classes. One that remains in my memory is Dr. Boas' course on the Kwakiutl language. Fascinated as I was by its structural complexity, I was depressed by my obviously inadequate ear, and this served as a deterrent to any further effort on my part to enter the field of linguistics.

No one ever suggested that I write up my notes or that I become a

Carrying the Saint from church to plaza before the Corn Dance, Laguna, N. M., September 1921.

The author in Laguna, 1921.

Spanish oven and household corral, Laguna, 1921.

Carl Leon, Laguna, 1921.

Dr. Franz Boas and guides, before ascent of Mt. Taylor, Laguna, 1921.

Navajo attending Corn Dance, Laguna, 1921.

Arbor, where officials sit and Saint is deposited during Corn Dance.

The Corn Dance, Laguna, 1921.

Women husking corn, Cochiti, 1921.

full-time student. Having learned in recent years how difficult it is to break in a new secretary, I can well understand that Dr. Boas had no wish to rock the boat. And I too was quite content to maintain the status quo.

7. AGAIN A FIELD-WORKER

In the spring of 1921, I was "invited" to go on a second field trip, again to the Southwest, and again with Dr. Boas—and this time with Dr. Parsons paying all my expenses. But before we left in early September, and in my capacity as secretary, I spent July at Bolton Landing on Lake George, where the Boases had passed many summers in a modest frame dwelling on the George McAneny estate (George McAneny's wife was the daughter of Dr. Abraham Jacobi, Dr. Boas' uncle by marriage and also his devoted friend). Some fifty feet up the hill was Dr. Boas' studio, and it was there that he and I worked most of the day.

My only household chore was to take care of my room. Henry, the Boas' second son, worked outside. All else was taken care of by Mrs. Boas, her daughters, Gertrud and Franziska, and a friend who was vacationing with them. At noon we returned to the main house. Before lunch there was always time for a swim off the McAneny dock at the foot of a long hill. (The climb back did not bother me. I had been inured to such an inconvenience by the seventy-nine steps—we had counted them carefully—leading from the beach at Sea Cliff, Long Island, to my grandmother's house, where I had spent many summers). After lunch Dr. Boas and I returned to his studio to work for several hours more. Dinner was early, and we usually went for a short walk afterward. Not infrequently, on our return, Dr. Boas would seat himself at the piano. Later we all sat at the dining table, over which hung a large acetylene lamp, the only one in the house that shed a light bright enough for reading. I don't remember playing games. Weekends we hiked—an activity I shared without much enthusiasm. Now I was truly "family."

However tough and exacting Dr. Boas may have been with his male students, within his family circle he was warm and loving. To be sure, he was the center of attention and, without any insistence on his part, things were done the way he wanted them done. Mrs. Boas had little if any interest in his intellectual activities, except where they involved his immediate comfort or general well-being. During my month at Lake George, I heard no peremptory orders, no loud words, no angry arguments. Voices were raised only in song. It was a happy and harmonious household and one in which I readily found a congenial place.

After some weeks in New York, I met Dr. Boas and together we travelled to Laguna. My few personal notes record no extended conversations regarding Pueblo life and society during our train trip west, nor do I remember any. What efforts there were at education seem to have been largely initiated by me, and they had little or nothing to do with anthropological inquiry. I tried to convince Dr. Boas that there was something worthwhile in jazz. His response: my taste in music was deplorable. And from my humming at odd moments—a habit my third-grade teacher deplored—and my limited repertory, mostly K-K-K-katey and a bit of Tchaikovsky, a composer Dr. Boas particularly disliked, I can hardly fault his opinion. But there was one subject Dr. Boas himself raised—dreams—to demonstrate that Freud's emphasis on latent sexual content was "ridiculous." To make his point, he would recite his dream experiences of the previous night. Having just read Freud's *Three Essays on the Theory of Sexuality*, I was convinced that Dr. Boas was making a very poor case for himself, but like a good Pueblo Indian, I said nothing.

AGAIN A FIELD WORKER

LAGUNA N.M. LATE SUMMER, 1921

This year we stayed in Old Laguna, boarding with the Indian postmistress, a tiny efficient person whose name I have forgotten. She lived alone in her immaculately kept house, spoke English well, and was a good cook. Her official duties were so consuming that we made no attempt to enlist her services either as interpreter or informant.

The first morning after our arrival we visited our friends of the previous year. In my notebook I mention particularly the Browns, Jennie Johnson, Alice Marmon, Mrs. Riley, and Old Kaciena. All of them were very busy preparing for the Saint's Day (St. Joseph's Day) festival scheduled for September 19. We were told that the Laguna Indians had changed their Saint's Day from March 19 (as given in the Catholic calendar) to September 19 because there was more to be grateful for after the harvest and their offerings could be more generous then. Despite important demands on her time, Kaciena was willing to work with me—money meant a great deal to her. Armed with a large kitchen knife, she directed me along the narrow trail leading from the village, stopping whenever she recognized a medicinal plant. In my notebook I wrote: "Perhaps last year I should not have been so at ease about this walk, wondering whether I would come back with or without my scalp." But this year I had no qualms, not even later, when, on horseback and in the company of Solomon Day, I left the village far behind.

I was, of course, interested most in attitudes toward curing, but

60

this was not a subject to be introduced quickly or directly, as I had learned in 1920. However, once an identification was made I did inquire about methods of preparing and using medications. Kaciena exhibited considerable reluctance in discussing such matters on two counts: first, because she feared, as do all medicine men, that power is lost when secrets are told; and second, because she feared that I would immediately use what she had told me to set myself up in the drug business. To pay her for her fear—and this is exactly how one of Dr. Parsons' informants put his request for more money—I increased the hourly rate enough to induce her to continue. But our peripatetic cooperation was short-lived. She suffered severely from rheumatism, and our daily expeditions soon became too much for her. It was then that I sought out Solomon Day, whose wife, Katie, had previously participated in our cookery sessions.

Solomon Day was happy to take over and, as already indicated, we adopted a new mode of travel. I had never been an enthusiastic hiker, but neither did I feel comfortable on a horse. Fortunately my animal was extremely good-tempered, and more than willing to advance at a slow walk punctuated by many stops. In the afternoon I submitted our plants to the "old women" for examination and comment.

Dr. Boas and I brought back a sizable boxful of these plants and had them identified at the New York Botanical Garden. Once this was done, I looked them up in a reliable pharmacopoeia. Many of them did indeed have medicinal properties; but only rarely did my Laguna informants use them in the ways established by modern medicine.[19] Twenty-one years later, and after I had returned to New York, I asked Dr. Boas if he knew what had happened to our plants. He wrote me shortly that they had disappeared. I gave my notes to Dr. Leland C. Wyman of Harvard, who, together with S. K. Harris, had published a Navajo medical ethnobotany in 1941.

During our morning rides I discovered that Solomon Day was more interested in hunting than in plant collecting and, glad enough myself to have a change of topic, I soon found time to interview him and Carl Leon, his good friend and much more knowledgeable informant, on Laguna hunting practices (see Dr. Parsons' undated letter to me, p. 24 above.)

Solomon Day and his wife, Katie, were quite "Americanized." Both were warm and friendly, Katie's intelligence well-blended with everyday womanly concerns. They had two children—a daughter, Lillian, who was away at school, and "Little Solomon," as he was always referred to, who was still too young to attend the village school, and who was watched over most tenderly by his doting parents. Carl Leon, their almost constant companion, was less well educated and much more intensely involved with the social and religious life of the

Pueblo. It is clear from my 1954 paper that I learned most about hunting practices from him.

It may not be amiss at this point to include letters written me by Solomon and Katie Day and Carl Leon while I was still working with Southwest data, and by the two men some 45 years later when, after a complete silence on all our parts and through the good auspices of Professor Thomas Sebeok of the University of Indiana, whose daughter had shared a room at Radcliffe with a Laguna Indian girl, I was again put in touch with them. (I had at various times tried both through the Indian Agency at Albuquerque and the Laguna post office to discover their whereabouts, but my letters of inquiry went unanswered until August 4, 1969, a year and a half after my last appeal and six months after Professor Sebeok had located my friends.)

As soon as I learned that both men were still living in Old Laguna (Katie Day had died), I sent them Christmas greetings and a small gift. Their response was immediate, heart-warming, and all too generous. All their letters (and Katie's) well demonstrate their integrity, their pleasure in old days, and a not unhappy adjustment to a changing world.[20]

City of Laguna, N.M.
Oct. 14th, 1921

E. Schiff
Dear Friend:
    You do not know how glad Carl and myself are when we got the strings of beads. We both thank you very much for them. Well we all hope that you got home safely. I bet you both were glad to get home because New Mexico is not like the city of New York. But do not forget the wild *wooly west*. I mean *God for saken land*. Well we all missed you both, we always talk about you and the Doctor *B*. We are all well here at home. There is to be another mask dance coming off Saturday Oct. 16-17. Come and look on. Well we all went on a picnic up the water cana [canyon?]. We stay there for three day that is my whole family. I mean the *D* family. But Carl and I did not see anything for there was lots of people their and making all kind of noise. Well you must write us a long letter and tell us all about your home time. The Doctor didn't even give us his address, so that we can write to him. Excause my poor hand written, also the pencil. No ink at all hope to hear from you. We all send our best regard to you. From the Day family and Carl. *God Be With you till we meet again.*

Mr. & Mrs. S. G. Day

(From the handwriting this was clearly written by Solomon Day.)

Laguna, N.M.
Jan. 3, 1922

My dear Miss Schiff:

Your letters came and also the gifts. We certainly appreciate them. And we thank you very much.

Big Solomon was not home when I got your first letter but he is here now. Lillian is away to school but Carl is here. Carl and Sol never went to hunt because Sol was not home and the game season was only ten days. The men that went out did not get any.

We had a little snow in the early part of last month, then from that time it was as pleasant as spring until yesterday. It turned so cold but no snow.

You seem to know just what little Solomon likes. He was so tickled over the gift you sent him and he said to tell you that he thanks you very much. I'll write again to let you know what Sol or Carl are going to do about going up the mountain for you.

They have been busy during Christmas and haven't had much time to do anything. This is just the time when all of the Indians in the Pueblo must observe the holidays by their dances christmas and the new year. Xmas weeks the dances are for four days. And the new year is on the 7th until the 9th. Then the dances are over with again for sometime. The last dances are more for the new officers for this year. These dances take place every year on the same date.

I wish you could [see] for yourself at just this time what my people do.

We all send our kindest regards to you. Carl joins in with the family.

Oh, yes we went to Acomia [Acomita?] the day after Xmas. Their dance up there was bigger than ours and prettier to me.

Goodbye.

Your friend
Mrs. Day

Laguna, N.M.
Oct. 1, 1922

Dear Esther:

Your letter came long ago and perhaps you think that I have forgotten already. The reason I did not write is because I have been sick for over a month. Carl and little Solomon went up to Mt. Taylor this morning on horses. How would you like that trip.

Big Solomon was at Grants where your train stopped. He was waiting for the east bound train and he got home that night about 11:30. He is at Winslow Arizona, working for the railroad company.

Nothing new around here. It is dusty and dry.

It seems to be getting cold, earlier than it ever did. No crop of any kind so I guess we'll starve this winter.

I promise to do better about answering your letters.

There was not much of a feast this year. All the young men, and boys went out to work in the strikers places, only old men are left.

Hope to hear from you soon. With kindest regards,

Your friend
Katie

Winslow Arizona
Jan. 7, 1923

My dear friend:

Your letter came yesterday and found us all well, way down here in Arizona. Carl is at home all alone. Little Solomon and I went home for Christmas and staid until the dances were over. We found Carl well. He had been at the sheep camp since we left, but we shall see that he gets a share of your gift. Thank U for your kind rememberance.

I have wondered what happened to you. I spoke of you just the day we were leaving for home, thinking that I would send you something but my husband said to wait until we hear from you.

Quite a good many of the Laguna people are here working for the Santa Fe R.R. Co.

We have not had any snow here. It is like early spring. But it was very cold in Laguna. But it is dry as ever.

During the summer, they only had one cutting of hay. No wheat nor corn. Then the strike came on. In that way the people are saved from starving and the State highway are working through that part too. Uncle Sam is also putting dames [dams] and ditch in that part of the Indian lands so that is quite a help. Otherwise I don't know what we would be doing.

Little Solomon goes to the City Public school here with the white boys and Mexicans and he likes to go to school. Of course it is quite different from the little Day School he has been going [to].

Little Solomon sends his kindest regards to you. And he also wants me to tell you about the distance to the school. It is almost as far as New Laguna from Old Laguna.

We shall be glad to hear from you from time to time. Kindest regards to you from all.

Your friend
Katie

Laguna, N.M.
March 10, 1923

Friend, Miss Eseter Schiff,

Just a few lines to you. Please let me know how are you. Bye this time I hope you are the same way as I am. I think you remember me. Im all way thinking of you. Well please if you have any pictures, send them I want to have one of your nice pictures.[21] I think that I have shown [?] by the length of this letter that [I] have not forgotten you. This is all.

Give best regards to all.

From Carl Leon

And after 45 years from Carl Leon and Solomon Day:

Old Laguna
December 24, 1968

Dear Mrs. E. Schiff Goldfrank

Grandpa has asked me to write this short letter to you. Your Christmas card has found him well and fine. He thanks you very much for the holiday remembrance gift. Grandpa's home and retired from the Santa Fe Railroad. He has been participating in our Indian ceremonies around Laguna. He probably will dance New Year's Eve. Right now he says that the people are heading to church of the village, for Xmas Mass. Laguna has changed a lot since you were here he says.

He says he wants to make you some Indian moccasins as a gift, so would you please send the measurement of your foot size.[22] This is about all he wants to say.

For myself I'd like to thank you for remembering him on this fine occasion. Together we send our Season's Greeting and wish you a Happy and joyous New Year.

Mr. Carl Leon's Grandson

Sante Fe, N.M.
Jan. 23-69

Mrs. E. Goldfrank

Yours letter came to me on Dec. 23-68. I am here in Santa Fe N.M. We come up here to live with granddaughter Jullia Harriar. She is working here in Santa Fe for a long time. My wife pass away from us Dec. 25 at 9:30 p.m. 1964[23] here in the Indian School hospital it is now five years ago this last Xmas. We come up to Santa Fe every winter. Jullia dose not want us to live in Laguna during winters, there is just two of [us] my daughter Lillian and myself. My son Solomon Day, Jr. is living in Carson City, Nevada. He is married. Well Ester I sure was glad to get a letter and the money and am thanking you a thousand time. When we got back to Laguna, I got the letter and I was supprised to hear from you. I thought you had forgotten us. When Carl Leon come to my house we still talk about you and the Dr. you was with. Well I went back to work for the Santa Fe Railroad Co. to Nove 13th 1936 when I retired from the Company and we came home back to our beloved home, and I start working on my old houses. I tore down all the old walls and build the new walls every thing new. I got a nine room house with two celler rooms, and I get my money every month while I am seating on a good feather cushion Ha-Ha. Ester If I sent you a string of toques [turquoise] bead will you wear [them]? Write again for I love to heare from you. This is our address here in Santa Fe N.M.

Solomon Day Sr.
1224 Lagun Ave.
Santa Fe, N.M.

PS I step on my glass now I am in a fix so excause my poor written next time I do better. Close here.

Love & regard to all of you
I am still your friend by-by

S. Day Sr.

Santa Fe, N.M.
Jan 31-69

My dear Friend

Yours Letter came me this morning by the mail man I was sure glad to hear from you and glad to know you still remember me. I myself also still think of you, before I got the letter from you. Esther never will I forget you, when Carl come to my house we always put your name in our talk. The trip we took up to Mt. Taylor it has been along time ago. Oh yes, the picture of yourself was gladly received by me, Savoy [someday?] I wish you could come west to visit the people of Laguna, peoples, I sure love to see [you] come bad [back?]—write once in awhile and let me know how you are. Last fall I had a chance to go to New York. One of my sister's daughter is living there at Hartford new york. She also married a college professor. She want me to take to her house to make my home, but I said too far. Maybe next time when you come to visit I'll go with you. I'll sent you torquese beads. When I go to Laguna I'll by it for you. If you dont want to keep it throw it into the Atlantic Ocean. I want [to] make [you] a Indian sqwa [squaw] sister. I will come to close here. By & by.

God blessed you all
Solomon Day Sr.

I continued to hear from Carl Leon and Solomon Day, Sr., usually however, through the good auspices of a grandchild or some other surrogate. Solomon's last letter in his own handwriting was dated June 4, 1970 and sent from Laguna. It reads:

My dear Esther:

I am going to write a few lines to you. Sorry that I didn't write to you for a long time, but I haven't forgotten you and the time you and Prof. were here in Laguna. Remember [when] the rock fell that was on the hill and the cave taking off the sand [indecipherable] you got it all over your stocking going through the fields. My deares[t] I sure would like to see you again. I too am older at 91 years. Well I still travel on the Sante Fe R. R. free. If my wife was still living we would to [go?] as far as Chicago and [you] can come as far as Chicago to meet there, but she had pass away 1963, Dec. 25 at 9:30 pm. I sure missed her. I am very lonesome. No more a mate. If I can find another mate at the same age just to talk to each [other]. But not what a man likes out of woman. No *more*. Well my good [friend] write and let me know where you are, a new address and a new name [?]. Next [time] I write I'll write more. Close here.

Love to you all. Let me hear from you. By By

Solomon Day Sr.

Carl Leon's last letter reached me shortly after Christmas 1972 and, like most of his others, was written by a grandson. A picture of Carl was enclosed, standing in full Comanche dance regalia and much as I had seen him in 1921. It was taken on Christmas Day and the letter informed me that "Grandpa was dancing Christmas Day and Christmas Eve." The following year my Christmas letters to him and Solomon were both returned. Each was marked "deceased".

To get back to Laguna in September 1921. Everyone was looking forward to the feast day on the 19th and everyone was expecting guests. The women had been cleaning their houses for days, whitewashing inside walls, sweeping dirt floors, cooking and baking as many as 30 to 40 loaves of bread a day in the Spanish ovens outside. They also made *piki,* the ceremonial wafer bread, using only blue cornmeal, the batter being spread on a heated grill and removed quickly and, hopefully, without breaking the paper-thin slice. The men plastered the outside walls anew and cleaned off the roofs, which, except for a few prestigious sloping ones of tin, were flat. They also brought in the lambs and cattle to be slaughtered, and for four nights before the feast they met in a house near the plaza, belonging to the oldest maternal family of the corn clan, to rehearse the songs and dances to be given on the feast day.

Considerably before the 19th, friends and relatives began arriving from nearby pueblos—Pohuati, Casa Blanca, Parajo—and not so nearby Isleta. The Navajo came too, some of the men on horseback, a wife often riding behind, but most of them crowded into covered wagons with their women and children, their dogs running alongside, trying valiantly to keep up. Once settled, the men circulated in the village, selling their attractive Navajo jewelry and fine rugs to anyone who wanted to pay cash, but usually bartering them for bread and chili, most of which was eaten during their stay in Laguna. I recently gave my first purchase—a modest bracelet of three thin silver coils studded with three small turquoise insets—to my godchild.

Two days before the feast the Mexicans arrived. To the delight of the children—and the adults—they set up a carousel. By the 18th there were any number of small stands selling cold drinks, ice cream, and melon; stalls for games, offering the usual assortment of prizes; and a large tent that served as a dance hall—in fact, a veritable country fair.

Before 7:00 on the morning of the 19th, the Comanche dancers (their costumes a Plains adaptation) assembled on the west side of the river, and a little after seven, they came riding slowly into the village. At their head strode their leader in a brilliant red suit and carrying the American flag. Behind him, abreast and on horseback, rode five dancers, clothed in black, with white fringe edging their sleeves and trouser legs. Their faces were painted red and they wore gaudy head-dresses of black-tipped eagle feathers. (Carl Leon was one of them.[24]) Three drummers, also abreast, strode behind the riders, each of them carrying a double-headed drum about a foot in height. Accompanying this cavalcade was a clown astride a small black jenny that he prodded into bucking and performing capers. He wore a long black coat, tufts of sheep's wool on his head, and a black cloth mask trimmed with white whiskers (presumably to approximate a Mexican). When the cavalcade reached the village, its members retired to "their" house near the plaza, from which they would emerge when they were to dance and to which they would return when their dance was over.

At 9:30 the church bell rang. The carousel stopped, the fairgrounds were deserted, and the Mass began. The priest, in a golden stole and flanked by a Franciscan and a choirboy, took their places in front of the altar. On either side stood a sexton—both Indians, and one the most eminent shaman in the village.

The church was packed with Indians and Mexicans, all decked out in their finest. For days everyone in Laguna had been making new dresses, blouses, and shirts. There were new store-bought overalls, shoes, and stockings for the boys, and for the women new shawls and large silk handkerchiefs to be hung down the back for propriety's sake. Silver necklaces, rings, bracelets and earrings in abundance were brought out, to add to the festive occasion. The Navajo alone did not enter the church.

After the sermon, which was delivered in Spanish, the two sextons removed St. Joseph from his niche and handed him over to a woman standing by. A second woman was given the pedestal to carry, and a third a crude figure of Jesus. The shaman-sexton led the procession, ringing a silver bell, his mate close behind him holding a tall candlestick. The priest and Franciscan followed the women with the Saint and pedestal. The villagers and their guests followed them.

Making its way around the south side of the village, the procession entered the plaza from the east. In the middle of the north side, a bower had been erected. Corn stalks covered the outside, the entrance marked by young poplar trees, the inside by fine Navajo blankets. Inside, also, were wooden benches for the village officials, and at the rear a table ready to receive the offerings. The tall candlestick was planted in front of the bower and St. Joseph was deposited on the table along with four lighted candles.

The governor of the village then addressed the large and mixed audience in Spanish.

"Today," he said, "we come here again to the feast of San José, thus is his name. It is good thus, that we see one another again in good health up here in Laguna. It is good today that we remember again the old ways for his sake. You have come here from all around. Therefore it is nice that we see one another today. Now go ahead. Let us be happy. You will take San José; all those who are honest will carry him and you will pray to him, where his father God is above in heaven. Indeed he is his father. Long ago he did everything that (God) wanted him to do. He took the name of God and Mary's child here in this world where he was born. Therefore this feast will be celebrated. On the 19th of this month it will be celebrated. Therefore we shall be happy and those who are honest will carry him, and you will pray afterwards. You will ask for good health and that the stock will be well and that our property will be plentiful and that we shall have a good winter and that the new year shall be good again in the future. Thus I want you to do, my people, all of you who are Catholic and Christian. Thus you will do my people. Now go ahead and prepare yourselves. Carry our San José and God's child. Now my people be good. You will carry them. Thus I advise you."

These words were followed by short speeches delivered by the lieutenant governor (teniente), the war captain, and the fiscale, all of them admonishing the people to do as the governor had requested. In my "Notes on Two Pueblo Feasts" (1923), I also stated that the governor asked that all "put away the firearms" (foreshadowing present-day campus procedures?). But this must have been told Dr. Boas as an aside, since it does not appear in the translation of the speeches quoted above that he generously gave me. (For slight variations, see his *Keresan Texts*, p. 211ff.)

No sooner were these speeches concluded than we heard the beating of drums and the songs of the Comanche performers. Two clowns preceded them, dressed in khaki trousers, leggings, and dark shirts. They also wore black masks outlined in white, a white cross on the forehead and a vertical line marking the back of the nose, from the tip of which hung a black tab. Like the clown on the jenny, they had tufts of sheep's wool on the top of their heads. One of the clowns carried a whip, which he used with great abandon to push back those who dared approach too closely. One flourish came within inches of hitting me—needless to say I stepped back hurriedly and stayed back. (This was my first personal experience with physical coerciveness in Pueblo society, and it clearly points up the untenability of Benedict's thesis regarding its "Apollonian" character.) The other clown carried a lariat, which he used to snare those who, according to his lights, stood too close to the dancers. Immediately behind these two clowns—in actuality they were police officers, quite like those other clowns and war captains who guarded the masked Kachina dances and priestly retreats from evil spirits and over-zealous observers—came three more dancers, two wearing outfits made of American flags, one carrying a shield in one hand and a wooden spear in the other, the second an axe. The third, also a man, who danced between them, was dressed like a Pueblo woman, buckskin leggings and a black manta covered with a cerise blanket. But "her" hair was arranged in Plains style—a braid hanging over each shoulder and a green band circling her forehead, two feathers standing upright at the back. In each hand "she" carried a wand tipped with two eagle feathers. As they danced, the four drummers, in circle formation, sang and beat time.

I shall not describe their dance in detail, but it is worth noting that this Saint's Day festival was a rich amalgam of Pueblo, Plains, and Christian elements. Professor William L. Leap has recently written that, contrary to much that has been said regarding the superficial integration of borrowed elements, many external features have become important integral parts of Pueblo Indian ceremonies. He illustrates his point very successfully by reporting on a funeral in Isleta that was explicitly said to be an "Indian" and not a "Christian" funeral. But among other things, this "Indian" funeral utilized in a significant way such undeniably Christian features as the cross, candles, and "holy" water; the saying of a rosary by the mourners; and the offering of a prayer exhorting the "Almighty" to overlook any omissions or incorrect actions (Leap, ms.). True, Leap's example is drawn from Isleta, and the funeral ceremonies pictured in *Isleta Paintings* dramatically confirm him; but there is enough evidence from other pueblos to generalize his point. It has often been said that two heads are better than one. Why then should it be surprising to find that the Pueblo Indians, who live in a harsh environment, believe that two religions are better than one, and that better yet is the incorporation of effective alien "medicine" into native practice? At noon, the dancers, led by the clowns, left the plaza, and everyone went home to enjoy the midday meal.

Some hours later, the villagers and their guests reassembled, and the Darawee was performed (this is the corn dance referred to as Yakohano by Dr. Parsons in her letter above, p. 24f.) A group of older men, in ordinary trousers and shirts, and usually wearing colored bandoleers, entered the plaza first, singing and gesturing to the accompaniment of a single drum. Then came the dancers, two men followed by two women, then again two men followed by two women, until all the participants were assembled. The men were variously costumed. Some appeared in ordinary trousers and shirts and sometimes a vest, some in the short white embroidered skirt quite like those worn in the masked Kachina dances, and some with a foxtail hanging from their belt. Their hands were painted white, sometimes in a design, their faces red and white. In the right hand they carried a gourd rattle, in their left, a tassel of corn.

The women wore traditional Pueblo clothing, the black manta and the silken handkerchief at their back. They were heavily bedecked with jewelry of silver, turquoise, and shell. Their hair was laced with red braid, in each hand they held a corn husk, and, as apparently befits womanly behavior even in a matrilineal society, their steps were less vigorous than the men's.

The Darawee continued for about an hour, during which time the women threw bread, corn, and fruit to the dancers. A not inconsiderable amount was deposited inside the bower, presumably for consumption by the village officials.

The Darawee was followed by a Comanche dance and, after a short intermission, by another Darawee. As this was nearing its end, the Comanche dancers again entered the plaza and the two sets of dancers, each doing its own thing, continued to the end. When the dancing was over the governor delivered a second speech, his aides, as before, adding a few words. The sextons and the appointed women picked up the figurines of St. Joseph and Jesus and, accompanied by a few devoted followers, redeposited them and the tall candlestick in the church. So ended St. Joseph's Day—and the Laguna Indians' harvest thanksgiving on September 19, 1921.[25]

The following week Dr. Boas and I witnessed a similar celebration in nearby Pohuati, and years later I saw the corn dance, with certain variations, at Cochiti and Santo Domingo. A country fair accompanied each of them, but when the dances were being performed, both audience and participants exhibited great earnestness in the evident hope that by their correct actions they could bring about a better life for themselves and their society.

Before leaving Laguna in late September, Dr. Boas was determined to reach the top of Mt. Taylor. This mountain, it will be remembered, was one of the most sacred places of the Laguna villagers, the home of the moisture spirits where from time to time offerings were deposited in a pit at the summit. In the summer of 1920, Dr. Parsons and Mr. Lafarge had made the trip on horseback without Indian guides and, after a day's hard riding compounded by torrential rains, returned exhausted and deeply disappointed. They did reach the top of Mt. Taylor, they did locate the sacred depression, but within it there were no offerings, no prayer feathers, no prayer sticks—only empty beer cans, tossed in presumably by the surveyors who had been working there shortly before.

It was probably their failure to find any sign of Indian relations to the supernatural that made Dr. Boas so eager to try his luck. And despite my ineptitude on a horse, there was never a moment's doubt but that I would accompany him. This time, however, we would have Solomon Day and Carl Leon with us—both enthusiastic about spending a day on the sacred mountain.

Dr. Boas and I were driven to the foot of Mt. Taylor by automobile. Our Indian friends were already there, each with a fully saddled horse and a .22 rifle. The horses were for Dr. Boas and me, and we duly mounted them. Solomon and Carl immediately started up the trail on foot, so swiftly, in fact, that we often lost sight of them as they made sorties through the woods in search of wild turkeys, which they did not find.

Shortly before noon we came within view of the summit. The grade became extremely steep. Our horses couldn't go any farther, and neither could I. Dr. Boas waited until our horses were tethered and then followed our loping guides on foot. They waved to me from their sacred vantage point, and I waved back wanly, still bothered by the altitude and watching for snakes in the grass or some equally unwelcome animal. From their gestures I realized that they had found nothing in the depression—not even the beer cans of a former year.

When they returned we ate our sandwiches and immediately started our descent. For some reason, going down seemed harder to me than going up. It was slower, our horses were less sure footed, and after considerably more than an hour of what I felt to be intolerable suffering, I decided I needed a respite. I had to get off that horse. And I did. Relaxing my muscles—a means I had been told saved drunks from hurt when they fell—I released my stirrups, made myself into the smallest ball I could, and slipped happily from my mount, rolling quickly down a quite steep incline to get far away from threatening hoofs.

I was completely unharmed, but my escorts were panicked. They tested me all over—arms, legs, back, head—and found me all of a piece and quite complacent. Their fear gone, they had no pity. They shoved me into the saddle and we made our way silently down the mountainside as the shadows lengthened. It was dark when we reached bottom, and I thankfully climbed into our waiting automobile. Solomon and Carl led the horses away.

That night I ate no supper—not even standing, as Dr. Boas suggested. But I did persuade our hostess to ready gallons of hot water and fill the large round tin basin that served us as a tub. I can't remember ever having a bath feel so good.

Dr. Boas thought me quite a sissy. I don't believe he had been on a horse for years, but he was no tenderfoot, and while the long day had left him tired, he was not at all sore. We never referred to my engineered fall, but he never again suggested that we travel together on horseback. Yet, despite its discomforts, we both felt that the trip had been worthwhile.

Whether we made our visits at the wrong time of the year or whether the influx of "foreigners" was the deterrent, I cannot say. But from our experience it would seem that Mt. Taylor, though still celebrated in myth and mentioned in ritual, had largely become a happy hunting ground in a completely mundane sense, even for the Laguna villagers.

COCHITI, N.M., 1921

Dr. Boas and I left Laguna for Cochiti after the dance at Pohuati on the 26th of September, or it may have been early October. I can't remember our means of travel, but we probably went by train to the station nearest Peña Blanca, where the post office was located and the Catholic priest resided, and which in 1921 was the jumping-off place for Cochiti, on the other side of the Rio Grande. How we crossed the river that first time I can't remember either, but it was already autumn and the river was probably low enough to ford. Ruth Benedict, writing to Margaret Mead on August 29, 1925 from Peña Blanca, tells that she was staying there with a Mexican family in "a clean room under a tin roof" (Mead, 1959a: 294), on September 1 that "it looks as if I had to go to Cochiti," because the Indian who came didn't "know enough," (295) and, on September 3, that "the cart came, and we lunged across the river and up to the charming pueblo" (298).

I do remember entering the village in a cart drawn by a team of horses. When we left in June 1922 (after our second visit to the pueblo), we also set out in a horse-drawn cart, this time accompanied by at least five members of my "family," which made things tight but jolly. At the river Dr. Boas and I climbed into a flat-bottom rowboat, which I did not totally trust, for reasons that appear below. But we made the crossing without mishap. I have a snapshot, which I must have taken since I don't appear in it. But Dr. Boas does, dressed as befits a famous professor of anthropology about to reenter the "civilized" world—dark suit, white shirt, tie, fedora, overcoat on his arm, and his sacred briefcase resting against his left leg, our younger Indian oarsman standing as if at attention, the older one, content to sit, no doubt worn out by his exertions. The Rio at this point is quite broad, and in 1922, after the spring rains, which must have been heavy, quite unruly.[26] But while it raised problems for travel, it gave assurance of a well-watered crop and good harvest.

Cochiti lies about 30 miles southwest of Santa Fe and a similar distance from Frijoles, where the people of Cochiti claim their ancestors lived hundreds of years before the advent of the Spaniards in 1540. Cochiti, like Laguna, is a Keres-speaking village. In 1921 its population was something over 200. In 1952, Lange put it at 444 (Lange, 1959: 426).

I was impressed with Cochiti's modernity, "the new one-story buildings, the tin roofs, the calico mother-hubbards." But while I saw no women wearing "the orthodox Pueblo costume, black manta, calico slip, woven belt" on ordinary days—which many women did in Laguna—at ceremonial times, and I had my only opportunity to observe this shortly after our arrival when the community harvested the cacique's corn, the orthodox Pueblo costume was again the order of the day. (In my monograph I date this event as 1922, but it was surely 1921, for it was in that year that we were in Cochiti at harvest time.)

Cochiti has been ridden by factionalism—apparently a chronic disease in all pueblos, to judge from the ethnological and archaeological evidence. In 1921 there were two major factions in the village: the "conservatives" and the "progressives." That this division was by no means recent can be seen from Bandelier's journal of October 24, 1880 (Lange, 1959: 14). Where the acceptance or non-acceptance of Catholicism was involved, it probably dates from the entry of the Spaniards into the region. But it is of interest that Fray Alonso de Benavides in his memorial commented as early as 1630 on the continual strife between "warriors and sorcerers" in the Pueblos (Goldfrank, 1945c: 3).

The "conservatives" believed that they could best be served by their traditional hierarchy and societies—of course, with adjustments to assure the continuance of their native ideas and practices. The "progressives" considered many of these ideas and practices a deterrent to progress. They looked at first to the Catholic religion for inspiration and education, and later to the U.S. government. For the most part, they accepted the annually elected officers of the pueblo, such as the governor (who most anthropologists believe was chosen to front for a native hierarchy, and particularly for the cacique, in dealings with the Spaniards). But when Dr. Boas and I arrived in Cochiti, it was the "judge," a man of their own choosing, and not the governor, whom they recognized as arbiter in matters of law and order.

In 1921, the leader of the progressive faction was John Dixon[27] (also known as Juan de Jesus Pancho, although I never heard him referred to thus). He was one of the first three Cochiti Indians to graduate from Carlisle, the Indian school of higher education in Pennsylvania. In 1921 and 1922 when Dr. Boas and I were in Cochiti, he was the "judge." Lange states that this office was created in 1921 and abolished in 1923, but when we first arrived in Cochiti, John Dixon seemed well established. "In the winter of 1922," I wrote in *The Social and Ceremonial Organization of Cochiti*, "Alcario Montoya, who has been governor of the Pueblo several times, along with some other Indians from Domingo and Isleta over whom John Dixon also has jurisdiction, made the journey to Washington to have him removed. The trip cost the pueblo some hundreds of dollars of public funds and was entirely unsuccessful, as the Bureau of Indian Affairs had no intention of removing anyone so imbued with their point of view, even though it made for constant friction and divided authority in the pueblo" (Goldfrank, 1927: 31). During both our stays John Dixon was Professor Boas' host and his major informant.

Also in this 1927 monograph I charted what I believed to be the structure of the traditional Cochiti society. I knew there had been changes since Father Noel Dumarest, the Catholic priest, had served the village around the turn of the century, and Dr. Parsons lists many adjustments in *Pueblo Indian Religion* (particularly pp. 1144 ff.). I cite just one case to show the value of restudying the same pueblo at different periods of time, even if, in the process, the investigator concentrates on what an anthropological major at Barnard College in 1968, in disgust, termed "pure esoterica."

In his notes edited by Dr. Parsons, Father Dumarest mentioned the nahia, the head of the warrior society, claiming that this officer was invested by the cacique and afterward was subordinate to him. In 1921, I was given an account which also mentioned that the nahia was invested in the cacique's house and was "dressed" by the cacique at the order of the war captains (at this time these annually elected officers were definitely considered lower in rank than the cacique); this operation completed, the cacique then became subordinate to the nahia.

Manifestly, Dumarest's informant and mine saw the situations of the cacique and nahia reversed. Lange states, "Present-day informants tend to support Goldfrank's position concerning the two offices of the nahia and the cacique," and he adds, "In rather typical pueblo fashion, it would appear that the two officers were essentially equal in over-all prestige and authority, with the cacique having the final word in matters of peace, or internal welfare, while the naihiya assumed charge in times of war" (Lange, 1959: 278).[28]

Eliminating for the moment the idiocyncracies of particular informants, I would like to stress that, besides adaptations due to drought, war, illness, or the extinction of a society (the Warrior Society became past history at Cochiti shortly after 1900), the strengths and weaknesses of personality can play important roles in how functions are redistributed or acquired—even in the "Apollonian" pueblos, as Benedict, Bunzel, and Goldman have characterized them—by the outright use of force.

Dumarest reports the following incident. He tells us, "The head of the *matalotes* [men who have killed one or more Navajo and brought back the scalps] is the leader in the war dances. The Cacique is not necessarily *matalote*, but he had the right in the war dances to assign each dancer his *malincha* or female partner. Recently, at Cochiti this right was usurped by the nahia who is also the head of the *matalotes*. He was on his way to fetch to the dance one of the women he had chosen when the Cacique met him and had him make the poor woman change from her dance dress and give it over to the woman the Cacique himself had chosen. The episode made considerable noise" (Dumarest, 1919: 200).

This time the usurper's maneuver failed. But it is hard to believe this was the only time in Cochiti's history that an individual took matters into his own hands to attain his ends. Certainly force would be a last resort in the pueblos, but there is too much evidence attesting to coercive and punishing action—even death—to claim that force is "alien to Pueblo society." Moreover, it should be remembered that when irrigation is large-scale (not necessarily in terms of absolute dimensions, but in terms of comprehensiveness) it produces a tendency toward centralized leadership, weaker to be sure in the western pueblos, such as Hopi and Zuni, where the permanent water supply depends essentially on springs, than in the eastern pueblos, where the Rio Grande provides a more permanent and adequate source. In Cochiti and Isleta, and elsewhere in the pueblos, the original structure seems to have emphasized dual leadership—the town chief (cacique) and the war chief.

In the 1920s this structure was greatly weakened in both villages. In Cochiti, the extinction of the Warrior Society in the early 1900s and what may have been an inadequate or aging nahia (as early as 1880 Bandelier wrote that the cacique was the "medicine man of war") provided the opportunity for the cacique to become the outstanding authority. Insofar as I was able to learn, this was accomplished—perhaps for the reasons stated above and because disciplinary action and the protection of ceremonies fell largely to the war captains—without any noteworthy opposition.

In Isleta matters were different. Here, after the death of Sun Arrow, the cacique in the 1880s, and the death of his legitimate surrogate in training, the war chief, ignoring accepted mores, assumed this position and abandoned his erstwhile functions to his assistant. In 1924 there were still many Isletans who refused to recognize the then cacique, and who, in fact, stated that the village had no cacique then or since the death of Sun Arrow (cf. Parsons, 1932: 256, n. 54; and Goldfrank, 1962: 8, n. 7; Goldfrank, 1967: 23).

Thus a trend led in one instance to acceptance of this succession, at least within the conservative faction, in the other to an ongoing dispute within the pueblo as a whole. In neither case is there any mention of the use of force—but that is a subject Pueblo Indians shun, particularly with outsiders, since cooperation is considered the wellspring of the good life. And in irrigation societies like the pueblos, cooperation is just that. White has said, in speaking of San Felipe, another Keresan pueblo, "Disobedience is sacrilege and heresy as well as treason" (1932: 11). His statement is equally relevant to Cochiti.

So factionalism was rife when we arrived in Cochiti in the fall of 1921, and Dr. Boas must have been fully aware of the situation when we went directly to the house of John Dixon, who, as leader of the progressives, could be expected to get us "settled" and find adequate informants for us.

Dr. Boas remained, as noted above, in John Dixon's house, using one of his two rooms as a combined bedroom and study and a place in which he could interview his informants—among whom, and primary, was John Dixon himself. I was installed in the schoolhouse, one room of which was given over to education, the rest to living quarters for the teachers, Mr. and Mrs. Ripley (pseudonyms), who were, I believe, in their mid- or late forties and childless. He was comfortably built and affable; she was gaunt and irritable. But she fed me well, and since I was rarely at the schoolhouse during the day, and our first stay in Cochiti was short—a little more than a week at most—I was not much affected by their quarrels or her querulousness.

Our first evening Dr. Boas and I walked around the village, past the Catholic Church, which was considerably larger than the one at

Laguna and, as we discovered later, much more conventional (it was open only Sunday mornings when the priest came over from Peña Blanca to say Mass). We also passed the two roundhouses, entered only through a hole in the roof, which was reached by a ladder; the Turquoise Kiva, symbolic of winter, was in the charge of the Koshari society; the Squash Kiva, symbolic of summer, was in the charge of the Kurena society. It was these two groups I termed managing societies in my 1927 monograph, and Lange, confirming me, stated that they "alternated annually in ceremonial supervision" (Lange, 1959: 285f.).

Most of the houses were of adobe, the material so eminently suited to the Southwest climate, but there was also a scatter of frame houses with tin roofs—more prestigious perhaps, but much hotter in summer. At one side of the plaza, there was a pump from which the villagers drew the water for their daily needs. Privies were routine, except when the open fields offered a more convenient squatting place.

The fields were a short distance from the village along the Rio Grande. The *Visitador*, Fray Francisco Atanacio Dominguez, who arrived in New Mexico in March 1776, wrote as follows regarding them:

> All important farmlands which this pueblo owns lie on the east side of the river, downstream along the river, extending the breadth of the plain and down to join those of the pueblo of Santo Domingo. There are some milpas on the bank on which the pueblo stands, and very few up to the north on both banks. All take water of the said river for irrigation through deep wide ditches. They yield very abundant crops of everything sown in them. There is an occasional peach tree. (Lange, 1959: 11)

I may add that there are some differences in reporting just how Cochiti's fields were located in relation to the river. I have a very poor sense of direction, so it is not too surprising that while I speak of methods of planting and harvesting, ditch digging and ditch cleaning, I never mention where the fields lay, although I knew they ran along the river bank. The rains too had their effects; a year of good rainfall, but not too heavy, might mean an extension of flood-farming, but even in 1921 before the ditches, etc., were vastly improved, major dependence on irrigation was essential for productive farming (see Lange, 1959: pictures between 296 and 297).

On September 5, 1925, Ruth Benedict wrote to Margaret Mead from Cochiti, "I want to find a really important undiscovered country." Mead adds, "She still thought that this was to be found by learning French or Russian 'well enough to be really at home in the verse';" And again, according to Mead, she "also wanted to find out whether she would have felt at home in a different period—in ancient Egypt, for example." Mead concludes that "through her first experience with anthropological materials she began to find answers to these two basic preoccupations" (Mead, 1959a: 201; see also Benedict's letter: 301).

As already indicated, Benedict's visit to Cochiti in the fall of 1925 was not her first field trip. And manifestly a few days or weeks spent in Cochiti in this and the previous year[29] collecting tales, many of which had in whole or in part been recorded previously by Dr. Boas (her acknowledgments are too many to cite) was surely not the answer to her search for an "important undiscovered country." But in a sense Mead was right. Through anthropological materials Benedict did begin to "find answers to these two basic preoccupations."

Quite clearly, the pueblos as she "found" them—one might better say as she understood them—were indeed an important undiscovered country for her, communities so different from "our dirty-minded, puritan-bred society" (Mead, 1959a: 140), which ruled out, on the basis of "logic," any "orthodox identification of capitalism and democracy" (152). For her, as she first noted in print in 1928 and more importantly in 1934 in *Patterns of Culture*, the pueblos were communities in which individual effort was concentrated on the collective welfare, in which sexual aberrations were of little or no concern, in which there were no reasons for disturbing rivalrous strivings, in which coercive authority was as inconceivable as the survival of a snowball in Hell.

In Cochiti, she writes, she had no difficulty in securing informants (probably because Dr. Boas had prepared the ground). But like most investigators up until the 1940s, including Dr. Boas, she did find "the taboo against imparting esoteric information to the Whites ... very strong" (Benedict, 1931: ix). And if, at the time her idealization of the pueblos was already taking shape (see Bennett, 1946), there is nothing to indicate this in her collection of *Tales of the Cochiti Indians*, dated 1931—three years after she first seriously stressed the "Apollonian" character of Pueblo society. But I am almost sure her manuscript was completed long before 1931. The Bureau of American Ethnology was notorious for its slowness in publishing, and Benedict's *Tales* probably shared the fate of writings by Parsons, White, et al.

My first morning after breakfast, I again wandered about the village—no informant seems to have been available for me and Dr. Boas was already working with John Dixon. In the plaza, drawing water from the pump, I saw a young woman, comely by any standard, who returned my greeting with a welcoming smile. A most encouraging gesture, I thought. I knew that women, and particularly young women, were not well informed regarding "secret" matters (men's business), but at this time I hoped to find someone willing to give me kinship terms that I could tie in with Dr. Parsons' genealogical work on Laguna (not published until 1923). And women the world over were—and are—notorious for their interest in small talk.

My presence in the plaza was no surprise to the woman at the pump. Any changes in village life, even those of small moment, quickly became common knowledge, and every household in Cochiti surely knew of our arrival the previous day and where we were staying. To encourage an exchange, I asked her if she lived near the plaza—carrying a bucket full of water would hardly be an enjoyable chore, however short the distance. She did live near the plaza, she said, and she asked me if I would like to visit her. Most pueblo people give the illusion of friendliness, whatever their real feelings. Anyone may be a witch, so best be nice to everyone. But her cordiality seemed real, and I gladly accepted her invitation.

On the way she told me her Spanish name was Isabel Diaz (pueblo Indians never address each other by their Indian names—one is the wife of so-and-so), that she was married to Pedro Ramirez (later I learned that she was his second wife and considerably his junior), and that they had two young daughters, Rita and Dolores.

Knowing that Dr. Boas was staying with John Dixon and working with him, she soon told me she and her husband were "progressives." Much later I learned that they no longer attended even the open performances in the plaza because when they had last done so, the dance "police"—counterparts, it would seem, of those I described for Laguna—had sought out persons who felt as they did and whipped them openly. And in 1929, I learned that she "was not allowed to see them any more," inferably not because she was a woman but because she was a "progressive."

Isabel spoke English well. She told me her mother had been born in a nearby pueblo, a member of a clan that was also represented in Cochiti. And since descent in both pueblos was matrilineal, clan membership in her new locale posed no problem to her. Nor did her marriage to Pedro, since he, as socially prescribed, belonged to a different clan. Isabel also told me that her parents were dead and that she had inherited her house from her father. In my Cochiti monograph (p. 27) I wrote, "Notions regarding property are undergoing gradual changes," influenced, quite clearly, by American inheritance patterns.

Isabel had sold her house to her cousin and her present home had been built by her husband. It was one of the newer types, a frame base with a tin roof and a nice yard in front. The main room, manifestly the master bedroom, boasted an iron bed, double and painted white. Behind this room was the kitchen, as I remember it, with only a kerosene stove, a few chairs, a table in the middle and floor, walls, and ceiling of wood slats. To the right was another room, a storeroom of sorts and presumably where the little girls slept on the earthen floor, wrapped, when the weather required it, in Navajo rugs for warmth and comfort. The privy was across a narrow road beyond the front yard.

Isabel was unusually outspoken, and this, I believe, was in large part due to the fact that before her marriage she had lived for some time outside the pueblo, with the family of a White doctor who seems to have had some government connection. It was not too long before I told her that I was interested in learning kinship terms, a task which I hoped would pose minimal difficulties, and we soon began to work on genealogies.

Once it became known that I was a regular visitor in Isabel's house, several of her female relatives put in an appearance, and while working in a pueblo is far from a bull session, there were often as many as three Indian ladies arguing over just what who called whom. This inevitably led to discussions of clans that were still in existence and those that had become extinct. In my Cochiti monograph I wrote, "I did not make a complete census of the village," but I did note "upwards of one hundred and fifty names with clans." And, most unexpectedly, I was given many Indian names. Moreover, "there seemed to be no objection to marriage into any of the clans, except one's own." I added, "often preferences arise in families and we find several members of one family marrying related members of another clan, or a man picking a second wife from the clan to which his first wife belonged." I cautioned that this last was "unconnected with any idea of levirate or sororate," but, as is the case in our own culture, "the result of a previous intimate relation with a certain family." I also noted that marriage was further limited by the influence of the Church, which prohibited the union of blood cousins and even the union of their children (Goldfrank, 1927: 13 ff.).

The terms themselves I found in a "transitional period" (19). Robin Fox (1967) is more inclined to believe that instead of clan degeneracy, there has been an incomplete development in this sector of society. In any event, certain typical Keresan Pueblo features were in evidence—a difference in the terms used depending upon the sex of the speaker and the principle of reciprocity. On the other hand, I also found that "categories differing from the expected usage" were in the process of being formed. For instance, in Genealogy I (Goldfrank, 1927: 121 ff.), the determining principle was the extension of father-mother terms to include all aunts and uncles, whether maternal or paternal, and, as would follow, the application of sister-brother terms to all cousins (19). Quite naturally the loss in importance of the mother's brother accompanied the deterioration in the importance of maternal clans; and this is documented even in my Genealogy III, which deals with a "family active in the religious life of the pueblo and well versed in native customs" (20, 122 ff.). And also, quite naturally, the discussion of kinship and clans soon led to a discussion of clan functions, such as clan adoptions, to assure the survival of a particular clan, or in return for clan action in effecting a cure. Clanship also had a role in the naming of the newborn infant.

Pedro Ramirez, who now and again came back to the house during the day, seemed eager to escape the female company. Sometimes during the growing season he even stayed the night in the bower-like shelter in his field. Except for short greetings exchanged with him and John Dixon, routine contacts with the Ripleys and walks in the early evening with Dr. Boas, my time was spent almost entirely with Isabel at her house, her young daughters nearby and a few, usually unexpected, female visitors. My considerable genealogical material provided a firm basis for my continuing investigations in Cochiti the following June.

As indicated above, Dr. Boas and I caught a glimpse of Cochiti ceremonial when the cacique's crop was harvested (in Cochiti both the planting and the harvesting were done for him by the community). The Kurena was the managing society at the the time. In the morning, the war captain announced that the cacique's corn would be harvested that day. Its members went through the village singing: two of them masked and draped in Hopi blankets, two also masked but virtually naked and carrying a Kurena whip, two unmasked but draped in blankets and carrying a comb, probably for some act of grooming, and two carrying black paint to be used in streaking the cheeks of those who participated. The women were also brushed with wands, an act designated by the same word that connotes "brushing off sickness."

About three o'clock in the afternoon the harvesters returned from the field. They were led by the war captain, his assistant, and the governor. Wagons loaded with corn drove up to the Koshari house (the cacique at Cochiti is a member of the Koshari Society). The Kurena stood at one side singing. The war captain, who was a Kurena, appeared in full regalia on the roof of the Koshari house, accompanied by some of his young helpers. Various officers made speeches.

A black manta belonging to the cacique (in Cochiti he is referred to as "mother," as is his sacred corn fetish) was spread on the roof. All perfect ears of corn were placed on it to receive his blessing. Later they were handed over to the Women's Society to lend out to women who were pregnant or sick or felt a need for special protection. The cacique and the three Koshari women who were his helpers remained inside the Koshari house. Smoke issued from the chimney, a sure signal that a ceremonial fire had been lit within.

After the perfect ears of corn had been "blessed" and disposed of, the rest of the corn was piled on the roof of the Koshari house. Each

Left to right (anthropological picnic): Nils Nelson of AMNH, unknown, Franz Boas, the author, unknown, Gertrud Boas, Robert Lowie, Pliny Goddard, William Ogburn, Gladys Reichard, Mrs. Nelson. Early Spring 1921?

Franz Boas, Alfred Kroeber, at ease, 1921 or 1922.

Portland Or. Aug. 7. 1922

My dear Esther,

I hope your trip is not as bad as you anticipated. How many miles of water or whatever to my L? The trip can be beautiful and not a bore (to use your terminology). We found Stepmeal at the Post Office all fine & the arrival of Norman Poor... the family in & out of meals... seems to be going well. We saved up Aug. 4, one day too late to celebrate with his godmother. We did & Emily Orin things the sweet boy; then is no use of going away. For tomorrow we have enjoyed an auto trip to Post Row along the Columbia, saying "Wish you were here & also"... but — our weather... the others... note is nice. So I suppose Tom think is just as good. Remember me & family to whoever you might be glad to meet. Wish (or do you say) you wish to go to meet Tom? Anyway I do will be glad to meet you Tom). Thank us for her letter. We shall postpone trip here until Wednesday

night. Kindest regards, little godmother next coupled her.

Yours, as ever
Emily Poor.

Dear Esther — such a waste of present writing paper — I must add a few lines and tell you that Portland is beautiful even though we cannot see Mt. Hood. Such weather is just too we are hanging around this hotel waiting for a train which they said will be on hand for us by evening. So when we arrive we will get a change of clothes. Papa Poor has been trying to find people who have gone out of town and I am spending most of my time writing letters till I thought we have been at them long ago. What do you say to all that — Catch and guess anything our family. We seemed to be locked to the anchor. This generation. You ought to have seen the same colors when we left — so clean and in order everything just as we found it. Well you get meat add a few words to Gladys' letter this well, don't take work with closely read cousins. Have lots of fun and Thanks of your mama. Emily Poor.

Kurena and every woman of the village was then given several ears of corn for seed. Any shortage would have been made up from the cacique's personal stock—a procedure on a small scale that is highly reminiscent of the ever-ready granaries of the rulers of much more populous hydraulic societies.

That is all we saw of Cochiti's extensive and complex ceremonial life in 1921. Dr. Boas and I left by train sometime in October feeling that we had made a good beginning, and we were already planning for our return the following June.

8. NEW YORK INTERLUDE

I passed the winter of 1921-22 much as I had passed the previous years—secretarial work, classes, Tuesday lunches; and I still was not asked to present my notes in any orderly fashion. But there was one difference: as the months went by, I realized more and more clearly that I wanted to study seriously, that the informal acquisition of knowledge, even the advantage of field trips, was not enough. When Dr. Boas told me he had been invited to give a summer course at the University of California, Berkeley, and asked me to work for him there after our June stay in Cochiti, I gladly agreed. But I also announced that at the end of the Berkeley session, I would like to resign my secretaryship. He didn't seem too surprised. He must have sensed my growing interest in an academic career. Although I am not entirely certain, I believe that before we left for the West, Ruth Bunzel had consented to replace me.

9. AGAIN A FIELD-WORKER

COCHITI, N.M., JUNE 1922

It is very different to return to a pueblo where one has friends or to walk in cold, with at best a suggestion from an Indian agent or the local storekeeper as to who might be a likely host or hostess. Dr. Boas' and my return to Cochiti was a homecoming, in the ordinary and not the Pinter tradition. (Mrs. Boas was to meet us afterward in Albuquerque, accompany us on a short trip to Frijoles Canyon and the Grand Canyon, and then be our housekeeper in Berkeley, where Kroeber had rented a small bungalow for us within walking distance of the campus.)

Dr. Boas had returned to John Dixon's house, and I to my same room with the Ripleys. Dr. Boas continued his interviews, and I mine with Isabel and her female relatives. But some things were not to remain the same. This year our stay in Cochiti was considerably longer, and Mrs. Ripley's behavior became more of a problem to me. She may have been passing through menopause, or perhaps both of us lacked sufficient adaptability. In any event, living at the schoolhouse became extremely unpleasant. I had written to Dr. Parsons about it. On June 15, 1922, she wrote me "Too bad about your nice room. . . Why don't you explain to Dr. Boas." Encouraged by her note, I overcame my reluctance to add to his problems. I told him I would like to live elsewhere and suggested that I might see whether Isabel and Pedro would take me in. Happily, they consented, and I spent my remaining weeks in Cochiti in their house.

It was a most rewarding change. We enjoyed each other, and after a short time Pedro, as well as a few male visitors, were willing to talk to me about matters beyond kinship. I believe everyone who offered information was related in one way or another to him or Isabel. Pedro was a man of great dignity, integrity, and few words, but I never doubted that he found me a not-unwelcome addition to their small household.

Despite my warm reception, my first night in the Ramirezes' house was not a comfortable one. I seem to be particularly attractive to bugs of various kinds, and that night I didn't sleep at all. I waited until the morning to register a complaint, and somewhat shamefacedly exhibited my welts to Isabel. I asked her if there might be another bed in the village less afflicted with wildlife. My request did not seem to embarrass her. Immediately, word went out of my need for a bugless bed—size and style of no moment. Within minutes, or so it seemed to me, several villagers with small cots were lined up in the Ramirezes' front yard. We spent the better part of the morning making a "scientific" examination.

Our method was simple enough. We tossed boiling water on the wooden supports and springs and watched. One by one all the cots were eliminated, to the obvious dismay of their owners. I decided that if I had to suffer bugs, I preferred Isabel's. That afternoon she and I went to work. We secured a can of Peterman's bug-killer at the village store; sprayed mattresses, rugs, and cushions; and settled the four legs of the iron bed in cups of repellent. (Isabel and Pedro had generously given me their bedroom—and this prized possession—and joined their daughters in the dark inner room.) Then we threw pot after pot of boiling water on the wooden floor, wall and ceiling slats—in fact on everything that would not be destroyed by this vigorous action. We had the great satisfaction of seeing bugs rush out from everywhere to meet a hot and sudden death. I remained in the iron bed, never quite relaxed, certain I was still being victimized—a flight of imagination quite contrary to the fact. For some time, that day at the Ramirezes' made history in Cochiti.

One Sunday afternoon, not long after our midday meal, news reached the village that the rowboat ferry between Peña Blanca and Cochiti had capsized and that the unlucky passengers were clinging to a tree-trunk in midstream. Everyone rushed to the river—men, women and children; even the oldest woman in Cochiti, and the richest (like the Navajo, her wealth was counted in sheep), removed her shoes and lifted her skirts high to keep them from getting wet as she sturdily crossed the newly irrigated fields that abutted the river.

Five or six people were sitting on the semi-submerged stump in rapidly flowing water. Even at a distance of some hundred or more feet we could sense their apprehension. Perhaps they were thinking of the man who, on his trip to the underworld, was taken to see a mountain of ice (an iceberg, his guide explained) where people who committed evil deeds while they were alive sit naked, "water dripping down along it and dripping upon the people" (Benedict, 1931: 255; from a tale recorded by Boas). Perhaps they were thinking of the "River Men" who visit the village in the spring, dressed like tramps and carrying quirts or whips, which they crack loudly. Lange reports that "a young mother discussing the 'bogeyman' aspects of the River Men told of how the younger children ran from their sight and of how her own nine-year-old son hid under the bed when he heard of their coming" (1959: 338). In my 1927 monograph (92 ff.) I note that the witches, so greatly feared by everyone, live in the river, and I record a tale of a boy witch, who, in an attempt to get a good friend to join the Witch Society, takes him down to the river for four mornings, gets him to drink its water and then vomit (this is also an initial phase of initiation into acceptable societies). The witch boy tells him of all the powers he would have once he joined the Witch Society. He would be able to "lie down with any woman, who would never know that anyone had been with her during the night." He "would be able to talk and understand all languages, even those of birds and animals and he could turn himself into a coyote, crow, owl, or any other animal, even a deer." He would be a successful hunter. They then go south to a nearby Mexican settlement, and here the witch-boy whispers something to his friend. It is then that the friend decides he will not join the Witch Society. I was not told the words he uttered, but from comparative tales (see Parsons 1939: 220 and n.) it can be inferred that what the witch-boy whispered to his friend and what frightened him away was the fact that, after joining the society, he would have the power to kill without fear of discovery.

Imbued with such beliefs and tales from earliest childhood, it is not surprising that despite the benefits derived from the Rio, the Cochiti Indians were not aquatic enthusiasts— and Indians watching the rescue preparations seemed as concerned as those stranded in mid-stream.

First, an attempt was made to reach the unfortunates by horse and cart. But the current was too strong and the driver had to turn back. Then a few of the best swimmers—there weren't many—tried to rescue one individual at a time. But this, too, was more than they could manage. Finally, a human chain was formed, led by the best swimmers, the less accomplished ones coming next, and those who couldn't swim at all remaining where they could stand. Eventually, the leaders reached the boat, righted it, and pushed it toward the stump. Gingerly the tree-bound passengers stepped into it and the human chain began pulling toward the shore. The viewers cheered as the drenched passengers mounted the bank, happy that no one had been relegated to a watery and unpredictable grave.

My relations with the Ramirez family became increasingly friendly. One day after we had been discussing methods of adoption, particularly clan adoption, Isabel asked me if I would like to be adopted into her clan. She would be my ceremonial mother and Pedro my ceremonial father. I was more than happy at this indication of their affection for me and quickly consented. Dr. Boas was not invited—just the Ramirezes and a cousin of Isabel's.

In Cochiti many ritualistic practices conform, with variations, to basic patterns. This is the case with clan adoption which, like adoption for cures and initiation into a society, closely resembles ceremonies performed at the birth of a child. In each of these situations, an individual's re-birth is being enacted.

When an infant is born the mother "lies in" for four days—four is the magic number in Keresan pueblos. She is then bathed and her hair is washed by a female relative. A shaman is called and, accompanied by family members, takes the infant out to the east "to the sun," sprinkles cornmeal in four directions, prays, and gives the infant a name or names as desired. The mother watches from the doorway.

Clan adoption involves an adult, usually, in this matrilineal society, a female who can be expected, through her children, to strengthen the adopting clan. It normally takes place in the fall. Mine was immediately exceptional since it took place in June, not long before Dr. Boas and I left Cochiti. Also, as noted above, Isabel had asked me if I wished to be adopted, although normally a person wanting to be adopted notifies the war captain, who then notifies the cacique, who then asks the war captain to make a public announcement. Clans may compete for the new member, but she will join the one that asked for her first.

Like most ceremonies, clan adoption begins with hairwashing, in this case by a female member of the adopting clan or, if there is no female member available, by the wife of the war captain or the wife of a male member of the adopting clan. Usually this hairwashing takes place at the house of the applicant's "ceremonial mother," who is always afterward referred to by her as "mother." Then, like the newborn infant, the about-to-be new clan member is taken out to the sun. Cornmeal is sprinkled toward the east and benefits asked. Her new clan is mentioned and she is given a new name. That night she provides a feast to which members of her ceremonial mother's clan (now also her clan) and their husbands are invited.

My adoption, as already indicated, deviated considerably from this pattern. There was no public announcement. But my "ceremonial mother," Isabel, washed my hair in her front yard, using a large tin basin exactly like the one I had so happily bathed in after my painful descent from Mt. Taylor. Pedro, my "ceremonial father," stood by, and present also were the little girls, Dolores and Rita; Pedro's daughter by a previous marriage, Maria; and Isabel's male cousin. Then Isabel turned toward the sun, sprinkled pollen, and mentioned my clan and my new name, "Wapurnitsa" (Abalone Shell). I can't remember whether I threw a feast, as I should have done. But I do remember that the day was one of great celebration, especially for me.

Shortly after Dr. Boas and I arrived in Berkeley, Isabel, responding to my letter, wrote that all of them liked the pictures I had taken. All of them, that is, except one. "You know which I mean." Almost surely, her own. She kept referring to my song that her step-daughter called "Esther's song." (As I explained above, I am not much of a songstress, and the only song I think it might have been is K-K-K-Katey.) Now, also, Cochiti's feast day was not far off, and all were getting ready for this "big day," plastering their houses, putting down new mud floors, whitewashing. Isabel added that the cacique's wife had given birth to a boy and that in jubilation the cacique gave "two long shots."

Pedro was busy baling hay (99 bales), and the men had gone on a hunt. She then asked me about the "pictures on the doorstep" I had taken on the day of my adoption and about those of her children grinding corn.

This newsy letter, with apologies "for making a lot of mistakes" and in the hope that "you will be glad to hear from me" was signed, somewhat unexpectedly, "Your mother, Mrs. Ramirez."

I heard from Isabel from time to time up until 1929, but then not until ten years later. I did not see her again until the summer of 1946 when I and my present husband, Karl August Wittfogel, spent several weeks in the Southwest. After that, she and I wrote each other regularly. We were close in age and were soon writing on an Esther-Isabel basis. In my Christmas note in 1972, I must have teased her for forgetting I was her adopted daughter. Her reply began, "My dear Daughter Esther." It was signed "Mother Isabel."

In this reply she bemoaned the difficulty of bringing up children. "It is very hard to make them obey. They do what they want to do." She added, "We cannot do like we did so many years back." Then she asked whether my children obeyed. Manifestly, even in her once-so-disciplined pueblo, the parent-child relationship was undergoing changes not too different from those occurring in U.S. society generally.

I am a poor correspondent, and eight months passed before I answered her plaintive inquiry. I told her that I kept the picture of her, her daughters, and me under the glass on my dressing table, along with those of family members, so that we were in daily contact. I told her that the ways of the world were certainly changing, but that, in looking back upon my own childhood, I could not say that I had always been obedient. I also asked her to go back to our Esther-Isabel basis, since my "mother" comment was just a bit of teasing. To no avail. Her quick answer began "Dear daughter." Again she referred to "the load parents have today." And she reminded me that I was her "daugher in cornmeal and the shampoo" since the day she had adopted me. This letter was signed "Mother Isabel."

10. ON TO BERKELEY, CALIFORNIA, JULY 1922

Dr. Boas and I met Mrs. Boas in Albuquerque, and then, backtracking, the three of us spent a day at Frijoles Canyon. We seem to have experienced the normal problems of automobiling at that time and in that area, for I have a snapshot of our chauffeur busily changing a tire on a narrow, winding mountain road, a steep cliff rising on one side and falling away sharply on the other to give us a fine view of the valley below.

As I have mentioned, the Cochiti Indians believe that their ancestors lived in Frijoles for centuries. The Canyon is not very long or broad. The floor had been excavated and a substantial complex of rooms exposed, indicating that the multiple dwellings were several stories high with setbacks not unlike those in certain of our modern high-rise apartment houses (it is still possible at Taos, N.M., to get an idea of how they were constructed). The cliffs rose precipitously on both sides of the floor, and on one side, near the top, a hugh cave provided the stage for important ceremonials. A round kiva had been constructed within it, and a ladder led to a lower level. Today ladders also make it comparatively easy for visitors to reach the cave, and it seems likely that the Indians had a similar device for entry. There are also several smaller caves (obviously once used as dwellings, to judge from the sooty ceilings), and stone extensions, presumably built like those in former times to enlarge the living space, have been added. But it is evident that the major part of the population occupied rooms on the Canyon's floor. Where their fields were placed or how they may have been watered cannot be determined from the numerous pictures I took that day. This fact again underlines the overwhelming interest in mythology, language, ceremonialism, and kinship in Southwest ethnological investigations in the early 1920s and the scant attention given to basic aspects of subsistence that make life possible in this arid landscape.

By 1939, attitudes had changed considerably. In the introduction to *Pueblo Indian Religion*, Dr. Parsons wrote, "To describe even a part of a culture is a dangerous enterprise; so interwoven is one part with another that the fabric tears when we begin to separate, leaving meaningless shreds in our hands. This is particularly true of those values and forms of religion, which is far more a dispersal of phenomena than, according to its etymological sense, a binding together; for religious facts get their value or weighting from the general life" (ix f.). In her Appendix, in listing "research desirable in Pueblo culture," she places after "comparative study of Pueblo handicrafts and arts" the short but important phrase "in fact, of the material culture in general, including land ownership and use." And in a note at the foot of the page she reports that "a study in Zuni economics is promised by Dr. Ruth L. Bunzel, who suggests that similar studies in owning and using property be made among Keres and Tanoans" (Vol. 2, p. 1211).

Dr. Bunzel did undertake such a study in Zuni in the 30s, but except for her chapter on economics in *General Anthropology*, edited by Dr. Boas and published in 1938, none of her data on Zuni economy as such has, as far as I know, appeared in print; neither in the weeks she spent in our company on Martha's Vineyard in the summer of 1941 nor subsequently did she discuss her findings with me or Professor Wittfogel, although she knew of our great interest in Pueblo subsistence economy.

After leaving Frijoles, the Boases and I returned to Albuquerque. The next morning we left by train for a short stopover (two nights and a day) at the Grand Canyon, which was certainly "grand"—and almost unreal when the lights of the dying day stained its great expanse. After a very early breakfast, the three of us walked down the trail to the edge of the short cliff that rose from the rushing waters below. I was not at all sorry that I had not accompanied Major J. W. Powell in 1869 on his famous exploratory expedition down the river in the small boat in which he and his companions put their trust. After our short examination of the scene, we walked back to the ranger's hut, where three sure-footed mules were waiting to carry us up the steep trail we had descended shortly before. That evening, with the other tourists, we watched spectacularly presented Indian dances. The next morning we left for Berkeley.

As I noted previously, we were housed there in a comfortable bungalow within walking distance of the campus. Dr. Boas went to the University daily, sometimes returning to lunch with us, sometimes not. Mrs. Boas and I, except for short shopping tours, remained at home. There were some evening parties—one I remember particularly at Alfred Kroeber's (he was not married at the time). Memorable was romantic-looking Jaime D'Angulo, the linguist and folklorist, who resented the anthropologists' "infernal curiosity and thirst for scientific data" that "kills" the Indians "spiritually first," and ultimately "physically" (see his May 19, 1925 letter to Benedict, in Mead, 1959a: 296). He sat on the floor the better part of the evening, strumming his guitar and singing song after song, to the delight of all who were not intent on serious discussion.

My last days at Berkeley had a certain sadness. I knew that, as a student, I would certainly be in contact with Dr. Boas, but I also knew that I would no longer be "family" as I had been at Bolton Landing or during these weeks on the coast, and this was a relationship that meant much to me. But on balance I thought the change I had determined upon would be a good one.

11. RETURN TO THE EAST

I had some misgivings about the long trip east. I was going directly to Twin Mountain House, an unpretentious hotel in the White Mountains, frequented by many persons associated with the Ethical Culture School and Society, and where I had spent my vacation the previous summer. But I quickly made the acquaintance of a young dress buyer for a San Francisco firm, and shortly we were joined by a charming and sophisticated Englishman and a much less sophisticated American in his mid-twenties who had been assigned the upper berth in my section. We were inseparable until Chicago. From the Englishman I learned that one could ask the chef to wire ahead and order guinea hens put on the train to be prepared for us that same evening. I had never seen anyone carve a bird more exquisitely than he. The young American was quite impressed by the company he was keeping, and when we reached Chicago he shyly pressed a small card into my hand and hurried off to make his connection. His card read:

"Dear Miss Schiff: You have been a perfect lady." I can remember no one before or since who honored me with a like message.

When I reached Twin Mountain House I found a letter from Dr. Boas. It read:

> Portland, Ore.
> Aug. 7, 1922
>
> My dear Esther:
>
> I hope your trip is not as bad as you anticipated. How many rubbers of whist or whatever it may be? The trip here was beautiful and hot as blazes (to use your terminology). We found a telegram at the Post Office telling us of the arrival of Norman Francis, the fourth boy in that generation. Everything seems to be going well. We arrived on August 4th, one day too late to celebrate with his grandmother. We had a lovely drive through the smoke-haze; there is no view of distant scenery. For tomorrow we have engaged an auto to go on to Hood Mt. along the Columbia Highway. Would you not like to be along, but—one mountain looks like the other and water is water. No, I suppose Twin Mountain is just as good. Remember me to Jeannette whom you will be glad to meet there (or do you say, *who* you will be glad to meet there?). Anyway (who will be glad to meet you there). Thank her for her letter. We shall probably stay here until Wednesday night. Kindest regards, little grandmother with crumpled hair.
>
> > Yours, as ever
> > Franz Boas

This note was written on two sheets of paper, ending at the top of the second page; Mrs. Boas filled in the remaining space. Her letter reads:

> Dear Esther — such a waste of precious writing paper — I must add a few lines to tell you that Portland is beautiful even though we cannot see Mt. Hood — But most disgusting we are hanging around this hotel waiting for a room which they insist will be on hand for us by evening. So when we arrived, no bath and change of clothes. Papa Franz has been trying to find people who have gone out of town and I am spending most of my time writing letters that ought to have been written long ago — What do you say to all these Scotch and Normans enriching our family — We seem to be doomed to grandsons this generation.
>
> You ought to have seen the bungalow when we left — So clean and in order, everything just as we found it —
>
> Well good-bye. Must add a few words to Gladys' letter. Keep well, don't shock aunts and cousins. Have lots of fun and think of your Mama Franz once in a while.

At the hotel I found quite a few friends and acquaintances who had been there the previous year. Among the latter was Walter Goldfrank. His "crowd" was considerably older than mine, but this year we spent a good deal of time together until he returned to New York a few weeks before I did. In October we decided to marry, and we did so in early December.

12. MARRIAGE AND ANTHROPOLOGY

My decision to take on a sizable ready-made family (as noted, Walter had three boys, aged 6, 9, and 12) understandably altered my study routine, which had just gotten underway. Of course, in the first weeks—the last of September and three weeks in October, I carried on as I expected to do. After I became engaged to Walter, I still thought I could continue my studies, but things didn't work out that way. I was without immediate family members, but my numerous aunts, uncles, and cousins had to meet Walter (they had objected to my going into the field with a man forty years my senior, and now they were not at all reticent in expressing their disapproval of my marriage to a man twelve years my senior and with three boys to boot). Walter also wanted me to meet his numerous family, especially his boys, and I had to dismantle my apartment and prepare to move into his. Our wedding was small, not more than ten people. My wedding dress was a suit (a very nice one, I thought) that I had been wearing for weeks. After a short ceremony and a moving talk by Dr. Felix Adler in his study, Walter and I left for a trip in the Caribbean. There was no wedding feast, not even a bottle of champagne. A Steinway grand, I had decided, would be a more lasting reminder of this important event.

I must have notified Isabel that I had married. Perhaps I even enclosed the engraved announcement. She wrote me almost immediately, and now as "My dear Mrs. Goldfrank." But formality was quickly abandoned. "What a surprise" the news of my newly acquired status had been to "the people" when she told them about it. She hoped that I had found "a good hubby" because she wanted her child to be happy, and being happy was the greatest good. She warned me that if her "son-in-law" was not a "good daddy," he could not be a member of hers or Pedro's clan. Again, she referred to my song and asked after Dr. Boas. Assuring me of her love and best wishes, and requesting "a bride and groom picture," she brought an end to her congratulations and admonitions: "Well sa-we-sha," she wrote, "it's time to be getting supper." Her signature: "Ma, Isabel Ramirez."

I hazard no interpretation regarding Isabel's methods of address and signature. But there can be no doubt regarding her warm friendship for "Mrs. Goldfrank" and her motherly concern for her "sa-we-sha," her child.

The winter of 1922-23 was a busy one for me—getting to know my new family, their problems and hopes, and running a much bigger household than anything I had known before. At the strictly domestic level, I was fortunate that the maid, who had been with my mother for eight years and with me for six, was willing to stay with us while we remained in New York. She married shortly after we moved to White Plains in June 1924, just a month after my daughter, Susan, was born. We remained in close touch with her until her death many years later. (Each Christmas she sent me a large box of sugar cookies made according to my mother's excellent recipe.)

The demands of my changed situation brought my anthropological studies almost to a complete stop. I managed to attend a few lectures and on occasion I joined the Tuesday lunchers. But my new life was so full and so fulfilling that I had no regrets at interrupting my incipient anthropological career.

Dr. Boas believed that his students should be self-starters, and once when I said to him that I thought if he kept hammering at me, I would get my notes out faster, he answered, "You have to do your own hammering." During my pregnancy, when I was more relaxed about my new family and my new tasks and spending more time at home, I began evaluating my data, ordering my genealogies and writing *The Social and Ceremonial Organization of Cochiti*.

Dr. Boas not only didn't hammer at me, he made no effort to get me to continue my studies systematically—in fact, he never even showed me his notes on Cochiti, which were used later by Ruth Benedict in her *Tales of the Cochiti Indians*. But this was not because he thought poorly of women students. To judge from my relations with him and his with Gunther, Reichard, Benedict, Bunzel, and Mead as well, he clearly put no roadblocks in the path of a woman student because she was a woman, but he believed marriage and a family came first in a woman's life; and however promising a woman student might be, he never encouraged her to limit or forsake familial duties in order to further her academic career. His attitude toward Ruth Benedict was the same, although her situation was the reverse of mine. She wanted to be self-sufficient and self-supporting, and while Boas recognized her talent and by this time surely knew that her marriage had been strained for years, Mead writes, "But in Boas' eyes, she was a wife, amply supported and with obligations of a wife . . . someone on whom he could not make extreme demands and for whom he need not be responsible" (Mead, 1959a: 343). Parenthetically, I may say that I do not think Boas ever made "extreme demands," nor did he shun responsibility if he thought the situation warranted it.

Dr. Parsons would have understood Benedict's desire to be self-sufficient and self-supporting. But temperamentally and scientifically the two women were far apart, and contacts between them were minimal. While Boas did nothing to influence me, Dr. Parsons soon drew me back into anthropology, as shown in her letter written in the summer or fall of 1924 asking me to go to Isleta.

13. ISLETA, N.M., 1924.

My husband thought I should go to Isleta. The family could survive without me for a few short weeks. For me Isleta would be a test, not of my ability to work in the "field"—this, I felt, had been proven—but to work in the field alone (at this time I did not realize how much support Dr. Boas' presence had given me).

Isleta is on the Rio Grande about 13 miles south of Albuquerque where I had asked the Indian Agency about living quarters in the village. I was given the name of one family, and it is psychologically interesting that, although I stayed with them for over a week, I cannot remember any of their names, first or last. When I arrived, they readily accepted me as a boarder. I had a small room separate from but within a few feet of their house, and they provided my meals, all at a very nominal cost. I was delighted with these arrangements—no problem about food and a modicum of privacy.

But Isleta was not Cochiti—and my Isleta "family" was not the Ramirezes. During our second visit to Cochiti, Dr. Boas and I had friendly, if not close, relations with quite a few of the villagers. What we were doing was no secret—and if most chose not to work with us, there was no overt and, I believe, little covert hostility. With John Dixon and the Ramirezes our relations were unusually warm.

Isleta was known to be a tough spot for anthropologists, and Dr. Parsons had never been able to work there with any great success. Although her "Notes on Isleta, Santa Ana and Acoma" were published in 1920, I doubt that she had stayed in Isleta any longer than she had in San Felipe the same year. In fact, she never discussed her early Isleta experience with me either before or after I went there.

Comparatively speaking, Isleta was a large pueblo; its population numbered over 1000. As many as 500 males might be commandeered by the leadership for ditch cleaning in the spring before the water was let in from the river (see Lummis, 1897: 111; Parsons, 1962: paintings 79-85).[30] Isleta is a Tiwan-speaking village, its language closely related to that of Taos, the picturesque pueblo so much frequented by artists and authors.

94

My "family" (I use this term with some hesitancy, in view of their behavior) consisted of a father, a mother, and two grown children, the son in his late teens, the daughter a year or two younger. All spoke English, but they kept me at arms' length and our relations remained formal. I may have eaten with them at times, but more often I ate alone, subsisting for the most part on a diet of bread and butter, boiled eggs, and tea—and this at my request, since it was easy to prepare whenever I wanted it.

I first tried to interest the mother in my work—asking for a story, any story, was my entrée. But she was not at all responsive, nor was her husband. During the first days they introduced me to no one. I wandered around the village like a lost sheep. One morning, I found some women coiling pottery near the round house. They tolerated my presence while I watched, but when I tried to make conversation, they shook their heads vigorously from side to side and indicated that they wished I would go away. One, finally, did tell me some tales. Also, a young blade, who spoke English, approached me and expressed a willingness to "help." I explained what I was interested in, and he obliged by giving me a list of clans—there were none in Isleta—but he spoke in considerable detail about the "onion clan," which has no analogue in the pueblos, east or west.

As day after day passed and I had nothing to show for my efforts, I became quite desperate, and limitations of time increased the urgency to get something done. I wrote Dr. Parsons, and she answered, as will be remembered, "Don't be discouraged." Luck again was on my side. Just when I was most dejected, the father of my "family" said he knew a good storyteller (of course, he knew him all along, but it was a full week before he mentioned him). He told me where he lived and that night I visited my one last hope.

Juan Abeita* lived alone. His daughter was away at school in Santa Fe. His wife may have been dead—he never mentioned her and I never asked about her. In his dimly lit single room, he began to give me bits of tales. I stayed with him for several hours and suggested that he come to my room the next night—I didn't like walking through the village in the dark, and his house was some distance from mine. He consented to this, but told me that the following day he would be leaving for Santa Fe to visit his daughter and he wasn't sure when he would be back. I was dismayed. I had finally found someone willing to talk to me, and he was going away within twenty-four hours.

But a bird in the hand is worth two in the bush. If one night was all he could give me, one night it would be. He came shortly after dark—this was November, so it wasn't very late. But he wanted to be

---

*This is the pseudonym used by Dr. Parsons in her 1932 monograph *Isleta, New Mexico.*

shielded from scrutiny and interruptions—he had his fears, and they were not without warrant, to judge from the letters written by the artist of *Isleta Paintings* more than a decade later. We took the sheets from my bed, fastened them across the windows, and locked the door. We sat on the floor so that we would cast no silhouettes. He talked and I wrote. To my amazement, he began with the secretly held Isletan emergence tale, the tale that tells how his people came from the lower world, who led them, where they stopped before reaching their present home.

My "family" certainly knew who my visitor was; but they wanted to know more. Soon there was a knock on my door. The daughter of the house asked to come in—she had to get a dress for the next day that was stored in a trunk in my room. I answered politely that I was busy and would give it to her in the morning. Minutes later there was another knock. This time it was the son of the family. He wanted his gun—an ominous demand, I thought. He was going hunting early the next day. Again, I refused to open the door and told him he could have it in the morning.

These interruptions did little to calm an already tense situation. It was midnight when my visitor rose to go and, taking a leaf out of Dr. Parsons' book, I suggested that instead of returning to the village from Santa Fe he meet me in Albuquerque at the Alvarado Hotel. When he said he would, I could hardly believe my ears. He left and it was long before I slept.

The next morning the daughter of the house failed to come for her dress and the son of the house failed to come for his gun. I rose early and told the parents I was leaving that day for Albuquerque. I gave no explanation for my change of plan—and they demanded none. I packed my suitcase and was sitting on my bed with the door of my room open when the son entered, ostensibly to help me get to the train stop. I thought this a good moment to ask him if he would cooperate with me, if he would keep a diary of important events in Isleta, the dates of various ceremonies and dances. Without mentioning any sum I indicated that I would be glad to compensate him for information he might send me. As I started to write out my address, he did what no other Pueblo Indian had ever done to me before—he threw me onto the bed and himself upon me. I gave him a good hard kick and he fled. I had had enough of Isleta. My adieus were hasty. Dragging my valise, I made my way to the house of a family I knew slightly who lived near the tracks, and there I remained until train time. They asked me no questions and I volunteered no information. The train arrived, and within the hour I was registering at the Alvarado Hotel in Albuquerque.

Again I had a worried night. Would Abeita show up, or would I be left stranded with no one else to turn to? Would I go home or would I return to Isleta and start over again? I could have slept peacefully. The next morning Abeita turned up as he had said he would. He was staying with friends nearby.

We had three sessions daily—morning, afternoon, and night—in my small hotel room. We worked hard. I wrote and wrote, but there was no opportunity to check anything he told me.

I left Albuquerque with some satisfaction. I had not accomplished all I had hoped to, but I did not feel that I had completely wasted my time or Dr. Parsons' money. Nor did she—the more so when a year later she found Abeita willing to work with her, too. I have friendly letters from him and his daughter, both written on January 19, 1925, hers from St. Catherine's Indian School in Santa Fe, his from Isleta, telling me about the swearing in of various village officials—the governor, the first and second lieutenant governors, and himself as sheriff.[31] He also reminded me that I had promised to send him some books. I am sure I did this, but I have no memory of their titles. Yet despite an encouraging ending to my sojourn in Isleta, I felt that for the foreseeable future my place would be with my husband and children in White Plains. When *The Social and Ceremonial Organization of Cochiti* was published, my life as an anthropologist seemed over.

If I was torn by any lingering doubt, it was completely dispelled when, at the picnic Dr. Parsons was unable to attend (Boas, Goddard, Malinowski, Benedict, and Reichard did), Goddard, pointing at three-year-old Susan, turned to me and said with special emphasis on the first word, "*That* is the best thing you ever produced." I thought he was right then and I think he was right now.

PART TWO

1. RETURN TO NEW YORK

Death the Reaper; Death the Sower. Walter Goldfrank died from a coronary thrombosis on a train en route to Philadelphia on a beautiful day in mid-September 1935. Two lives were over, his and mine with him. But mine would go on without him. I knew very soon that I couldn't remain in the blatantly domestic atmosphere of Westchester. Our eldest son had married, our second was working in Maine, our youngest was living in a carefree artistic world in New York. Sue and I were still together. Late as it was, she was accepted that year at the Fieldston School, established in Riverdale at the end of the 20s by the Society for Ethical Culture. Until some always helpful cousins of my husband found an apartment for us in New York, she stayed with my old friends the Willys Kents. Mrs. Kent had been a classmate of mine in the old Ethical Culture school. Mr. Kent was a teacher there and also director of the summer camp which was sponsored by the Society and which my daughter had attended for at least two summers. So Sue was among friends and near her new school, but it was several years later—and then only after seeing her Rorschach test, that I fully understood how traumatic a father's death could be to a much loved girl-child of eleven—despite the fact that my own father died when I was nine.

Left alone in the roomy old house, so shortly before filled with voices, I faced my future. Death the Sower. I moved to New York in mid-November and was immediately joined by Sue. But domesticity alone was no more satisfying in New York than it would have been in Westchester. After an absence of many years, I decided to return to anthropology and Columbia.

2. AGAIN THE DEPARTMENT OF ANTHROPOLOGY

In January 1936, the Department of Anthropology at Columbia was quite different physically and intellectually than it had been in

98

August 1922, when I resigned my position with Dr. Boas. Physically, it was much larger. It now filled the better part of a wing on the fourth floor of Schermerhorn Extension. Small rooms lined the hallway leading to the secretaries' office (Ruth Bryan took charge of department business and Bertha Edel served Dr. Boas in non-departmental matters). To the left was a spacious study occupied by Professor Boas, who was on the point of resigning (he did the following year). On the right was Ruth Benedict's still sizable but much smaller one. Behind Dr. Boas' study was the room occupied by Professor W. Duncan Strong, the archaeologist, and across the hall was the "laboratory." George Herzog was professor of linguistics and he and, I think, Bunzel used the small rooms behind Strong's. There were many more students, but my contact with them remained casual until more than a year later.

My welcome at Columbia was extremely heartening personally, but extremely guarded when I raised the question of my scientific reinvolvement. For Dr. Boas, I was still a beloved daughter, but, as in the past, he left decision-making to me. What I would do was my affair. He neither encouraged nor discouraged my return to anthropology. I soon realized that while he was still the head of the department, he was essentially the *éminence grise*, visible and felt, but only rarely accessible to students. I soon also realized that his long-time interest in race was now leading him far beyond the academic scene. Again, as he had during World War I, he had entered the political arena, but now his target was Germany—the Germany of the Nazis.

Like most New Yorkers at this time, particularly the Jewish and labor sectors, Dr. Boas was greatly concerned about the Hitler regime—its flamboyant nationalism, its attacks on racial minorities and independent thinkers in all walks of life. Having maintained with extraordinary passion his romantic attachment to Germany in the years prior to, during, and after World War I, he was now filled with revulsion toward the country of his birth. Having shown little interest in the Russian revolutions of 1917, he had, after Hitler burned his books, sought out an ex-leader of the American Communist Party to brief him on the fight against Nazism and determine how he could be fitted into it. (Personal communication.) Mead writes that in 1934 Benedict had complained, "He has given up science for good works." And indicative of her own attitude, she added: "Such a waste!" (Mead, 1959a: 348).

On this first visit to Columbia, I also spoke to Bunzel and Benedict. Bunzel had her Ph.D. and was, I believe, doing some lecturing. She was most warm in her expressions of sympathy, but she was skeptical of my finding a place at Columbia in anthropology. Ruth Benedict seemed to share her doubts, and she told me of a study of adolescents being directed by Dr. Caroline Zachry, a psychoanalyst for the Commission on Secondary School Curriculum. It was sponsored by the General Education Board of the Rockefeller Foundation. Given my years of raising a family—and my considerable experience with adolescents—Benedict thought Dr. Zachry might find a spot for me.

3. SITTER IN THE STUDY OF ADOLESCENTS

Amazing as it seemed to me then, and still seems to me now, Dr. Zachry immediately offered me space in their rooms in an old brownstone on West 90th Street and, to start with, suggested that I examine their recordings of interviews with students at several of the schools included in their study—some private, some public, some in New York, some as far west as Chicago. She also permitted me to attend a weekly seminar along with their paid professionals, mostly teachers, psychiatrically trained social workers, psychologists and a few others involved in special studies, such as Victor D'Amico, then head of the art department at Fieldston, who was making an inquiry into the relation of painting to personality. Margaret Mead, whose writings on adolescence were well known, had already briefed the group on field techniques and allied problems and, as I remember it, Morris Opler of Cornell University was the staff anthropologist when I joined. After he dropped out Jeannette Mirsky took over.[1] (I had known Jeannette at least since my junior year at college, when we were neighbors on West 83rd Street and her sister had married a relative of mine (we also were graduates of "Ethical," although we had not known each other there). Dr. Lawrence Frank of the General Education Board of the Rockefeller Foundation was *ex officio*, as was Dr. Vivian T. Thayer, then principal of the Fieldston School and later a leader of the Society for Ethical Culture.

Sometimes the seminars were merely a clearing-house for accumulated staff observations, but outside specialists often addressed the group. I particularly remember Professor Harold Lasswell (who spoke at least twice and at the time was still revelling in his self-created scientific jargon which, once mastered by the uninitiated, introduced them to many stimulating ideas), and Drs. Fritz Redl (a long-time student of youth problems in Europe), Edward Liss, and Erik H. Erikson, psychoanalysts. It was Erikson who admonished the participants in no uncertain terms not to overstrain their insights when making projections. "Don't forget," he said, "you are working with normal children." Nothing during the whole year was more to the point. Few of the workers had children of their own or had been exposed to the day-to-day advance of a child into adolescence within a home environment. I never entered the discussion at these seminars, but by listening I learned a good deal about trends in education, not the least of them the value (and non-value) of psychoanalysis for blind interpretation.

From the interview material I was able to recognize significant differences between the selected schools and between their populations. At Fieldston, the pupils were unusually articulate, as were the Fieldston parents, who consented to discuss their own and their adolescents' problems with members of the staff (I do not remember seeing parent interviews from any other of the schools). Also, it became clear that ties to Europe were the strongest among pupils in the Eastern schools. In the midwest, Latin and Greek were indeed dead, dead languages, and even French and German were of little concern.

As in my early Boas days, no one asked me to report on what I had learned. Again this was not an uncongenial arrangement. I had a place to go to regularly, an academic milieu, data at my disposal that was recent and relevant. Not until the winter of 1936-37 did anyone seem interested in what I had done or could do; and then it was my old friend Jeannette Mirsky who sought me out. (Perhaps I should mention here that there was one other person in the seminar who approached me for aid—a young staff member, learning that my daughter and I would be out of town asked if she could have my apartment on her wedding night.) But Jeannette wanted my scholarly collaboration. She had just been asked to do a background study of the Fieldston School and to analyze the data amassed on its senior-year adolescents. It was on this later assignment that she wanted my help.

4. REPORT ON FIELDSTON SCHOOL AND REPERCUSSIONS

Dr. Zachry was quite content to have us work together—in fact the only question raised regarding our collaboration was raised by us. Was it good to have two graduates of Ethical, and one whose daughter (mine) was then attending Fieldston, evaluate their alma mater's past and present? Our question was brushed aside. Jenny, as anthropologist on the job, was the given person to study a "culture"; Fieldston, for which there was such an abundance of interview material, was the given school to be studied first; and, all things considered, I was the given collaborator.

We worked hard that spring of 1937. I made a preliminary evaluation of the interview material, while Jenny reviewed Dr. Felix Adler's break with Jewish tradition, his founding of the Society for Ethical Culture with its overwhelmingly Jewish membership in 1876, and the establishment by the Society in 1878 of The Working Man's School. A decade or so later, at the insistence of Society members who wanted their offspring to share the educational benefits of the disadvantaged, the School for Ethical Culture was established, with its predominantly Protestant teaching staff, in largest part women born and raised in New England; its predominantly Jewish student body, mostly from upper-middle-class New York families of German background; and its scatter of scholarship pupils, some recommended by workers in one or another settlement house, some children of teachers (the major gentile element in the pupil population), and a few Negroes, almost all from prominent families.

Our report was completed in the spring of 1937 and mimeographed copies were made—a very small number of them, which was most unusual. In fact, there were not enough even for members of the staff, and we soon learned why. In our report we had made several points that Dr. Thayer had found unpalatable. We had stressed the linkage between the Society and the Ethical schools, with particular emphasis on Fieldston, of which he was principal, and we had noted that, despite a very real desire to encourage the autonomy of the latter, the ideological approach and values of the Society were clearly echoed in the classrooms—especially during the weekly sessions on ethics. We also noted that with the opening up of Fieldston, completed in 1929 at a very substantial cost, there had been a considerable change in the composition of the student body.

Fieldston, situated on a wooded slope in the Riverdale section of New York City, was still "the country" to the majority of students who lived with their families in midtown. This fine new school with good outdoor play space was certainly more attractive to older boys than downtown Ethical, but the fact that more students, both boys and girls, could be accommodated opened the door to many families (still predominantly Jewish) whose children would have found acceptance more difficult in earlier times when the school was much smaller. Moreover, the ethnic composition of New York City Jews had also changed radically since the establishment of the first Ethical school. From the turn of the century, there had been an increasing flow of East Europeans to New York, mostly poor. But as the decades passed many of them had become quite wealthy. To give their children a good education, and what many considered the best education possible, they wanted them to attend Fieldston. Some of these "newer" families, like a goodly number of the "older" ones, were socialist-minded, and they found the secularized religion of the Society for Ethical Culture highly congenial. Others, however, still adhered to the traditions Felix Adler had rejected long years before. Their sons were bar-mitzvahed, their sons and daughters confirmed. They observed the Jewish holidays; and whereas the "first families" of the Society prided themselves on inconspicuous consumption, to paraphrase Veblen, the new and largely *nouveaux riches* families of the late 20s felt no such constraint.

True, "the crash" brought serious financial and emotional problems to Fieldston as elsewhere, and we pointed out, on the basis of our data, that the children of the *nouveaux riches* families were more disturbed than the scholarship pupils, who had lost little in a material sense, since their families had little, or the children of the older Ethical families, who had been accustomed to living modestly whatever their means. By the mid-30s, when my daughter transferred to Fieldston from West-chester, the line between the children, and particularly the daughters, of the "older" and "newer" families was quite evident. The former were considered bluestockings, while the latter, besides adhering to Jewish tradition, were inclined to dress more expensively, to come and go by automobile rather than subway or bus, to give more elaborate parties. My daughter did a straddle. Many of the bluestockings were old friends, whom she had previously met at the Ethical summer camp, and naturally she continued these contacts. But the sophistication of the "others" (who, of course, also satisfied the high intellectual demands of the Ethical schools) was also appealing. Thus personal experience reinforced insights I gained from Fieldston's interview material.

But perhaps what disturbed Dr. Thayer most in our report was our discussion of the Negro issue. We felt that the Ethical schools deserved great credit for seeking out Negro children of ability and offering them what was generally considered an excellent education. Although they were warmly welcomed in the lower grades by teachers and classmates, adolescence in a co-educational school created many problems.

On the basis of our interview material, we recommended that when a Negro child was registered in an Ethical school, his (or her) parents should be told quite plainly that, eager though the authorities were to advance racial tolerance and understanding, they could not guarantee the behavior of their White pupils, particularly their White adolescent pupils or their families, and that, to forestall future traumas, Negro parents should encourage their children to maintain a foothold in the Negro community. It should be remembered that we came to this conclusion long before the concepts of Black power and the need for Black identity were part of our social vocabulary. But Dr. Thayer, I am certain, was already fully aware of the Negro issue and the delicate and disturbing problems it had raised for a "progressive" school like Fieldston.

That this was not a new problem is clearly shown by the following episode, which occurred in the 20s or shortly before. A dedicated member of the Society, a teacher at ECS, told me that her younger sister had, through the years, been a close friend of a Negro classmate (also a girl). However, certain strains developed between them in high school, although her sister's attitude remained unchanged. Yet when she invited this Negro girl to a party at her home, not only did the girl refuse to go, but her mother telephoned to say that she would not permit her daughter to attend a party given by a White classmate, since she did not want to expose her child "to one more unpleasantness."

That Negro-White relations were still a problem in the 30s is shown by a passage in *Emotion and Conduct in Adolescence,* published in 1940 and written by Dr. Zachry in collaboration with Margaret Lightly, as "Editor, Study of Adolescents." The text reads:

> Marion had attended a consolidated rural school continuously from the first grade. Throughout those years there had been a small sprinkling of Negroes in classes otherwise Caucasian. During the tenth grade Marion commented to a teacher that the two Negro students in her class now had greater difficulty in social relations than in elementary school years. Marion, herself, made it a point to continue to sit with these girls, but she felt their plight was a difficult one in the group. She thought it was too bad for them to have to be in a school where there were so few like them—where nearly everybody else was different. "They're entitled to the same as we in education," she said, "but I don't see what good a school can do if they're really unhappy." (1940: 365)

We know the first episode occurred in an Ethical school. The second so closely resembles an example given in our report that it surely occurred at Fieldston. (Although the school was described as "a consolidated rural school," the word "rural" seemed to be a not too unhappy euphemism for a wooded hillside in Riverdale.) In a 56-page statement entitled "A Description of the Study of Adolescents," issued by the Commission on Secondary School Curriculum as "Revision of June 1938," the various schools in the study are listed. One of them is described as "Private Progressive High School B, eastern city: class followed through grades 9, 10, 11, and 12," and the passage dealing with this high school again surely relates to Fieldston and to our report. Captioned "Introduction to the Social Background of Private Progressive High School B," it reads:

> The first part of this report outlines the history of the school and of its founding in terms of leading personalities, outstanding events, and basic ideology; traces the provenance of students' families and identifies the values stressed in the various cultural groups represented; and analyzes the changing composition of the student population itself. The second part is devoted to a summary analysis of the emotional security of thirty students chosen at random from among those on whom case materials are available at this school. This analysis is made against the general

background indicated in the first part of the report and in terms of such factors as the social and economic status of the student's family, his intelligence quotient, his ordinal position among his siblings, and his acceptance or rejection of the patterns of security or insecurity in his family group.(45 f.)

This is the only overall report on a listed school mentioned in the "Revision of June 1938," and ours was the only overall report on the table at this time. If I needed further evidence that it was our suggestion regarding the problem of Negro adjustment that had caused Dr. Thayer's major discomfort, this passage provides it. As far as the "Revision of June 1938" is concerned, the Negro issue was an un-issue. Moreover, our choice of students was in no sense "random"—it included *all* members of the class followed through grades 9, 10, 11, and 12.

I do not know when the weekly sessions of the Study on Adolescents ceased, but I remember attending none after Jenny presented our report. Several publications were issued later, but the only references to our work that I have seen are the Aesopian passages cited above. I had understood that Dr. Fritz Redl would prepare a summarizing volume, and when I learned he had not been given our analysis of the Fieldston data, I sent him one of my copies. In 1967, when I tried to retrieve it, he wrote me that he had not prepared any such volume, and that he could not locate my copy—hardly surprising after three decades. I had destroyed my remaining copy some years before in one of those excessive cleanups that result in more space but also—and almost inevitably—in regrets. In a long-forgotten carton, Jenny found a folder marked "The Fieldston Report, Spring, 1937." The folder was empty. The Rockefeller Foundation, the sponsoring angel, searched their archives diligently but could find nothing relevant except the "Revision of June 1938," which they kindly had xeroxed for me.

I have made no further effort to find a copy of our report. But the "Revision of June 1938" has convinced me that my memory of my and Jenny's joint contribution to the Committee on Adolescents is substantially accurate.

Early in 1973 I met Dr. Peter Blos at a cocktail party. He had been associated with the Study for Adolescents and in 1938 was asked to do what I thought Dr. Redl had been asked to do—describe and evaluate the work of the Study of Adolescents. This he did, but, as he told me, "in his own way." He was a clinical and therapeutic practitioner and he probably preferred to analyze a few case studies in great detail rather than make a comparative study of groups of young people from different academic environments. His book, *The Adolescent Person-*

ality: A Study of Individual Behavior: (1941), deals with four cases—two, a boy and girl still in high school, and two, also a boy and girl, who were dropouts and, as Dr. Zachry noted in her Foreword, "could provide data on the problems and responsibilities faced by young people no longer under school influence." Dr. Zachry also noted that the study had amassed some 600 interviews from high schools and colleges, both public and private, located in different sections of the United States, and that essentially the data so collected were "to serve as a diagnostic basis for education rather than treatment." In large part, these data were highly personal, and it is understandable that the Committee felt they should not be published as recorded or even after details regarding school and individual identification were camouflaged. However, at first it was still felt that the data might be made accessible "to a selected number of people for professional use."

In the end, it seems, they were destroyed—the reason: no institution was able to house so bulky a collection. No doubt all who participated in this six-year study (1932-38) learned a great deal—but the fate accorded its findings has, except in a very limited way, precluded later generations from benefiting from its insights and conclusions, regarding not only adolescents in the 30s, but also perhaps in the difficult 60s and 70s.

5. EPISODE IN THE SUMMER OF 1937

Accompanied by a friend whose husband was to follow a few weeks later, I went to England by boat in mid-July. We soon discovered that Dr. Abram Kardiner, the psychoanalyst, some of whose joint sessions with anthropologists as informants I had attended irregularly the previous winter, was a sailing companion. When he asked if he could occupy a deck chair adjacent to ours, we agreed happily. The five-day trip was smooth and afforded us many opportunities to share walks on deck and cocktail parties with him—the last being a champagne affair in the lounge thrown by "les girls."

After a night in Liverpool (Kardiner went on to London immediately), my friend and I hired a car, and for three weeks we toured England and Wales. Each afternoon around four o'clock, we asked a convenient policeman or representative of the Automobile Association to recommend a farmhouse or simple boarding house that would put us up for the night and feed us. We had no reservations anywhere, but we did have luck. No one believed us when we told them later that we had found the food in these non-tourist dwellings excellent—home-cured ham, fresh eggs, milk, wonderful thick cream, and fresh strawberries. What more could two wanderers ask for? When we were forced to stay in a hotel, as was the case in Warwick, we were treated, not unexpectedly, to overdone mutton and watery potatoes. In Stratford we got our last break. The hotel was full, but a helpful clerk suggested, with a considerable show of originality, a night club not too far from the Shakespeare Theatre. Here there was a room for us, very ample and decorated in the style of most powder rooms in expensive New York hotels. And it faced a lovely garden. We just had time to wash up, have a hurried tea in the garden, and rush off to the play. I don't remember what it was we saw, but on our return "home" at a very late hour, the owner of the night club was entirely ready to serve us an excellent steak, french fries, beer, dessert, and coffee. We spent the next days sightseeing, and no one suggested that we move to a more appropriate residence. My friend and I parted in London when her husband arrived, and I went on to Paris, where I met some of my American friends and also Raya Garbousova, the well-known cellist, who years later married a man with three boys. When she came to New York to give a concert, which I attended, she said to me: "I felt if you could do it, so could I."

I left for New York in mid-August, again by ship. But first it was necessary to go by train to Le Havre. I wrote the following piece about this ride shortly after I arrived home. I entitled it "Culture Takes a Holiday."

It was on the boat train from Paris to Le Havre. Arriving early, I had seated myself in the second class window seat indicated by my ticket and watched each succeeding passenger arrive. With considerable bustle, a short sturdy man, sixty, perhaps, examined all the numbers in my section and turning in dismay to his two grown sons and young daughter who followed him, indicated that they didn't have a window seat, but would have to dispose themselves on either side of the aisle. Father and son faced me across the table. The second son and daughter took their seats in the section opposite. And next to me the porter planted a well-worn valise.

No sooner settled than the father of the children rushed from the car to return a few minutes later proudly bearing a brown paper bag which he placed in the rack over his head. My first question as the elderly gentleman faced me was, "Where have I seen him before?" And as I examined his ruddy face, his large and worldly nose, his twinkling yet shrewd blue eyes, and the drooping mustache that hung from his lip, one side jauntily cut an inch shorter than the other, so bristlingly British, so plainly Bostonian, I realized that before me stood America's reincarnation of England's "Colonel Blimp."

107

The train left the station. Father pulled forth Voltaire's "Candide," the elder son Van Wyck Brooks' "Flowering of New England," the daughter Locke's "History of Morals," and the last member of the quartet screened himself behind a half-dozen newspapers, coming forth now and again to read some editorial to his father, to get his thought on some particular passage. A continual stream of small talk flowed back and forth; a potpourri of jests, gossip, politics and mythology. No member of the group recognized my presence, and at the first tunnel father closed the window without so much as a "by your leave." And it remained closed for the rest of the trip, although the day was warm.

At noon I ordered a sandwich and coffee and the porter laid a cloth over my place at the table. My luncheon arrived and was served to me. Father then removed his brown paper bag from the rack, flourished a bottle of *vin ordinaire* and four sandwiches at his children, much as the male robin returning to the nest of his young would toss the juicy worm from his beak. The wine was poured into a small metal cup, and passed from hand to hand, each bite of roll washed down with a gulp of wine, father's face glowing red at the economical and satisfactory lunch he had provided. Suddenly he exclaimed, "My Lebkuchen." All the children shouted in chorus, "You know it was stale three weeks ago in Nuremburg." "Nonsense," said father, "it's as good as new." Rising from his window seat, he pushed past his son and into the aisle. I was still eating my sandwich. But without a word or look in my direction he opened his valise, and after a bit of rummaging drew forth his toilet case and placed it on the table beside my small lunch. Then followed a shabby pair of bedroom slippers and finally in a mood of complete abandon, he brought forth his crumpled and used red and white striped pajamas. It was an intimate moment. The Lebkuchen was discovered; the apparel satisfactorily replaced; the lock snapped, and father returned gaily and triumphantly to his seat, smacking his lips over the crumbling cake.

My sandwich had lost its flavor and remained unfinished on my plate. As I left the train my glance fell on the worn valise beside me, and on the tag I read the name, ELLERY SEDGWICK.

I knew that Ellery Sedgwick was the editor of the then foremost literary magazine in America, the *Atlantic Monthly*. In years gone by I had sent several examples of my writing to the *New Yorker*. None had been accepted, but I thought this piece might, since here was a profile of a well known literary figure. But the above effort shared the fate of my earlier ones. The editor wrote that they excluded personal experiences that mentioned real names. I could understand their rejection on many grounds—but their explanation seemed strange indeed as I knew that since the mid-20s they had been publishing profiles which not only mentioned names but also, and not infrequently, unflattering tidbits about their subject's life and ways. However, much later an editor told me that they made a distinction between profiles based on freely given interviews and contributions that had not been sanctioned by the subject—and my piece certainly could be excluded on both counts.

The *New Yorker's* rejection notwithstanding, I still wanted to have a little fun out of my encounter with an eminent member of America's literati. I decided to send my "profile" to the *Atlantic Monthly*, and this I did with the request that it be printed in the section captioned "The Lion's Mouth," which concentrated on short items dealing with a variety of subjects. I added that I thought my piece would be of special interest to the editor.

On November 16, 1937, I received the following note:

Dear Miss Goldfrank:

You have an eye for drama and how you would have enjoyed a bit of character acting of the most naturalistic sort. Your sketch was shown to me and I began it without any conception of why I should find anything of personal interest. When I got to the third paragraph, my exclamation was, "How like *my* father!" and not until you detailed the books we were reading did the truth come home to me. I could not help having several copies made to send to my various children, so you can imagine them laughing in chorus all over the United States.

It is really a very amusing sketch and, I have no doubt, an accurate one. I only wish that I were not so self-conscious as to make it impossible for me to print it in the *Atlantic*. You have a turn for description and I hope that this will not be the last thing you will send us. I am sorry we did not talk on the steamer but then I should not have had this surprise.

Yours sincerely,
Ellery Sedgwick

As I said in the first pages of these Notes, Professor Baldwin at Barnard had little respect for my "daily themes," and I felt he was quite correct in his judgment. And while my Cochiti monograph, written in the mid-20s, has stood the test of time well (although when Fred Eggan told me long years ago he considered it the best of the short pueblo studies, I felt he was giving me more than my due) there is little to be said for it from a literary standpoint. However, working on the Fieldston report with Jenny the previous spring had not only sharpened my understanding of the school's background and relation to the Society for Ethical Culture, her proficiency as an author[2] taught me a good deal about the art of writing. Ellery Sedgwick's letter confirms this conclusion. But even after our exchange I never again submitted anything to a literary magazine. However much my writing may have improved, I have been content to send my contributions to professional journals where acceptance depends more on substance than on style.

6. STUDENT IN ANTHROPOLOGY AT COLUMBIA UNIVERSITY

In the fall of 1937, I began to attend classes at Columbia more regularly. Dr. Boas had resigned, but he still occupied his old study. Shortly afterward, Ralph Linton was appointed the new head of the department. But Benedict retained her old office space adjacent to the secretaries and near Dr. Boas. Linton was settled in one of the small rooms down the hall.

Benedict had known for quite some time that Columbia did not want a woman as head of the department, and Linton knew that she and Professor Boas had opposed his appointment—as Mead put it, because "we had felt that Ralph Linton's thinking and interests were, in certain respects, close to those of Ruth Benedict, whereas sociological and structural emphasis were needed to give balance to the department" (Mead, 1959a: 350). Linton was the last candidate to be opposed—among several others, Malinowski was perhaps the most outstanding. Had he, one wonders, also been turned down because his thinking and interests were, in certain respects, close to those of Ruth Benedict?—which indeed they were—or because both Benedict and Boas hoped that they could pull the rabbit out of the hat, that they could by repeated rejections erode the resistance of Columbia higher-ups to the point where they would settle for a woman, and that woman Benedict.[3] If Boas and Benedict harbored any such illusions, they were finally dispelled when Columbia dropped the academic plum in Linton's lap.

Benedict's resentment is understandable, but it was most unfortunate for the cause of departmental harmony, and particularly for the students who, in the years following Linton's appointment, were sharply divided between "his" and "hers."

The more advanced graduate students and the junior faculty supported Benedict. Those who leaned toward Linton were largely the more recent starters, but while they found him an excellent lecturer and knew that his *Study of Man* was highly praised, they were never quite on balance. Much later, some of them told me of their ill-ease during their term of study. One said, "It was as if I was walking on a tightrope, always fearing I would make a misstep and antagonize one or the other—and I needed my degree."

Two years after Linton's appointment, the department war was still being fought. On October 24, 1939, Boas wrote to Benedict, who was on sabbatical leave in California, "I wonder whether Bunny [Ruth Bunzel] sees all the affairs in the Department without bias. Of course, she is very much troubled. I suppose it is quite true that Linton and Strong have too much undergraduate outlook. . . . I think we could stand some more positive knowledge, but I should be very sorry if the main spirit of the Department were changed" (Mead, 1959a: 415). And the war continued unabated until Linton left Columbia in 1946 to become Sterling Professor of Anthropology at Yale.

I was spared the students' worries. I did not want a degree. I was forty years old (the average age of the students was about twenty-five). I had been in the field four times. I had published and I felt confident that if I had anything worth saying I would find a platform from which to say it. And I didn't want to teach. My overriding concern was to flesh out my early field and family experiences, and since I was not working for a degree, I could be selective. Indeed, to many of the students I must have seemed little more than an aging dilettante.

I ignored physical anthropology, linguistics, and archaeology, except for one course given by Duncan Strong on the Indians of the Plains. My major interest lay in theory and ethnology and, with respect to the latter, particularly in problems of social organization (which followed naturally from my work in the 20s) and of personality and culture (which through Benedict's *Patterns of Culture* had greatly stimulated research in this field by anthropologists and psychologists, and especially psychoanalysts).

I cannot say just what years I took what courses. But I know that I studied theory with Benedict and A. Irving Hallowell, who came to Columbia from Philadelphia once a week during at least one winter and who first introduced me to Carpenter's ideas on animal learning and organization and pointed out their implications for primitive—and more advanced—societies. With Benedict I also studied comparative social organization (which included systems of kinship) and mythology. I took no course with Linton—largely because of a parochial disinterest in the areas he was drawing on—essentially the Marquesas and Madagascar. However, beginning in the winter of 1937-38 and for several years running, I regularly attended the popular sessions he conducted jointly with Abram Kardiner at Columbia on personality and culture.

As already indicated, Dr. Kardiner had previously conducted sessions of a similar nature without Linton at the New York Psychoanalytic Institute, but I did not attend the one at which Bunzel and Benedict had reported on Zuni (I may have been ill or out of town). In *The Individual and his Society*, Kardiner gives a resumé of what they said. His own interpretation of Zuni personality in no way deviates from theirs (1939: 111 ff.).[4] Not everyone present was as uncritical. I was told later that Dr. Lawrence Kubie, the well-known psychoanalyst, had maintained that the Zuni dreams collected by Bunzel did not fit the Apollonian image she and Benedict were projecting. Some years afterward, Bunzel showed me these dreams, along with Kardiner's interpretations, which she considered unsatisfactory. I begged her to publish them without his comments since she felt that way, but like her extensive notes on Zuni economy, they have never to my knowledge appeared in print. I quite agreed with Dr. Kubie that these dreams revealed highly aggressive personality traits that did not fit Benedict's Apollonian construct of pueblo society.

The first year I attended the Kardiner-Linton sessions I sat among the students, but after my summer with the Canadian Blackfoot (the Blood tribe) in 1939 I was invited to join Linton and Kardiner in the first row along with special visitors and anyone who had reported on field work—among whom were Clyde Kluckhohn (on the Navajo), Benedict and Bunzel (on Zuni), Cora Du Bois (on Alor), and Carl Withers (on "Plainville," a pseudonym for an Ozark community). I was also asked to discuss my field impressions, but I felt I had not as yet done enough research to place the changes I had noted in a broad historical context. I therefore suggested that I might give my analysis later, but I never did. However, as my work progressed I had informal and rewarding talks with Linton. He was particularly intrigued by the incipient class structure my data revealed, and his emphasis on the institutional aspects of change was extremely attractive to me. In his Foreword to Kardiner's *The Individual and his Society*, he stated, "The construct of non-material culture . . . has an exceedingly wide scope and it is advantageous to break it down in various ways when working on particular problems." After noting that a number of anthropologists, and especially Benedict and Mead, were emphasizing "behavior patterns readily ascertainable from the overt expressions, and the ideas and attitudes which motivate these behavior patterns," he pointed out that Kardiner "employs the concepts of *institutions* and of *ego* or *basic* personality structure." Kardiner's concept, Linton continued, "represents the constellation of personality characteristics which would appear to be congenial with the total range of institutions" (Kardiner, 1939, VI). Here the word "total" is of the greatest importance, for it was the type of selectivity in Benedict's *Patterns of Culture* that, without doubt, had heightened the dramatic impact of her conclusions, but that, also without doubt, had led her at times to ignore the very institutions that indicated an altogether different societal structure than the one she underscored.

To be sure, like many others, I had found Benedict's concepts as developed in *Patterns of Culture* extremely stimulating, but since my return to New York, I had been arguing vehemently against her view of Zuni society, relying on my observations in Laguna, Cochiti, and Isleta more than a decade earlier. Benedict never denied my facts, but they left her thesis untouched. Her answer: "You have never been in Hopi or Zuni." And on this point she was eminently correct. Another decade passed before I felt able to counter publicly her picture of Zuni society. And although her image of this society continues to influence the thinking of many non-anthropologists, almost all anthropologists, even those who find inspiration in her presentations, and I am one of them, reject her highly oversimplified and misleading interpretation of Pueblo society (see Bennett, 1946; Hoebel, 1954; Dozier, 1961, 1970; Barnouw, 1949, 1972).

In the early 40s I took a course with the sociologist Robert K. Merton who was strongly influenced by both Marx and Freud—a combination that fitted well with my early interest in economics and my now interest in personality and culture.

As for my co-students, a notable number of them have attained high positions in the academic world—at least one became a dean, one the head of an important university institute, one a university president—and several found large audiences for their anthropological writings. But while I shared classroom experiences with them at this time, often joined them for lunch at a crummy stationery store on Amsterdam Avenue, and invited them to hold meetings of the Anthropology Club in my apartment (at one of them, Goldenweiser, who was the honored guest, apparently delighted the company even more with his playing of Chopin than with his anthropological discourse) and early in 1940 gave a small party that some half-dozen of them attended, I never became intimate with any of them except Jeannette Mirsky, whom I had known for many years and who had completed her doctoral requirements except for her thesis.

My major contacts were with Benedict and Bunzel and, of course, Boas, all of whom belonged to my anthropological past. Again I was invited to be a weekly luncher;[5] now our meeting places were closer to Columbia, the Japanese restaurant, Aki; the Columbia Faculty Club; and the staff dining room at Barnard. Only rarely were we joined by Museum personnel. Margaret Mead was in the field during much of this time; Nelson came rarely; Goddard was dead; Lowie, Spier, and Gunther were in the West. But in these first years after my return Boas, Benedict, Bunzel, Reichard, Herzog, Strong, and Parsons were the regulars and, as formerly, there were the irregulars—essentially anthropologists from other universities in New York and elsewhere.

In August 1935, the Soviet Union, frightened by its aggressive neighbor, called for a united front against Hitler. The League Against War and Fascism was established and I, and almost everyone I knew, joined it. In the department both staff and students became politically involved, especially in the anti-Hitler fight. Later I learned that not a few of the students had been members of a Communist cell—influenced by Bernhard J. Stern, professor of sociology, who inducted Granville Hicks of Harvard into the Communist Party and later became the editor of the Marxist journal *Science and Society*. No one ever asked me to join this Communist group, although it was clear that I was anti-Hitler and pro-Republican Spain. But it was also clear that I had no love for Communism as a system of government, and the less so the more I learned about Stalin's methods of accusation and liquidation.

It was, of course, nothing new for Dr. Boas to choose popular platforms for expounding his scientific and political ideas. In 1936, the year I returned to New York, he published in *Time, The New York World Telegram, The New York Times,* and *The Nation*, his titles being respectively "National, not Racial," "Descent Unimportant in Tracing Gestures," "Urges Tolerance Here," and "The Individual Counts."[6]

In 1938, in a speech delivered at a meeting of the Anti-Nazi League in Carnegie Hall, his topic was "Intellectual Freedom in Nazi Germany." It was first printed in the Bulletin of that society (No. 2: 7) and then in a revised form in the *Independent Journal of Columbia University* (5, No. 6: 1.4) under the title "The Death of Freedom." Also in this year he published "An Anthropologist's Credo" in *The Nation*.

In 1939 Dr. Boas seems to have become more openly active in Communist-dominated and Communist front organizations. In September 1935, Dr. Henry Linville had walked out of a convention of the American Federation of Teachers, and the following month the New York Teachers Union split, the right wing calling itself the Teachers Guild, the left wing retaining its original name. The membership of the truncated Teachers Union, still Local 5, almost immediately assumed a "new look." According to Robert W. Iverson, who made a detailed study, *The Communists and the Schools (1959)*,[7] its "gates were flung open to a 'mass membership'; the dual groups of unemployed and substitute teachers and the Classroom Teachers Groups were now disbanded and their members welcomed into the Union. The result was a spurt in the membership of 1,200 after the walkout in September 1935 to 3,500 in April 1936" (100). A most immediate effect of the new administration "was the 'politicalization' of the local." The *New*

York Teacher replaced Linville's *Union Teacher* and a "program of 'affiliation'" was launched, leading to linkages "with fronts such as the League Against War and Fascism, the National Negro Congress, the American Labor Party, and the North American Committee for Spanish Democracy" (101). In 1936 an attempt to contain the Communist influence in the American Federation of Teachers failed. Professor Jerome Davis, "who was then fighting his dismissal from Yale, was elected President of the A.F.T.," and its organ, *The American Teacher* "was moved to the offices of the *New York Teacher*." A "rank-and-file" member of Local 5 "was made editorial secretary, and the 'new look' appeared in the next issue of the 'A.F.T. Journal' " (104). By 1938 "Communist control of the New York Teachers Union was clamped tight" (111), and "the numbers of unionized college teachers in New York City had grown to such a point as to justify the creation of a separate local" (114). Thus "local 537 was founded, and a battle for control immediately ensued." This battle the Communists won (144), and it was this union that Boas joined.

In 1939, his statement on taking this action was reproduced in *The American Teacher* (23, No. 4) and his picture appeared on the front cover. That same year *The American Teacher* published two more of his articles, the first, under the title "Democracy and Intellectual Freedom" (23, No. 6, 1: 9-10), reproducing an address he had given at a meeting sponsored by the Lincoln's Birthday Committee for Democracy and Intellectual Freedom; the second, entitled "Teachers Must be Free to Educate Youth" (24, No. 1: 12), reproducing in a condensed form the keynote speech he had given at the American Federation of Teachers Convention in Buffalo on August 21.[8] On the previous February 14, just two days after his Lincoln's Birthday speech, Boas' statement on "Intellectual Freedom" appeared in *The New Masses* (30, No. 8: 17), a journal that was widely considered Communist controlled. On March 10, in an address delivered at a meeting of the New York chapter of the American Association of Scientific Workers, Dr. Boas was already maintaining that "a bigoted democracy may be as hostile to intellectual freedom as a modern totalitarian state," and his reference in the preceding sentence to "the early New England settlers" and "the restrictive policies of some of our states" clearly underlines which democracy he felt was "bigoted" (Boas, 1945: 216). He gave no corresponding hints regarding the identity of "the modern totalitarian state" he had in mind.

In the late summer of 1939, to judge from his Bibliography in *AAA Memoir* 61, he sent a letter to the editor of *Equality*, seemingly another of those newly established journals that were then dotting the landscape. It was printed under the heading "In regard to the policies and program of the American Committee for Democracy and Intellectual Freedom" (1, No. 8:40).[9]

At the close of his speech to the Lincoln's Birthday Committee for Democracy and Intellectual Freedom, Dr. Boas declared, "Today we can express our convictions only in words, but you can rest assured that we shall create an organization to strengthen democracy, that steps have been taken which will lead to the realization of this end." And later in 1939, the American Committee for Democracy and Intellectual Freedom was officially set up. Dr. Boas became chairman and Moses Finkelstein, a Ph.D. candidate in the Department of History at Columbia, secretary. In 1938 Finkelstein (he later changed his name to Finley) was holding meetings of a Marxist study group at his apartment near the University,[10] and not surprisingly he was the Committee's major policy formulator.

Late in August 1939, the democratic world was shaken to the core by the Stalin-Hitler Pact. In America, the hard-line Communists immediately flaunted their buttons bearing the slogan "The Yanks are not coming," but many long-time Communists abruptly severed their ties with the party, and many non-Communists who, despite their knowledge of the purges and the harsh treatment accorded political dissidents in the forced labor camps in the Communist fatherland, had been supporting one or more of the rapidly proliferating Communist front organizations because of the USSR's anti-Hitler policy, now withdrew completely from these organizations (Howe and Coser, 1962: 392, 398 ff.).

Not so Dr. Boas. On October 24, 1939, he wrote Ruth Benedict, who was in California:

> I was so glad to get your letter of September 26. . . . You want to know what I think about world affairs? I have given up speculating about it. It seems to me fairly clear that Hitler is now a pawn in Stalin's hands, and that Stalin would like western Europe and Germany to bleed to death. Only I do not know whether he would like that to happen for the sake of his own power or for the sake of communism. So far as our affairs are concerned we sail under false colors. If we want to have absolute non-interference we have to forbid all trade in any kind of war-material, no matter how innocent it may look. But can we? Our farmers and merchants would raise such a howl that we would be in the war before we knew it. Nobody would be willing to do the reasonable thing and distribute the burden so imposed upon the whole nation. The embargo on arms is a purely sentimental affair. I think it would be wise to keep it in view of the future. I remember too well American bombs and bullets being called "Wilson's prayers for peace." I should not mind it, if I had any trust in

England's and France's democracy. They do not fight for ideals but to retain power. Under these conditions the whole embargo question as it stands does not seem to me worth all the excitement. What is important is a rigid cash and carry. I am a little worried about the complaint that nothing is happening at the West front. Obviously they know that an attack would be terribly costly and fruitless. It will be a war of exhaustion. I am more interested in our own civil liberties and, as you know, I am in that fight. Just now we are attacking the Chamber of Commerce of the State of New York, who want to see our free high schools chopped off, religion introduced, etc. I wish I had more strength, but I cannot undertake any work that requires physical strength. My heart simply won't stand it. . . . (Mead, 1959a: 413f.)

Dr. Boas clearly saw the advantages Stalin expected from his pact with Hitler. Russia's western flank would be secured, and the Germans would be encouraged to turn against the West—which they did in the spring of 1940. But where in this letter to Benedict are the harsh words Dr. Boas leveled against Nazi policy in pre-Pact days, where any criticism of the Soviet Union for joining the German imperialists? Indeed, the only harsh words in this letter are aimed at England and France. Boas did not trust their democracy: "They do not fight for ideals but to retain power," and so for now we should not lift the embargo, we should be concerned only with "our own civil liberties."

In "Education and Democracy," which appeared originally in *The American Teacher* in September 1939 and in condensed form in *Race and Democratic Society*, Boas wrote, "It has always seemed to me that, if I agree with a person in regard to one specific problem in which we wish to cooperate, his political, religious, or social views in regard to other matters are irrelevant" (202). And the Pact did not change his attitude. In the spring of 1940, I drove Dr. Boas from Columbia to his home in Grantwood, N.J. As we sat in the now defunct 125th Street ferry I noticed that he had a copy of *Friday* under his arm. I asked him somewhat rudely, "What are you carrying that thing around for? Don't you know it's a Communist front magazine?" He faced me unblinkingly and said, "I will go along with anyone who is fighting for what I am fighting for."

Both statements are more than astonishing when we remember that they were made by a world-famous scholar who had never stopped admonishing his students to refrain from giving an answer to a problem until they had carefully examined and weighed all matters impinging upon it. One cannot doubt, in view of his letter to Benedict, that Boas, if not familiar with all factors involved in the Pact and pre-Pact policies and actions, was familiar with many of them, and these of major importance. Certainly it was admirable to maintain "our own civil liberties," but Boas' decreased criticism of Nazi Germany, his lack of criticism of the Soviet Union, now allied with the Germany he had been attacking since 1933, his denigration of the institutions of our own country and the aims of our long-time friends, France and England, had interesting analogues in the Communist Party line of the time, not only in the United States, but the world over. Enough here to quote Mao Tse-tung, who, when Stalin joined hands with Hitler, declared in an interview with Edgar Snow, "Germany gave up her anti-Comintern Policy." And this he followed with the assertion that "the center of world-reaction now lies in England."[1 1]

Hitler's bombing of the Low Countries in the spring of 1940 did not alter Boas' position in any notable way. As Howe and Coser tell it, "At a mass convention held in Chicago on September 2, 1940, the American Peace Mobilization was born," and Dr. Boas, along with well-known Communist sympathizers, was included among its leaders. Its major public "stunt" was keeping "a 'perpetual peace vigil' in front of the White House" (394). And on September 6, Dr. Boas wrote in *Friday*, "We want to defend our democratic institutions based on intellectual and spiritual freedom of the individual. . . . Let us be ready to maintain our democratic ideals in these turbulent times! Let us shun war unless it is carried to our shores" (1, No. 26: 2). And two weeks later, again in *Friday*, he wrote, "A bigoted democracy may be more intolerant, more oppressive than any other form of government"; and to illustrate the deficiencies of our system he mentioned particularly the plight of the "undernourished ill-clad child of the slums, the isolated child in a remote valley, the negro children in the South"—all of them indeed harrowing. But so was Germany's devastation of the West, a fact that did not deter him from writing a letter to the editor of *PM*, which appeared in that newspaper on October 4 under the caption "Britain's War Aims" and which again spelled out his misgivings regarding the intentions of this suffering country. It hardly needs pointing out anew that whatever Boas' reasons for his selection of topics and the course of his argument, these sentiments accorded perfectly with the Communist line during the days of the Hitler-Stalin Pact.

Then on June 22, 1941, the Pact was at an end. Hitler's armed forces invaded Russia, Churchill made his famous "blood, sweat, and tears" speech in support of the USSR, and the "perpetual peace vigil" was permanently abandoned. The *New Masses*, which during the Pact had, like Mao Tse-tung, found the center of world reaction to the west of Germany, wrote on July 1, 1941, "The mortal issue is joined . . . the armed forces of German imperialism, representing all that is twisted, and brutal, medieval, and obscurantist, sinister and reactionary and evil in a world system which is writhing on the eve of its doom—has attacked the villages and homes, the fertile fields, and ingenious workshops of the new civilization." And it asked "Everybody who stands for defense and the flowering of American democracy, who stands for civil liberties, who stands against anti-Semitism and for the unity of Negro and white"—in fact, everybody who had been emphasizing just the issues that Boas had been so concerned with during the Pact—to join in "our common job, to see the situation with ruthless clarity, to act upon it, to further the unity of the people at the expense of the confusion and disunity of the oppressors."

Here the *New Masses* was proclaiming the new Communist line, but it was taking no chances of being misunderstood. In the July 29 issue that contained a piece on race by Dr. Boas as part of a symposium on the subject (probably planned weeks earlier), the editors wrote, "It is now nearly five weeks since Hitler launched his murderous assault on the Soviet Union. At one blow the entire character of the war has changed . . . everyone now wants Hitler stopped. They want fascism smashed, they want the world to be free forever from this scourge." And then they added somewhat plaintively, "There are those who do not yet understand that it is necessary to give swift substantial aid to the Soviet Union and Britain. Some, like the *New York Times*, would give all help to Britain and ignore the USSR. Others, like certain progressives, would help only the Soviet Union and ignore Britain." They concluded, "The war now raging in Europe is a just, progressive war." And on November 7, 1941, on the anniversary of the Bolshevik takeover of power from the short-lived and Western-oriented Kerensky government, Professor Boas sent what, as far as I can ascertain, was his first "Greeting to the Soviet Union"—a gesture so welcome that it appeared on that day in a "Special Supplement" of the *Embassy of the Soviet Socialist Republics Information Bulletin* (16, cited in Boas Bibliography: 108).

In December 1942, Dr. Boas participated in a Forum organized by *PM* on "What are we going to do with the Germans?" It went as follows:

Dr. Boas: What we must remember about Germany is that Hitler has been in power for not more than nine years. It will be ten years next Spring. Now ten years is not so long a time in the life of a nation and there is still a whole generation in Germany that has grown up and worked both under the old Empire and the Republic. Suppose we go back to 1914. That would be 28 years ago. Take a person who was 20 years old then and grew up under another tradition. There is a very considerable number of persons of this age who are now inactive. We ought to strengthen that element and do whatever we can to bring them into power. This, of course, is not an easy job, but it can be done.

We ought to give as much initiative as possible to that group and to use as little outside pressure as possible, because they would simply react to outside pressure as they did the last time. The more we police, the stronger would be the reaction, and, I think, so far as possible it should be avoided.

Question: Will a certain amount of force be necessary?

Dr. Boas: Yes, certainly. Disarmament has to be supervised, no doubt about that, but it should go hand in hand with general disarmament. As far as internal affairs are concerned, the more we leave to the Germans, the better it will be, for the simple reason that force will cause resistance.

Question: How deeply into the German ruling class will we have to cut to eliminate Fascism in Germany?

Dr. Boas: The whole present ruling clique ought to be eliminated.

Question: In what way? Tried, executed, put into concentration camps?

Dr. Boas: No, in insane asylums.

Question: What about the Prussian Junkers and Army leaders?

Dr. Boas: You cannot trust them insofar as the question of democracy is concerned. But you can trust them so far as decency is concerned, unless they have pretty much deteriorated in the past ten years.

Question: Do you think there is hope for a democratic Germany?

Dr. Boas: I don't see why not. Take the whole development and the rapidity of the change from the Republic to the Nazis. I don't see why a turn like that should be permanent. The Nazis have been in power only nine years. There must be very large numbers of Germans who grew up under different traditions.

Question: What about the young Nazis?

Dr. Boas: Of course, those who were pampered in the Nazi school of leaders are hopeless, except a few here and there. I know young people in general. I think there must be considerable numbers who resent Nazi compulsion and a fair number of individuals—I would not say how large—who, after the pressure to which they have been exposed, would go to the other extreme and long for freedom.

Question: You think education would bring them back?

Dr. Boas: Not all of them, but a sufficient number. In regard to the question, "What to do with the Germans," it is very decidedly my opinion that we ought to see to it that the older generation is helped as much as possible, by helping them to get into power.

There is a great danger that the Germans in the areas where they live in enclaves outside of Germany will be exposed to bitter revenge on account of the ruthless persecution of other nationalities by the Nazis. This should be avoided. I cannot see any solution of this problem except by a general policy of transmigration, notwithstanding the hardships it would imply. (Boas, 1943)

Here again we see Boas the scientist differentiating subtly and in historical depth, rejecting such then-popular concepts as "total guilt" and "total punishment" for a whole people, however revolting and ruthless their government had been. His aim: "To seek truth for truth's sake"—as he had demanded so often during his long career.[12]

Throughout his life, Boas had been involved in controversy, and even his last words proved no exception. In 1959 Mead wrote, "On December 29, 1942,[13] Boas was giving a lunch for his old friend Paul Rivet at the faculty club at Columbia University. A glass of wine in his hand, he said, 'I have a new theory of race . . .' and fell back dead" (Mead, 1959a: 355).

Such a statement from Boas' lips at this late date would have been more than sensational no matter when or where he made it. But Mead shows no interest in what her famous teacher may have had in mind. Her very next sentence reads, "There was now no senior person alive to whom Ruth Benedict looked for guidance in the choices she made as to the role which she, as an anthropologist and citizen, should play in the world."

After considerable search I have uncovered no source for this alleged last statement or any comment on it. In his 14-page essay "Franz Boas as Physical Anthropologist," Herskovits (1943) makes no reference to it, nor does J. M. Tanner (1959) in his 36-page essay, "Boas' Contribution to Knowledge of Human Growth and Form," nor does Stocking (1968) in his 30-page essay, which deals in unusual detail with Boas' ideas on race and on his conflict with the geneticists. Moreover, in the Foreword to the collection of Boas' more "popular" papers, published in 1945 under the title *Race and Democratic Society*, Boas' son, Ernst, writes that his father "had reviewed and approved the selection of articles that are included in this volume, and had carefully reread and edited the first twelve papers." Number V, "Racism," was originally published in *Asia Magazine* in May 1940 under the title "Racial Purity." A footnote in *Race and Democratic Society* states that it was "slightly revised, November 1942" (Boas, 1945: 28)—that is, just a very few weeks before Dr. Boas died. Except for the title, I found only one place where it had been altered, and this involved only a single sentence. In *Asia Magazine* this sentence reads, "Our conclusion is that the claim to biologically determined mental qualities of races is not tenable." The first sentence in the final paragraph of "Racism" reads, "The claim is not tenable that mental qualities of races are biologically determined" (Boas, 1945: 37).

I asked Dr. Harry Shapiro, who has been engaged in organizing and annotating Dr. Boas' papers on physical anthropology (still an on-going operation), what difference in thinking the changed wording connoted. He saw none, but suggested that Boas may have considered his earlier phrasing somewhat ambiguous, and may have felt that his point emerged more clearly in the revised form. Both in his article in *Asia Magazine* and in "Racism," the following sentences remained unchanged:

> Much less have we a right to speak of biologically determined superiority of one race over another. Every race contains so many genetically distinct strains, and the social behavior is so entirely dependent upon the life experience to which every individual is exposed, that individuals of the same type when exposed to different surroundings will react quite differently, while individuals of different types when exposed to the same environment may react the same way.

Dr. Shapiro also told me that he had attended a luncheon given by Dr. Boas for "his old friend," Paul Rivet, at the Columbia Faculty Club the week before Dr. Boas died and that then Boas had said nothing about "a new theory of race." From the way in which Mead reports Boas' last luncheon, it seems legitimate to infer that she herself was not present when Boas "fell back dead." Nor, it seems, was Ruth Benedict or Ruth Bunzel, both of whom Ruth Bryan, Dr. Boas' long-time secretary, assured me, early in 1972, she had contacted by telephone to announce the sad but hardly unexpected news of his death. (Dr. Boas was 84 years old and for some years had not been in good health.) And she could not recall, when I questioned her further, any special luncheon or the name of any person he had been dining with on this last day of his life.

To be sure, Boas was not without a sense of humor. But for him race had been a major area of study for more than half a century. Knowing the passion with which he had argued his view throughout the years, it is inconceivable that, with or without "a glass of wine in his hand," he would have made so momentous a claim so casually. Moreover, the lack of corroboration of his alleged last words, or any substantiating evidence in his notes, or any discussions that would have led a friend or colleague to suspect a radical change in his position, or, most convincingly, the fact that in the month preceding his death he had approved the selection on race included in his posthumously published *Race and Democratic Society*—make it more than moot that whoever "heard" Boas' last words as given by Mead, misheard them.

Serious scholars may wonder why I have chosen to list these Boas writings of the 30s and early 40s. I have done so not only because Dr. Boas, though retired from his professional post, continued to influence the intellectual and political climate in the Department of Anthropology after my return to Columbia, but also because I believe both the titles and their timing give crucial insights into the thought processes and personality of anthropology's most eminent figure. To some, it will be no surprise that a man of such great scholarly accomplishment, methodological meticulousness, and flair for leadership could, once his emotions (Godwin would have said his "passions") became involved, place in limbo or blot out altogether the scientific principles he had proclaimed for decades and was continuing to proclaim. But in two periods of his life—1914 to 1919 and 1933 to 1942—this is what Franz Boas appears to have done. "A man of unimpeachable devotion to his ideals." Yes—but a man who, in moments of extreme love or extreme hate, invoked these ideals ("democracy and intellectual freedom," "the individual counts," etc.) unevenly and, at times, even in contradiction to his own scientific standards and core beliefs.

During these years Benedict and Bunzel went along with Boas uncritically. Benedict had come a long way from her "What a waste" comment in 1934 (on his concern with politics), to her participation—and active participation—in the American Committee for Democracy and Intellectual Freedom, of which Boas was chairman. Mead, in discussing Boas' and Benedict's positions during this period, writes,

> Boas believed that he would be able to spot a Communist at once by his lack of intellectual independence which, he felt sure, would show through everything. He remained scornful of attacks on many of the causes with which he associated himself, his uncompromising attitude insulating him from any education on the subject of Communist methods. Ruth Benedict was a little more in touch with the tone of the times. She knew that some of the people with whom she came in contact were Communists, but she too refused to believe that what these doctrinaires advocated needed to be taken seriously. If she had ever had a friend who became a Communist, she would have shrugged her shoulders as she had done when close friends turned to Christian Science or Anglo-Catholicism or psychoanalysis. So she was no less scornful than Boas of the attacks, which she herself knew enough to recognize came not from the Right but from the disgruntled and unorthodox Left, which sought to discredit generous human causes by giving them a Communist label. (Mead, 1959a: 349)

And to point up Benedict's later more critical attitude she added:

> Only after her experience in Washington—after tussles over clear-
> ing assistants and briefing sessions on security—could she be per-
> suaded to take even the ordinary sad precautions of the twentieth
> century, such as writing to a committee for Wallace, which had
> used her name without her permission, and keeping a copy of her
> letter of protest.

And then reverting to Benedict's earlier attitude, Mead concluded:

> But before the war [obviously during the Stalin-Hitler Pact] in
> the battles against race hatred, discrimination, and limitations
> of freedom of speech and of the press, she and Boas marched
> ahead, hardly vouchsafing a sidelong glance at those who were
> willing to let a good cause go by default if by chance the "Stalin-
> ists" had also espoused it.(Mead, 1959a: 349)

On the basis of what Mead says of Benedict's tolerance of the
conversions of her "close friends" to this or that ideology, it seems
reasonable to assume that Benedict would have been equally tolerant if
those who "espoused it" had been Stalinists without quotation marks.

Fully aware of the Boas-Benedict-Bunzel hostility to him on the
academic level, Linton chafed increasingly at non-academic activities he
felt obliged to attend. He told me how much he resented going to the
money-raising front dinners at which Boas was the guest of honor, but
in view of Boas' position in the department he had felt compelled to
attend. Completely unsympathetic to these activities, I encouraged
Linton to shun them in the future. I had told Boas why I wouldn't go,
and he had shown neither surprise nor resentment. I was still a
daughter—and, from his standpoint, not far removed from a rebellious
adolescent. But despite our unbridgeable political differences, our deep
affection for one another never lessened. He was the only non-relative
on my side that I invited to my wedding to Karl August Wittfogel in
1940, and his family asked me to join with a very few others from
Columbia in viewing his body at his home in Grantwood, N.J. With
Linton things were quite otherwise. His presence at the Boas dinners
did nothing to narrow the breach between them, and when he stopped
going to them no one commented on his changed behavior.

Among the students, many had strong Communist sympathies and
took great satisfaction in Boas' political stance. There were, of course,
some, like me, who were critical of both great totalitarian powers—Nazi
Germany and the Soviet Union. But, on the surface, relations among all
of us remained friendly.

8. WE LEARN ABOUT RORSCHACH TESTING

In the early spring of 1938, or a little before, Ruth Benedict asked me if I would like to join a small group interested in learning about Rorschach testing from Bruno Klopfer, a recent German émigré from Fascism, a Jungian, and a keen student of Hermann Rorschach, the Swiss scientist who had invented the so-called Rorschach ink-blot test for interpreting personality. The group had already met several times, but this did not deter me. I immediately said yes.

When I appeared at the next session, the members of the "class" were already assembled—all five of them: Caroline Zachry (the classroom was in the same brownstone that had housed the Study of Adolescents and which also served as Dr. Zachry's domestic and professional residence); Wilma Lloyd, her close friend and housemate; Ruth Benedict; Ruth Bunzel; and William Whitman (regularly called "Bill") who had been doing field work in the pueblo of San Ildefonso, New Mexico, and was writing his Ph.D. dissertation (it was published posthumously in 1947 as *The Pueblo Indians of San Ildefonso*). This small company was ranged about a rectangular table—Dr. Klopfer at the head (as I remember him, he was about 40 years of age, rather short, slightly built, his eyes behind glasses, intelligent and probing), Dr. Zachry beside him, the two Ruths on their left, Wilma Lloyd facing them, Bill to their right. Having been duly introduced to Klopfer, I took my seat next to Bill.

After a moment of silence, Klopfer turned to me and suggested that since it would be a waste of time for the others to rehash what had been discussed previously, I should then and there not only examine the ink-blot cards but give my reactions to them. In short, I should learn by doing—and doing in a way that, as I discovered later, was never suggested in serious Rorschach testing. Innocent that I was, and not wanting to acquire a reputation for contrariness at this, my first meeting with the group, I acceded to his request.

Rorschach has written,

The subject is given one plate after another and is asked, "What might this be?" He may turn the plate as he likes. . . . So far as possible, but avoiding any suggestions, of course, the subject should be made to give at least one answer to each plate. Ordinarily notations are taken just as long as answers are forthcoming. It has not been found useful to fix a time limit to the interpretation. The important thing is to have the experiment performed without compulsion as far as possible. . . . Apperceptions are created by the appearance of sensations and recollections of groups of former sensations which are recalled by us and

125

give rise to a complex of recollected sensations whose elements by their co-existence in former experiences received a particularly strong coherence and a separation from other groups of sensations. In the apperception, therefore, are contained the three processes of sensation, recollection, and association (Sicha, n.d., p. 1 f.).

These statements by Rorschach should be enough to suggest how revealing answers to the ink-blots can be.

Beyond the suggestion that I take the test, no compulsion of any sort was exerted on me. Also, as Rorschach intended, I was given all the time I wanted, no limit was put on the number of my answers, and I was shown one plate after the other and asked: "What might this be?"

The ten plates used in the test are on heavy white cards about 7″ x 10″, some of the ink-blots only in shades of black, some in shades of black with a little red, and some in pastels. A subject's answers are evaluated according to number, the use of color and movement, and how much of the blot is included—the whole, a large detail, or a small detail.

I took up the first card without hesitation. Soon the pauses between my responses became long. I had not read what Rorschach had said about "recollected sensations" and their impact—but my slowness was surely revealing. In fact, my answers consumed the whole of the evening and much must have been learned about me that I would rather have kept hidden. In any event, no one commented on my performance when I released the last card. Klopfer offered no interpretations either then or later. Indeed all acted as if they had not been present during this session that obviously was so embarrassing to me. (Years afterward a friend gave me another Rorschach test—in private this time—and while I believe my answers did not differ too greatly from those on that memorable evening in 1938, I gave them much more quickly and without suffering any comparable malaise.)

One afternoon late in the spring of 1938, when our Rorschach course was over, Ruth Benedict and I were walking toward Broadway (I believe we had been attending a meeting in the Zachry brownstone). Without preamble, she said, "You know Klopfer took my Rorschach," and without any comment on my part, she continued, "I gave only one answer to each card and each of them was a whole. Quite schizophrenic." After a short pause, she added, "Klopfer was amazed at the complexity of my integrations of color and movement."

By this time I as well as Ruth understood the implications of these statements. We had been told that the average response per person was somewhere in the neighborhood of forty; that one response to a card usually indicated, as she herself had volunteered, a schizophrenic personality—that is, the personality of an individual who had evolved a

A. Home on the range, Summer 1939, Blood Reservation.
B. Mother and favorite son, Summer 1939, at the Sun Dance, Blood Reservation.
C. At the Sun Dance, Blood, 1939.
D. At the Sun Dance.
E. Raising the pole for the Sun Lodge.

Ruth Benedict (second from right) on arrival at the Blood Reservation. Pictured with her are, from left, Marjorie Lismer, guide (?), Gittel Posnansky (Steed), Robert Goldfield (Steed).

Medicine Man's Rival—Blood Blackfoot, 1939.

Outside the homestead: the author and neighbor, 1939.

scheme of life or system that was so satisfying or so compelling that there was no need to consider any elements beyond those already included. Under such circumstances the fact that each response was a whole would not be too surprising. Moreover, we had also been told that whole responses indicated ambition (and, of course, the greater the number of wholes, the greater the ambition) and that an intricate weaving together of color and movement responses (reflection of sensation and association) within a single whole indicated unusual ability to coordinate elements of very different kinds within a single frame. In fact, in just ten responses to a set of ink-blots, Benedict revealed a considerable part of her complex and fascinating personality. In just ten responses she provided the key for a deeper understanding of her scientific approach and thinking.

Before I wrote my paper on "Socialization, Personality and the Structure of Pueblo Society" (1945b), Ruth countered my anti-Apollonian examples by saying, as I mentioned previously, "You have never been in Hopi or Zuni"; and after the appearance of my paper, which dealt mainly with Hopi and Zuni, she countered my anti-Apollonian examples by saying, "I'm so bored with the pueblos." Ten years after *Patterns of Culture* was published, and after there had been much discussion and criticism of its substance, she could still see no reason why she should have added a new introduction to the paperback edition, either to defend or to modify her original position.

The telling word-picture so basic in a good poem—and Benedict's correspondence with Edward Sapir shows how intensely she felt about a poem being good—had its analogue in her descriptions of cultures: the pueblos are Apollonian; the Aztecs are Dionysian; the Dobuans see human nature as fundamentally treacherous; the Kwakiutl measure their success by the humiliations of their fellows (all in *Patterns of Culture*); the Chippewa *"can not kill the father"* (Barnouw, 1949: 241); the Blackfoot always dance on a knife-edge (said to me and repeated later to Barnouw, ibid.). Thus again in just ten responses we learn why these characterizations, once they were articulated by Benedict, remained forever unchanged.

9. 1939–SUMMER: ON THE BLOOD (BLACKFOOT) RESERVATION IN ALBERTA, CANADA AND ITS BY–PRODUCTS[14]

In the spring of 1939 I heard that Ruth Benedict was organizing field work among four groups of Blackfoot Indians—one in the United States (the Southern Piegan, with whom Clark Wissler had more than two decades earlier worked so effectively) and three in Canada (the

Northern Blackfoot, who were already being studied by Lucien Hanks and his wife, Jane Richardson, whom I had known while she was getting her Ph.D. at Columbia; and the Northern Piegan and the Blood, neither of whom had been studied systematically by anthropologists). The four groups, who shared a common language, were to constitute a laboratory for testing various theories regarding the effects of different histories (U.S. and Canadian policies) and different environments (physical and cultural).

Ruth was fully aware of the distance between her and my interpretations of pueblo society and of my refusal shortly after my return to Columbia to edit, at her request, notes on the Dakota assembled by Ella Deloria because I felt Deloria's merging of time periods and the resulting lack of distinctions between pre- and post-buffalo days gave what I already believed was an unrealistic picture of Sioux social history and development. Despite our disagreements, Ruth welcomed my suggestion that I join one of her groups. I would have a free summer (my daughter would be away in camp for two months), I would be of little or no extra expense (I was ready to pay my train-fare both ways, and living costs, I knew, would be extremely modest), and, perhaps most important from her standpoint, I had considerable field experience and had published.

Immediately she suggested that I might stay with Harry Biele and Marjorie Lismer on the Blood Reservation, and before she left New York she indicated that she thought I might coordinate and correlate the findings of her various researchers.

The U.S. group comprised Rae Walowitz and Gitel Posnansky and one other young woman, whose name escapes me and whose sojourn on the reservation was short. Rae was accompanied by her husband, Max Geltman, who became well known as a writer on political and ethnic questions; Gitel by her husband, Robert Goldfield (later they changed their name to Steed), who taught in a New York public school. Neither Geltman nor Goldfield had any conventional anthropological training. They came to know the Indian informants, but I was told they did not interview them officially.

The Canadian group comprised Oscar Lewis, who, accompanied by his wife, was to study the Northern Piegan, and Harry Biele and Marjorie Lismer, who, as noted, were to study the Blood. Except for me and the Hankses, the working members of these groups were all graduate students in the Department of Anthropology at Columbia, and none had had any field experience.

Harry picked me up in Browning, Montana, in a car he had bought from his father for $45. Rae told me that the car in which she and Max had traveled to Montana had also cost $45, but that they, and no doubt Harry as well, had been given additional funds for travel. Having driven across the border, about eight miles beyond Cardston, Alberta, a truly Western settlement with one broad unpaved street studded with hitching posts and small shops and an incongruously large Mormon Temple looming in the background, Harry and I arrived at "our" log cabin, where we were cordially greeted by Marjorie. Here as in my Blackfoot monograph (Goldfrank 1945c) I use pseudonyms for our close friends and informants whose confidences can in this way be protected, at least to some degree.

Our cabin was a sturdy affair. It was the permanent home of the George Pointed Plumes. He was the son of Pointed Plume, wealthy measured by Blood standards and a "chief," as he told me later. George's wife, Edith, was the daughter of William Curtis, a highly literate half-blood, and his full-blood wife, Julia. William had frequently consulted Wissler's various works on the Blackfoot, some of which he owned.

The George Pointed Plumes had six children, ranging in age from thirteen years to two months. Myrtle, the eldest, had lived since she was five months old with her grandfather, Pointed Plume. She had returned "home" shortly before I arrived. Things had not been going too well between the "old man" and his wife of many years, and Myrtle was far from pleased with her change of residence. "The family," according to her Curtis grandmother, "said she was spoiled," Pointed Plume having made her a minipoka—a "child of plenty" as the Blackfoot translate this term—by a series of give-aways in her name.

A give-away honored and raised the status of the person in whose name it was offered, and validated the wealth and position of the giver. Both George Pointed Plume and his brother James had in their early years also been made minipokas by their father's "generosity." Myrtle was the only one of Pointed Plume's grandchildren who could boast a similar status. To throw a give-away was a costly business, and honoring had to be continual.

"True" minipokas—and they could be of either sex—were watched over carefully, usually by an older member of the family. The boys sought each other out as playmates, and if a non-minipoka edged into their group, he would not be accepted as an equal. He would be the one to take orders, to retrieve the practice arrows the "children of plenty" shot into the air, and to serve on demand as their housemate.

When Myrtle was two years old and Fanny, the next in line, two months old, Pointed Plume had honored them jointly in a give-away, but this double gesture was never repeated. Obviously, one minipoka grandchild was all he could afford. It may be that this one honoring—and no doubt it was not allowed to be forgotten—was a sufficient acknowledgment of her grandfather's devotion to mitigate any envy Fanny might have felt for her "true" minipoka sister. In any event, the next younger sister, Rosalie—and her grandmother Curtis' "favorite," as we were quickly informed—was never honored by a give-away singly or jointly, and her hostility to the proud and "spoiled" Myrtle was certainly neither hidden nor lessened by the loving attentions of her Curtis grandmother. Their younger brothers Harold (aged 6) and Otis (aged 4), were completely indifferent to Myrtle's favored status. They were much more interested in exhibiting their prowess on horseback. And Constance was, as could be expected, concerned with nothing beyond the satisfaction of her infant needs.

Obviously the George Pointed Plumes had been induced by the Indian agent, after negotiations between Columbia University and the Canadian government, to permit us to use their cabin for the summer months. To give us sole possession, they had moved into a large tent some thirty feet behind and to the side of their erstwhile dwelling, and had quickly constructed a privy for our use.

Our cabin had a modest kitchen, with a wood-burning stove that drew so poorly we had to depend entirely on a gasoline-fed two-burner that served us unbelievably well, both in the cabin and during the ten days we spent in tents at the Sun Dance at the end of July and beginning of August. I mention the kitchen first because the only way to get into the cabin from the outside was through the kitchen door. Immediately behind the kitchen there was a sizable living-dining room, which, as if that weren't enough, also served as Harry's bedroom. To reach the bedroom that Marjorie and I shared—and later also Ruth Benedict—we had to pass through our living-dining room, and if Harry was already settled for the night, our eyes were modestly turned away from his couch.

For drinking water we had to travel more than a quarter of a mile to a shallow well, and since we got it by the barrel-full we always went by car. (Although I could drive, I never touched a wheel in all the weeks I was on the reservation—and this was no deprivation, since I felt I had done my share of taxiing by depositing children all over Westchester for thirteen years.) We filled our barrel bucket by bucket and, fearful of pollution, boiled and filtered every drop of it. Needless to say, we used it with the greatest restraint—the severest drain, aside from small basins of water required for our morning ablutions and minor dishwashings, being Harry's insatiable desire for coffee.

It was nine weeks before any of us had a tub bath. We did swim from time to time, at some distance from our cabin in a shallow rivulet that rippled happily over a very rocky bottom. For light we depended on kerosene lamps—and my memory is that this seriously discouraged night work and, for that matter, reading of any kind. But our days were long and busy, and when darkness fell we were quite ready to take to our beds. We needed no bugle to signal "lights out."

The Pointed Plumes' tent was the only dwelling within sight of our cabin. The Curtises' comfortable wooden house was almost a quarter of a mile down a fairly steep slope. A nearby stream had stimulated a slim growth of trees, and this shaded setting contrasted sharply with our uninterrupted grassy surroundings. Only to the west of our cabin, and some twenty miles away, was the broad expanse of high plain interrupted—and then most magnificently—by the snow-capped Rockies that changed color with the passing hours. As the sun began to set and the pink glow of twilight deepened into the blue shadows presaging night, our working day was over except for preparing our evening meal and washing up. Harry could never understand why I did not want to have steak three times a day, seven days a week, when it cost us, in this cow country, only 28 cents a pound! Although Marjorie and I were equally impressed with this modest price, we continued to insist on more variety—but we still had plenty of steak.

Except for Edith, her younger sister, Marian, and their brother, Joe, all of whom were married, five of the Curtis children (from Tom, in his late teens, to Sidney, who was about 9) were still living with their parents. There was, however, a constant coming and going between households. Joe visited his parents quite frequently, and I met Marian during the week she stayed at her parents' house before she returned to her "jealous" husband. Marian also, and quite regularly, provided a haven for Tom when he became dissatisfied or discomforted at home. Indeed, it was not at all unusual for children of the Blood, even quite young ones, to leave their parents' home and "visit" with a sympathetic relative—usually an older sister, aunt, or grandmother—sometimes for hours, but not infrequently for days and even months.

Edith was very close to her mother (hardly a day passed when they did not see each other, and I never heard a cross word between them); and her children were always welcome at the house of their Curtis grandparents. The older Pointed Plume girls and the younger Curtis boys were almost of an age, and "play" between them often emulated the more intimate—and sometimes the more violent—moments of adult behavior. As Alexander Henry wrote in his Journal, 1799-1814, the Blood "are much given to gusts of passion, a mere trifle irritates them and makes a commotion which a stranger would suppose must result in bloodshed." But, he added, "The matter is soon adjusted and their passions quickly subside" (Goldfrank 1945c: 88).

In good part this was true in 1939, but "commotion," both then and earlier might result in bloodshed. Previously, it had been common practice for a husband to cut off his wife's nose if he found her *in flagrante*, and he would watch with unconcealed satisfaction when his "comrades"—and his agemates who were joined by their membership in one or another of the men's societies—publicly ravished her. By 1939, thanks to the Canadian "establishment," the lot of the Blood woman had improved considerably, although cases of wife-beating were not unknown. But even when there was no physical abuse, little was forgotten or forgiven. I was told by one "happy" wife that her "happy" husband still angrily recalled her flirtatious behavior during an Owl Dance some twenty years earlier. And adjustment often took the form of separation. It is not uncommon for a man or woman to "marry" three or four times—and for many children the parent role was filled by their grandparents.

Indeed, jealousy has been the prime source of quarrels between men and women among the Blood, and the behavior patterns of elders, as in our society, have an early impact on children. One sunny morning Harry brought his newly found friend, a medicine man 77 years of age, to visit us. Pictures were being taken, and the old man asked Harry to snap one of him and me alone. A harmless enough request, I thought. But when he casually put his arms around my shoulders as he stood behind me, the six-year-old, who had come to feel during our weeks of close association that I was his special possession, angrily removed the old man's encircling arms and replaced them with his own.[15]

His mother and other family members laughed heartily—and approvingly. Didn't this six-year-old's reaction show that he was well on his way to becoming, in the traditional and admired sense, a Blood man? Yet despite quarrels and separations, enduring marriages were by no means infrequent.

In contrast to my experiences in the pueblos, I had no difficulty in finding responsive informants, and, for the most part, at our very doorstep. The structure of Blood society encouraged individual initiative. Of course, there were rules of desirable behavior, but in 1939 even those most stressed were often breached.[16] It was not unusual for a man to completely ignore the mother-in-law taboo (the prohibition of facing or speaking to a wife's mother directly) or to make sexual allusions in the presence of a sister or a brother's wife. Indeed, in the latter case, he was believed to be "in earnest."

Understandably, I began working with the Curtis family—William, Julia, and their daughter, Edith Pointed Plume—but soon Julia told me that their friends the Ned Sloanes were coming to stay with them for some time and that Ned, particularly, was eager to talk with me.

The Ned Sloanes were financially strapped because of Ned's incapacitating illness (which he referred to euphemistically as "rheumatism"), and working with me would be a source of income (not a great one, to be sure, but a dollar earned for a three-hour session twice a day was surely better than talking for nothing, especially when talking was one of the few activities he could participate in without assistance). And talk he did, with gusto, and about many matters that for most

Blood would have been prohibited between a man and a woman.

Ned Sloane was a half-blood. His paternal grandfather had joined the Mormon Church, and Ned's father had left Salt Lake City at nineteen to make his way to Montana. He met Ned's full-blood Indian mother at a trading-post and married her "the Indian Way": he gave three horses to her relatives. Ned's mother died in childbirth, and not long afterward his father left the reservation to be a government scout in Lethbridge. His contacts with his young son were few.

Ned was raised by his maternal grandmother. They spent two years on the Blood reservation and then stayed with his uncle in Two Medicine, Montana, until he was six, when he and his grandmother returned "home." The following winter he was sent to the Dunbow Industrial School, a co-educational Catholic boarding school, a hundred miles away. In his eleven years there, his grandmother came to see him once or twice and, all told, he had four visitors. But what Ned learned during these eleven years served him well, especially his mastery of English.

Ned Sloane spoke freely of his young days on the reservation and of his school years. He never ran away, as not a few of his fellow students did. He was a good athlete, played in the band, and was rewarded for good behavior by being appointed a monitor. He then carried a "black book" in which he noted, and reported, the misdeeds of his fellows. "They often ganged up on me," he commented. But their hostility gave him little concern. Increased power over others more than compensated for any loss of popularity.

Returning again to his first "home," Ned, like his father, became a government scout and interpreter at Stand-Off—a not unlucrative vocation that insured a modicum of prestige to those who had been denied traditional roads to wealth and esteem. And since Ned had lacked both horses (the most favored means of exchange) and cattle (cattle-herding had replaced buffalo hunting as the pre-eminent economic pursuit), he had gladly accepted the government's gift of land with the condition that he farm it. The following decades were good to Ned, but the intensification of his disabling disease brought many changes in his way of life, and few, if any, were for the better.

Ada, Ned Sloane's half-blood wife, was a handsome woman somewhat younger than he, who had married him when he was a good catch. In 1939, despite his worsening physical condition, he still created an impression of vigor and self-confidence. The jaunty angle at which he wore his hat when he was being driven to Cardston clearly reasserted an early and, from what I learned, a justified image of himself.

Ada's beauty was joined to a dignity that never forsook her, at least not in my presence, no matter how inconvenient (or pleasant) the care of her husband might be. In addition to the many demands made upon her by her ailing husband, she cared for her blind mother, who lived next door, and often for her little granddaughter.

Marjorie and Harry rarely worked at home. Marjorie spent many hours at the Agency Headquarters recording data on bands, place of residence, and household membership, which she later supplemented from interviews with one or another of our Indian friends.[17] Free to drive where he wished, Harry made many informal visits to various parts of the reservation, but he also worked intensively with one medicine man and gathered considerable new information on the Horn Society, whose members bought and sold the greatly valued "sorcery sticks."[18] For me, these arrangements were ideal. Except for lunch, and not always then, I worked with virtually no interruption, with an intelligent informant, who was willing to talk on many subjects—tabu or not.

About mid-July, Ruth Benedict came to stay with us. When she arrived in the company of Gitel and her husband, Bob Goldfield, and certain others, she was pale and preoccupied (see snapshot, taken shortly after she arrived—facing p. 127). We soon learned why.

Some weeks before, while driving over a rough road to get camping paraphernalia from the Geltman's, Bob had lost control of his car on a sharp turn, and the Indian who was guiding him was killed. Understandably, this accident interrupted formal field work in the area where Gitel and Bob had set up their camp, although Benedict did what she could to reestablish her group's relations with the dead man's family and the community. Also reports had to be made to on-the-spot authorities, to Professor Boas, and to Columbia University. Actually, reactions on the reservation were surprisingly mild (the victim was far from popular, having shortly before returned there after serving 20 years in Leavenworth for the murder of nine of his Blackfoot fellows). And once the funeral was over and suitable gifts were made, a side of beef among them, field work seems to have gone ahead pretty much as planned. But, as director of the Blackfoot Project, Ruth's burden remained a heavy one, and the change in her locale, although obviously welcome, did not completely dispel her concern. Shortly after Bob and Gitel left us, she complained of a severe migraine, and for days, except for meals, short periods of consultation with one or another of us, and sporadic efforts to work on the book she was writing on race—a subject she found "boring"[19]—she lay on her bed. At first I thought her malaise was due to menopause, but before the summer was over I came to understand that, while this might have been a contributing factor, it was probably not the decisive one. Years later I learned from her story of her life that from her earliest days withdrawal had been her not infrequent response to strain (cf. "The Story of My Life . . ." in Mead, 1959a: 108ff.).

The Sun Dance, which was being held at a considerable distance from our cabin, began at the end of July and lasted for some ten days.[20] It was the great event of the year. It gave us an unusual opportunity to meet many members of the Blood and their friends from different and sometimes distant sections of the reserve and, more important, we were permitted to witness all public ceremonies.

We still had to "keep house," so to speak, but more accurately we, like everyone else, camped out. I have a vague recollection of Harry's making several trips from our cabin to the Sun Dance area, loaded down with paraphernalia—two tents, one for "les girls," one for himself (which he shared with our indispensable two-burner gasoline stove), a minimum of cooking and eating utensils, enough comestibles to withstand possible emergencies, and basic articles of dress and personal hygiene. I don't remember how we obtained our drinking water, but there must have been a reliable spring nearby. Bathing was no greater problem here than at "home," and our comfort stations were the numerous bushes that dotted the slope leading down to a small river. They were open to the curious on every side and almost always a group of young boys was lined up on the opposite bank enjoying choice seats at what was certainly not "The Greatest Show on Earth."

When we arrived at our destination we found quite a few tipis, some painted, some not, and numerous modern-style tents edging an oval field that would be the scene of important ceremonies in the days to come. Housing arrangements were dictated in greatest part by band affiliations—each band being assigned a particular location. After we paid the expected visitors' fee, including a substantial gift of tobacco, the officiating authorities permitted us "outsiders" to set up our tents close to those occupied by the Curtises. Inside the oval there were two very sizable tipis. The larger one would be the scene of more important ceremonies. The smaller one would, among other things, serve as the meeting place for negotiations preliminary to the transfer of the Long Time Pipe.

Earlier in the year a young and ambitious farmer, downed by illness and believing himself "at death's door," had dreamed he should vow a sacred pipe, and on the advice of experienced elders he vowed the Long Time Pipe, known as one of the "strongest" and, perhaps for this reason, one of the most expensive. Some years before the present seller had paid fifty horses for it, and the one before him a hundred. In 1939 it went for a mere twenty horses and some goods. To us the price agreed upon seemed high but, in Blood terms, the young man was getting a real bargain. In the final public phase the buyer, mounted on a painted horse, the pipe bound to his back, rode up to the entry of the smaller of the two tipis on the oval. The seller then emerged, making his way down an aisle flanked by eager observers, carefully examined each of the horses being offered in payment—obviously to assure himself that all was in good order, that there was no hanky-panky or visible defect. This was no paranoid reaction. Not infrequently in the past, payment had failed to meet specifications. The deal was then called off completely or postponed until satisfactory substitutes were found. But in 1939 all went well. The seller got his twenty horses and the young farmer rode away, the proud and confident possessor of the Long Time Pipe.

Certain Sun Dance activities we were not permitted to see, some we were unaware of, and some overlapped.[21] But we did see wagonloads of logs and leafy branches being hauled into the area where the Sun Lodge was being erected. Only a woman who had been chaste before marriage (no easy attainment in Blood society) and had never been a partner in an adulterous relation after marriage (no easy attainment in Blood Society either) could vow the Sun Lodge. However, I was told that many eligible women shunned this privilege and its traditional accompaniment, the purchase of the *natoas* bundle, because the costs were often beyond their resources and, in addition, the care of the bundle was an exacting one. In fact, the woman who had vowed it in 1929 was still waiting for a willing and sufficiently well-heeled tribeswoman to bid for it. In 1939, interest in the Sun Lodge proceedings was low indeed. To his dismay, the "transferrer" received only two horses for his efforts, and the crowd had learned in advance that there would be no giveaway of any account.

Many who might have attended found the Owl Dance a more inviting attraction, with its on-the-spot opportunities for flirtatious signallings and their not infrequent aftermath, hidden intimate relations. However, in the early afternoon, when the center pole of the Sun Lodge was in place, the audience increased considerably. Now the women—who months before had "vowed the tongues" to be offered to the Sun in gratitude for favors received and hoped for—were ready to perform the final act. Again the demands were high. The preliminaries had been intricate and even dangerous, for if a vower made an error in performing the rituals required while preparing the tongue offerings or was suspected of having indulged in extramarital adventures, she would be forced to leave the vowers' tipi and under no condition be permitted to make her offering to the Sun.

Some women felt their virtue would be enhanced if they named a male—or males—whose amorous approaches they had summarily rejected. And usually there was no argument. But I was told there had been times when the vower was openly challenged at this crucial moment and if the accuser could make his accusation stick, the woman would quickly withdraw, her shame never forgotten. In 1939 the final ceremony successfully followed prescribed patterns. If any mishaps had occurred during the preliminary activities, we never learned of them. (For comparative data see Wissler, 1918: 234-40.)

But much more eagerly attended was the public transfer of the membership and insignia of the Horn Society.[22] As already noted, this was considered the most dangerous—and most prestigious—of the age-grade societies, without doubt because in many instances the transfer of membership included, through further vowing and additional payment, the transfer of a "sorcery stick." Inside the large uncovered circle the sellers and transferrers were closely bunched and, also inside, the buyers, usually accompanied by their wives and certain other relatives, found their places. Beyond them the expectant crowd sat or stood, and many were packed uncomfortably close into horseless wagons in order to enjoy a less impeded view.

From the start, the interest was great, as yards of textiles and other goods were presented to the sellers for the purchase of memberships and insignias of office. It reached its height when the richest man on the Blood reservation moved forward to make his payment. As he rose, his handsome half-blood wife, who had spent some years among the Whites, asked her male neighbor with what was surely an assumed innocence, "What do I do here?" A short time later, and clearly with no instruction from him, she walked the long calico aisle without the slightest show of uncertainty or insecurity to receive her husband's ceremonial insignia.

At the conclusion of the afternoon exchanges, the new members of the Horn society paraded their newly acquired standards. But the moment of greatest tension and greatest excitement came after nightfall, when the sorcery sticks were transferred. Except for those directly involved, each person attending the Sun Dance was compelled to remain inside his or her tipi. For this was no ordinary exchange. This was no simple payment of horses and goods. This was the greatest trial for the buyer, who, without any show of emotion, had to remain seated in the society's chosen tipi, under the continual gaze of his fellow members, while his wife and the seller of the sorcery stick were taking a "ceremonial" walk around the campground and, at appointed places (we were told four) would consummate the purchase of this powerful instrument by prescribed acts of sexual intercourse.[23]

In a society where jealousy is omnipresent, this part of the Horn ceremony is considered one of the most difficult moments in a husband's life. In fact, some men have never joined the Horns because they felt unable to cope with this demand. Some, if they were rich enough, found relief by the purchase of a surrogate "wife" through whose cooperation their ownership would be recognized.

The last ceremony we witnessed, and I believe it was the last to be given in 1939, was performed in the larger of the tipis in the oval. It was obviously the final gesture of dedication to the Sun. Virtually everyone came—men, women, and children, members of the Blood, as well as Indians from neighboring tribes and Whites. Those who could find no place in the tipi sat on the ground outside—they were by no means few and, at times, we were among them—peering under the tipi flaps to get a glimpse of what was going on inside. Attention was largely riveted on the center pole, and I have a vague memory of horned headdresses on several dancers, and also of women actively participating.[24]

The Sun Dance came to a close, and like everyone else, we gathered up our belongings and headed for "home." It was a pleasure to lie again in a comfortable bed, without nocturnal visits of untethered and unmuzzled dogs, no doubt hoping to satisfy their hunger for food as well as affection. By the next day all was as it had been. We cooked, we cleaned, we continued interviewing informants.

Not all my notes are dated, but those that are indicate that at the Sun Dance I had some sessions with the Curtises, and I seem to have met George Pointed Plume's father there, whether for the first time or not I am not sure. Soon after our return, Pointed Plume and his "new" wife and her infant daughter by a previous marriage came to visit George and Edith. They set up their tent slightly below and some 50 feet from our cabin and about the same distance from the George Pointed Plumes' tent.

I immediately spoke to Edith about talks with her father-in-law, and since he had time on his hands—his sons were satisfactorily attending to the family's economic enterprises (tending the wheat, haying, and cattle herding)—Pointed Plume was entirely willing to work with me; and since he spoke little English, Edith suggested that her mother act as his interpreter, which she did.

The Ned Sloanes had returned to their own home after the Sun Dance, so there was no embarrassment of informant riches, and again, collaborators were available at my doorstep. Ruth continued working for the most part on her book on race, and Harry and Marjorie went their separate ways, as formerly.

As already noted, and fortunately for me, insofar as my understanding of Blood history and social norms were concerned, Pointed Plume and Ned Sloane occupied opposite poles in Blood society. Pointed Plume was a full-blood, his name usually prefaced by the word "Big" (which implied status as well as size). He claimed to have been a "chief," as his father had been before him, and that, like his two sons and his granddaughter, he also was a minipoka. He had joined the Pigeons, the Braves, the Brave Dogs, and the Horns (twice), had bought a medicine pipe and three bundles, and had been the major contributor when his sister vowed the Sun Lodge. Moreover, he was one of the few wealthy Blood (measured by the number of horses and cattle owned) who had also taken advantage of the government's offer of farmland. And it was this last decision that tided him over the serious drought years of 1919 and 1920, which destroyed most of the animals on the Blood reservation.

In *Changing Configurations* . . . (1945c), I note that those Blood who, in addition to their cattle wealth, had had the foresight to accept the government's land offer and, through the sale of the wheat they grew on it, had been able in a few short years to rebuild their herds of cattle and horses, could still validate their positions and maintain their influence through traditionally favored means of exchange. And I also noted that the children of these enterprising traditionalists were marrying off their children to the children of those half-bloods who had grown wealthy because their successful farming of the land granted them by the Canadian government had enabled them to build up herds of horses and cattle from scratch. This had permitted them to participate, insofar as they cared to, in the old ways of gaining prestige or in "the American way" (living in sturdy and better-furnished houses, acquiring better and varied farm implements, better saddles for riding, and conspicuously better clothes for their children). In short, these children of the newly rich were proudly considered by themselves and their families as minipokas, "the American way."

I was introduced to Pointed Plume's "new" wife, but she neither visited me, near neighbors though we were, nor did she suggest that she might become an informant. Pointed Plume, however, came to our cabin regularly and seemed to enjoy his sessions with me, as did the willing Julia Curtis. In recounting what Pointed Plume said about his favored upbringing, his chiefly status, his long-time and active participation in Blood ceremonies, his "generosity"—and his excellent economic situation—she may well have felt a not wholly disinterested pride. Hadn't Pointed Plume's son married her daughter? Hadn't he made a minipoka of her oldest granddaughter? And on his part Pointed Plume certainly enjoyed recalling his comfortable and cherished childhood, his participation in his father's activities, his own successes. Never did he speak of sexual matters, either in relation to himself or others. What I learned about his relations with his handsome second wife, who had brought the two young sons of his first wife to manhood after their mother's death, I learned from others.

Almost as soon as Pointed Plume and his "new" wife arrived, we were told things were not going too well between them. In fact, they were barely settled in their tent when we heard he had beaten her because of her "intimacies" with a young man who had separated from his wife and was on his way to visit relatives nearby. The "new" wife's denials did nothing to appease the angry Pointed Plume, and she soon picked up her child and belongings and left him to the care of his son and daughter-in-law. In a few days she was back again. Yet gossip had it that at "a mere flip of her cigarette" Pointed Plume would have happily returned to the woman whose life he had shared for two decades.

Not many days later both Pointed Plume and his "new" wife pulled up stakes. I never heard from or saw either of them again, but while Pointed Plume worked with me his domestic ructions never disrupted our interviews. He was both eager and meticulous in giving any details he considered important and appropriate for me to know.

Our time on the reservation was coming to an end and Ruth, who had for years enjoyed "playing" with kinship terms, asked me to get some Blood genealogies in the days remaining to us. This I tried to do and, as previously, my informants, particularly Julia and Edith and one or more of their relatives and close friends, were cooperative. But the results of my efforts did not satisfy Ruth. She complained that some of my reciprocals did not match as they should. And this was true. The problem arose, I believe, not only because the Blood kinship system was highly complex, but because it was in transition. Traditionally, and still among most of the members of the tribe, particularly the older ones, age was a most important criterion. But times were changing. A father's older brother might still be called "grandfather" by the younger brother's son. But not infrequently, and when interviewed alone, this same younger brother's son might call his father's older brother "uncle," as is the custom with us. Yet despite our disagreements I continued to work on Blood kinship until the end of my stay.

After nine weeks on the reservation, I was not at all unhappy to leave. I had amassed a great deal of information and maintained excellent relations with my Indian informants and their families, with one exception—a not too-well-liked sister-in-law of one of them, who, several years before, had been a major contact for a White woman of recognized artistic talents. I had made no effort to interview her formally, because of her hostility to my major informant, but one afternoon, finding her in our neighborhood, I did ask her to join with a number of women engaged in a bull session in our cabin to discuss female "business"—conception, birth, etc. I served tea and crackers, a gesture of hospitality I had sedulously avoided until then, and after I left the reservation I learned she had claimed that "in my Jewish way" I had offered my company only our cheaper crackers while keeping the more expensive ones for myself. I am neither secretive nor sensitive about my origins—and this was the only remark of its kind that came to my ears. I felt then, and I feel now, that this was her way of expressing her anger at my failure to recognize her status (her husband was a "chief") and her obvious abilities. Need I say that in our meager household we had no ordinary and extraordinary crackers. Whatever I offered my visitors was all we had.

Shortly after Pointed Plume departed and a week or so before I planned to greet my daughter on her return from camp and Ruth planned to go West to visit her sister in California, all of us at the cabin decided it was time for a swim in that rocky rivulet that ran through the Mennonite compound. We were just emerging from the cool waters when a young boy arrived with a message for "Dr. Benedict," asking that she contact the long distance operator in New York as soon as possible. All of us were apprehensive that it might be bad news. Why else call from New York and request an immediate reply? We hastily donned our robes and drove up to the main Mennonite house.

Ruth went directly to the telephone—one of those old-fashioned instruments that had probably been hung on the wall decades before. It was placed just inside the entry, and Marjorie, Harry, and I stood on the narrow wooden platform just outside. We stayed close at Ruth's request. After an exchange with the operator the call came through and we heard Ruth say with considerable surprise and relief, "Oh, Reggie" (this, of course, is not the caller's true name). When she joined us she said, "It was Reggie. He is flying out from New York tomorrow and wants me to meet him at Lethbridge. I told him I would." (I knew who "Reggie" was and that he had been seeking a divorce on grounds involving some members of Columbia's Department of Anthropology.) Ruth volunteered no further information, and none of us asked any questions.

Early the next morning Harry drove Ruth to Lethbridge. I do not remember whether he met Reggie that day (he certainly was not present during their pre-arranged interview), and, on returning to our cabin late in the afternoon, Ruth's only remark about the day's happenings was, "Reggie asked me not to discuss what we talked about." Ruth appeared completely at ease as we watched the sun set, and in the next days life remained serene, except, of course, for the news of the Stalin-Hitler Pact. But about three days before we planned to leave, Ruth again complained of migraine and lay on her bed, as she had when she first joined us. Again I thought it was a menopausal reaction.

The day I was planning to return home, all of us drove into Browning, the small town on the U.S. side where Harry had picked me up weeks before. Marjorie and Harry would be returning to the reservation, I was leaving for New York that afternoon, and Ruth was planning to stay with members of her U.S. "laboratory" before entraining for California to spend a month with her sister.

Both Ruth and I, who wore our hair short, felt a desperate need for haircuts, and we finally located a men's barber shop. The barber did not seem at all disconcerted that we were female. There were the usual barber-shop chairs facing mirrors and a few stools against the opposite wall for watchers and waiters. There were no waiters and I was the lone watcher while Ruth was having her hair cut (mine had already been done). Suddenly, and still facing into the mirror, Ruth said, "I got a letter from Margaret [Mead] a few days ago. She is furious." Then Ruth, usually so restrained, took off her "mask," and I quickly learned the cause of her malaise these last days at the cabin. "You know," she said, "when I met Reggie he asked me some questions related to his divorce action. I felt I had to answer them. I couldn't lie."

I could see Ruth's agitated expression reflected in the mirror as she talked, but she did nothing to hurry the barber and he went on snipping away with complete unconcern. Ruth continued, "Reggie asked me to put my answers in writing and add my signature. He assured me that what I had attested to would remain secret. Now Margaret writes that my statement has become known. She could not understand how I could have signed my name to such a thing and she predicted dire consequences for me. I could be called as a witness in the divorce proceedings, my character would be impugned, my professional career endangered."

I listened to Ruth's worried words but refrained from commenting. I had often seen her turn off an unwelcome request with a lift of her brows, a curl of her lips, or reliance on her long-time and well-known hearing difficulty, although to judge from later comments, she had often clearly understood what had been said. Not that evasion is a crime. Almost everyone, and I include myself, has met an unwelcome situation or question by resorting to it, and each of us has his or her own criteria for invoking it.

Benedict gives us some clues regarding her own criteria in "The Story of My Life. . . ." There she writes, Mother who, she tells us, she had "violently repudiated" in her young years (Mead, 1959a: 98)

> thought that I was playing in the elder patch, which was allowed, but I set off for the flat,[25] which was a long excursion across the railroad tracks. When I got down there, I found Grandfather was haying on the flat, and he did not know I had run away. Now my Grandfather was the one person who stood out for me above all others. . . . That day on the flat Grandfather welcomed me royally. He took me on the haywagon to load the hay, and into the barn, while he threw over the sweet-smelling load. When they came up for milking I rode up on the empty wagons. But here was a difficulty, and I had to tell Grandfather that Mother didn't know I'd gone to the flat. He smiled down at me and said, "Well, if she doesn't ask, we won't tell her." It was a high point in my life. I had a secret with Grandfather, and I could see that he liked it as

well as I did. Pretty soon I strolled into the house from the elder patch, and Mother asked me, "Were you playing in the elder patch all this time?" I said yes, and it didn't bother me at all; why should it? But that evening after milking, when Grandfather came in for supper, he lifted me up to his face and whispered to me, "Did Mother ask?" What could I do? I said no, and he smiled at me again. But I ate no supper. I had lied to my Grandfather, and that was a different matter. My Grandfather, I suppose, belonged to "my life"; anyway he was one of my self-elected loyalties, and I had been false to it. Life was more complicated than I had supposed, and somehow, somehow after that I must plan so that I wouldn't have to *lie to Grandfather*. [26] (Italics in original.) (102f.)

Certainly a revealing passage. To lie to someone you have "violently repudiated" didn't bother Benedict "at all." But to lie to someone who stood out for her "above all others"—"that was a different matter."

I caught my train East soon after we left the barber shop. Some days later Ruth went to California. Originally she had planned to stay there for one month, but it was April before she returned to New York. Reggie's divorce was a *fait accompli* and Ruth's career was in no way blighted by what she had said and done in Lethbridge. However, immediately after my return to New York, Margaret Mead telephoned me—this was the first time she had ever done so. She asked whether she could come to my apartment and talk over what had happened on our reservation. We did not bother to discuss aspects she was already familiar with, but I told her quite frankly what I knew (Ruth had exacted no promise of silence from me). An hour or so later, Margaret rose to leave. Her parting remark to me was, "I can't understand Ruth."

In New York I soon began ordering my notes by topic and informant. In a letter from Pasadena, dated October 18, 1939, Ruth wrote me:

Esther darling,

I began to copy the kinship charts when your letter came and I got stuck on the woman's paradigm. I am not satisfied with it at all, but I mustn't put off sending you the man's paradigm. I'll work on the woman's and put it in an envelope in a day or so. . . .

Are you working on Blackfoot? I wish I was there. But it is wonderfully peaceful and leisurely out here and I work in great tranquility. The RACE book is getting along well; at least I'm keeping up with the number of words per day I set myself. The whole subject is such a bore!

Write me when you can. I feel very far away, and I think of you lots. All my best wishes,

Ruth

I do not remember ever receiving these paradigms, but several of them were included in Ruth's notes sent me by Margaret Mead in April 1972. Except for listing kinship terms on cards, I had ceased working with Blood kinship altogether. But it was my good fortune that my *Changing Configurations.* . . (1945c) and the Hanks and Richardson *Observations on Northern Blackfoot Kinship* (1945) were published in a single volume. The Hankses had a section headed "Variations in Terminology." Their data made quite understandable the difficulties I had met with in my own short-lived inquiry.

To judge from her October 18, 1939 letter, the pleasant moments of our Blackfoot sojourn remained uppermost in Ruth's memory, and, despite our differences regarding kinship, she obviously hoped it would be possible for me to continue my study of the Blood. In her letter dated January 22, 1940 and also from Pasadena, she wrote:

Esther dear,

I was so glad of your letter and I am pretty shocked to see how long it's been since it came. . . .

I've been chuckling about the little twosome to the Blackfoot for next summer. Of course I think that you and Harry are the two to go on with Blackfoot, and it's right and proper that the two best people should be able to stand each other when they both know the other's work is good. . . .

. . . Has Oscar got anything written up? I haven't answered his letter, but at that time he didn't speak of having anything ready. I miss not talking Blackfoot with you all. And who sees "vested interests"? It seems a far cry. But I suppose people used to analyses of our culture might feel that any "wealth" society even though it were Blackfoot, must have vested interests. It seems to me misleading.

. . . I'm having such a good time working without interruption, and I don't doubt I am getting soft. But I like it. Just the same, I miss you all a lot. Don't forget what I look like; I'll want to be recognized when I get back.

Affectionately,
Ruth

And then she added in handwriting:

I'll be back in April. Give my love to the Blackfooters. Tell Harry to write me!

There had been several points in my field notes that I felt needed clarification, and my reading of the historical sources, especially the Sessional Papers of the Dominion of Canada, were of great help. It was from them I learned that, in 1877, the Canadian government had granted two cows to a family of five and three cows to a family of five to ten. During the previous decade, the buffalo had been decreasing rapidly, and for 1878 the "winter count" of one Blood reads, "This was the year the buffalo went out of sight." But despite this catastrophic development the former hunters, according to the Agency reports, found it highly distasteful to care for cattle, to milk them regularly, and then turn over their calves to the government until their number equalled the number originally granted their families. The Blood either slaughtered the cows that so complicated their traditional mode of life or gave them away as part payment for bundles, society memberships, etc. In 1884-85, the Indian Department sold off the few that remained, thus eliminating, as their report stated, "another source of expense and anxiety" (*Sessional Papers of the Dominion of Canada*, 1884, 3, No. 4: 83).

But the horses continued to multiply and, by 1894, they had become such a nuisance that the government offered to exchange twenty cows for twenty horses (ibid., 1897, 11, no. 14, XVI). The Blood who were rich in horses (and 100 was the number usually given to indicate that a person was rich) would still have enough horses to continue to enhance their prestige and validate their generosity. Not a few accepted the government's suggestion. All in all, an offer of twenty cows for twenty horses—particularly after almost two decades of lean hunting—was certainly not to be scorned. So the rich Blood got richer (until the drought of 1919-20) and the poor remained as poor as they had ever been, except for those who had been willing to farm.

In view of Ruth's comments on "vested interests" in her January 22 letter, which obviously referred to remarks made by Oscar and also by another of her students, Bernard Mishkin, who had done field work among the Kiowa in the summer of 1935 and had written on *Rank and Warfare among Indians of the Plains* (1940), it is not surprising that when I told Ruth, upon her return to New York, about the new way in which earlier wealth differences had been maintained and, from a financial standpoint, even increased, she shook her head and responded, "That just can't be so."

During Ruth's absence I had also been working on the case histories of Ned Sloane and Pointed Plume. I had used the information they had given me, but had not always quoted them verbatim, and I had included relevant comments made by others. Ruth thought I should have reproduced what they themselves had told me and only in their own words. So I started out anew on Ned Sloane, but what I wrote following her suggestion seemed to me stilted and at times forced. In the end I stopped working on these histories, although Ned Sloane's was already quite advanced.

And this may have been for the best. Both histories, I still believe, provide fascinating insights into Blood personality and the ways in which traditional attitudes survived—or not survived—in a quickly changing society. But having recently reread what I wrote three decades ago, I have no regrets that the histories have remained unfinished and unpublished, either in the form I employed originally or in the one requested by Ruth. Even though I had used pseudonyms for these major informants, in my 1945 monograph, they would have been only a thin veil easily penetrated by members of the tribe, and, in the case of Ned Sloane, would surely have embarrassed not only his immediate family but perhaps Ned himself.

On the very day Ruth wrote me about the possibility of my returning the following summer to the Blood reservation, I met Karl August Wittfogel for the first time. Ruth had referred to him at a weekly luncheon in the faculty dining room at Barnard more than a year previously. She had said, "There is a scholar studying Chinese society who believes that the turntable used in pottery-making may well have been the forerunner of the wheel." Ruth mentioned his name but not what I learned later—that she had chaired a meeting sponsored by the Institute for Social Research, that Dr. Boas had been present and that Wittfogel, a long-time member, had been the principal speaker. Pre-Columbian pottery was uniformly held to have been shaped entirely by hand. Ruth's comment aroused little interest in me. I cared little about details of material culture and, in fact, as I learned later, Wittfogel's comment on the possible origin of the wheel was a bit of exotica definitely peripheral to the main lines of his thinking.

I had invited some students of anthropology to a small party I was giving on January 22. Joe Bram, who was somewhat older than most of his colleagues and considerably younger than I, asked whether he could bring along "a beautiful blond." I, of course, said yes, and when I opened the door, there he stood with his "beautiful blond," who turned out to be Karl August Wittfogel—six foot three and wrapped in a most generous topcoat made for him in China, where he had spent two years before the outbreak of the Sino-Japanese war in 1937.

Wittfogel had barely crossed the threshhold when he asked me, "What about irrigation in the pueblos?" And this, I soon learned, was basic to the main line of his thinking. He had met Joe in Provincetown the previous summer and Joe had mentioned my work in the Southwest. After a week of exchanges on this all-important subject, as well as on others, needless to say, Karl August Wittfogel and I decided to marry—a step we took on March 8, 1940. So when Ruth returned to

New York in April it was not long before she again met the scholar "who had been studying Chinese society."

Ruth was still eager to have the major findings of her four Blackfoot "laboratories" in print. On July 25, 1940 she wrote me from Shattuck Farm:

Dear Esther:

I've had letters from June and Jane in answer to mine about the plan of the book. They're delighted to have Oscar do the historical backgound. The main problem is that I wrote them that the outline couldn't possibly be followed and documented in the space allotted to each chapter. They write, "By all means let's get this thing done once for all, and if it's too long to be acceptable as a Psych Monograph, we'll trust the publication elsewhere." But I hate to pass up this opportunity for publication, and if we made a selection among the points raised in the outline we might still get out a good monograph for the Psych series. You've been working with the outline. Have you any suggestions? The monograph should be, in general, the likenesses and contrasts of the different reserves and the relation of these findings to the old culture. . . .

Are you and Karl August enjoying Provincetown? Summer has only just arrived here. My love to you.

As ever,

Ruth

I've written Harry and Oscar

In an undated letter, written in July and shortly after the birth of a child to him and Jane, June Hanks wrote me regarding the projected Blackfoot publication and included a lengthy statement detailing how the data might best be approached. A first part was to present descriptive material and the two major subsections under this heading were The Administrational System and The Economic System.

A second part was to deal with the effects of the economic and social systems. It had four major subsections: The Effects on the Social Structure of the Group, The Effects on the Relation between Individuals, The Effects on the Relation to Things, and The Effects of the Individual's Relation to Self. Under each of these subsections there were further subdivisions—in several cases as many as seven—and each author was to deal with these many topics in twenty-eight pages!

I have no copy of my answer, but I feel certain that my reaction to this outline must have been quite similar to Ruth's. On July 22, 1940, three days before Ruth sent off the above letter to me, I heard from June again. This time he wrote:

Dear Esther:

May I tell you of the change in the plans with respect to our mutual publication. First note the Table of Contents. Oscar Lewis will probably write the introductory chapter and the Piegan chapter. Ruth Benedict will write the concluding chapter. Jane and I shall do the Blackfoot of our reserve together.

Next at Ruth's suggestion we are going to remove the arbitrary limit of 30 typewritten pages.... Our instructions as to length then become: As brief yet as inclusive as possible....

Our best to you,

June Hanks

Although not attached to the second letter, I found the following undated memo among my papers.

The Psychological Effects of Certain Economic and Administrational Systems on the Blackfoot Reserves (not a title).

Table of Contents

An Historical Introduction to Blackfoot Culture—Chapter I by Oscar Lewis(?)

The Economic and Administrational Influences on the Blood Reserve—Chapter II by Esther Wittvogel [!]

The Northern Blackfoot Reserve—Chapter III by Jane Richardson and L. M. Hanks, Jr.

The Northern Piegan Reserve—Chapter IV by Oscar Lewis

The Blackfoot Reservation of the Southern Piegan—Chapter V by Rae Walowitz

An analysis of the foregoing data—Chapter VI by Ruth Benedict

No such book was ever published. But it is more than possible that when I began writing *Changing Configurations* (1945c) I was not unmindful of June's first outline. And I made it quite clear that professionally I did not intend to use the name "Wittfogel," whether spelled incorrectly or correctly.[27]

Although this joint publication never materialized, some parts of the projected volume did appear. In 1942, *The Effect of White Contact upon Blackfoot Culture,* by Oscar Lewis, was issued. This was his doctoral thesis and it contained no references to data he or any other "Blackfooter" had collected during the summer of 1939. Only in his 1941 paper, "Manly-hearted Women among the North Piegan," did he refer to the 1939 data. The Hankses, who, as already noted, were not in the field in the summer of 1939, presented the results of their several visits to the North Blackfoot Reserve in a number of publications

(Hanks and Richardson, 1942, 1945, 1950; Hanks 1954).

In December 1941, at the Annual Meeting of the AAA, I read a paper entitled "Administrative Programs and Changes in Blood Society during the Reserve Period" (Goldfrank, 1943d). After I finished, Philleo Nash, later Commissioner of Indian Affairs in the Kennedy Administration, who was to speak on "Historical Changes in Klamath Social Structure" in this same session, suggested that since so much of my data paralleled his, there would be little lost if his paper was omitted from the crowded morning schedule. Of course, his generous gesture was quickly rejected. There were indeed similarities between our communities, and I was happy to learn about them—and about the dissimilarities as well.

The need for data from different tribes for purposes of comparison was underlined by Clark Wissler, whose review (1947) of my *Changing Configurations* stated, "Fortunately for us, while the writer is ever ready to interpret her data, she gives most of her space to well-chosen statistics and case histories. Thus the reader can reject her assumptions of cause and effect and make his own interpretation.... The nearest comparable studies are Keesing's work on the Menomini, a central Algonkin woodland culture, and Margaret Mead's study of the Omaha." He concluded, "There is certainly room for more such factual studies."

This largely positive review from the pen of the leading authority on the Blackfoot Indians was highly gratifying. Equally so was the response of George Devereux, an anthropologist who had done field work among the Moi in China and among the Mohave and Hopi in our Southwest. While studying at the Menninger Clinic in Topeka, Kansas, as a prelude to becoming a psychoanalyst, he was asked, because of his field experiences, to do what he could to dispel the stubborn neurosis of an American Indian, a veteran of World War II and a member of a Plains Indian tribe—not the Blood. To protect the patient's identity, Devereux has designated this tribe as the "Wolf" tribe.

Knowing my *Changing Configurations,* Devereux asked me, in March 1949, to read and comment on his manuscript of some 400 pages. This work, published in 1951 as *Reality and Dream: Psychotherapy of a Plains Indian,* was a trail-blazing effort in transcultural psychotherapy[28] within the context of Plains Indian society, and it included a verbatim transcript of the intensive sessions he had held with the patient.

I was pleased to comply with Devereux' request. The few chapters I had seen previously had assured me that this work would be an outstanding contribution to culture and personality studies and to comparative studies, in which I had become increasingly interested because of my work with the Chinese History Project directed by my husband. As the completed book shows, Devereux drew in great part on the writings of R. H. Lowie (Crow), G. MacGregor (Sioux), C. Wissler (Blackfoot), G. B. Grinnell (Cheyenne), A. L. Kroeber (areal studies), and A. I. Hallowell and W. LaBarre (psychologically oriented anthropological studies). I would certainly be in good company, and during an unhurried summer in Cornwall, N.Y., I read the manuscript pages Devereux had sent me, the last on June 5, 1949. I then wrote him quite informally what, from my knowledge of the Blood, I considered relevant. Wissler's criticism notwithstanding, I did not shun interpretation.

Devereux most generously acknowledged my labors, "Mrs. Esther Schiff Goldfrank, a leading specialist on Plains Indians, painstakingly checked the manuscript from the ethnographic point of view, and provided extensive and significant comments, many of which were incorporated into the manuscript in the form of footnotes identified by her initials (ESG)" (p. xxi). In his chapter on "Transference and Kinship Behavior," he reproduced in the text a long passage from my letter dealing with parent-child relations and the roles and attitudes of Blood men and women (1951: 63-65, 1969: 114-17). In the paragraph immediately following, he wrote, "It must be admitted at once that Goldfrank's characterization of the emotional climate prevailing in the Blood Blackfoot primary group seems to be *partly* contradicted both by her own published data . . . and by what has been published about kinship behavior obtaining in at least one other Plains tribe. Indeed, many accounts of the Plains kinship behavior have stressed the good relationship obtaining between a man and his female blood-kin, and the presence of considerable rivalry between men. This *apparent* contradiction stands in need of a detailed analysis, especially since it is felt that Goldfrank's summary is both correct, and fully applicable not merely to the Blood Blackfoot, and to the Wolf Indians whose kinship behavior is known to resemble that of the Blood Blackfoot, but probably also to almost all typical Plains Tribes."

A decade after the summer of 1939, three more of my papers on the Blood appeared in print (1952a, 1951b, 1952).

It is good to know that others have been carrying on research among the Blood and related peoples. One of them, whose achievements are well known, wrote me not long ago that he had just reread my *Changing Configurations* and found it both "informative and lively." On this comforting note I end my saga of the Blood.

10. 1939-FALL: THE ANNUAL MEETING OF THE AAA AND LESLIE A. WHITE

At this meeting, which was held in Chicago from December 27 to 29, evolution was a major topic of discussion. On the afternoon of the 27th, Alexander Lesser spoke on the "Present Status of Evolution in Anthropology," and the whole afternoon of the 28th was given over to a symposium "On Method and Theory in Ethnology." Ralph Linton was chairman and Leslie White, the first-named participant, spoke on "The Evolutionary Approach" (American Anthropologist, 1940: 320f.). To the best of my recollection it was after Lesser had finished reading his paper that Leslie White made his first frontal attack on Boas and the Boas "school" for their fight against the concept of societal evolution which had been advanced among others, by Lewis H. Morgan, whose *Indian Journals,* 1859-62 (1959), *Systems of Consanguinity and Affinity* (1871), and, most especially, *Ancient Society* (1877) had brought him widespread acclaim as a pioneering and important voice in American anthropological studies. But while such avid students of society as Marx and Engels had found inspiration in Morgan's writings, Franz Boas, on the basis of his and his students' fieldwork, had for years been insisting on the untenability of Morgan's simplistic developmental scheme, and here Boas had a valid point. Unfortunately, he threw out the baby with the bath. White also had a valid point—the need to reassert "the evolution of culture" (the words in quotation marks became the title of his 1959 book). His scheme, which is as simplistic as Morgan's and seems close to Engels' view as expressed in his book *The Origin of the Family, Private Property and the State*—but actually is not (see Wittfogel, 1957: 385 and 1972: 64, 78)—is, however, quite in line with the unilinear concept propounded by Soviet ideologists until today.[29]

In his Chicago 1939 attack White spoke with extreme passion, his tone strident, his language intemperate. My memory is that he spoke off-the-cuff. I took no notes and, insofar as I know, there is no printed record of what he said at this time. But a few excerpts from his writings published in the decades following reaffirm important aspects of his then attitude and argument.

In "Energy and the Evolution of Culture" (1943), White writes, "The anti-evolutionists, led in America by Franz Boas, have rejected a theory of evolution in cultural anthropology and have given us instead a philosophy of 'planless hodge-podge-ism' " (355). In support of his view, White then mentions Robert A. Millakin, "a distinguished physicist," and George G. MacCurdy, "a distinguished American scholar" (356). In *Human Origins* (1933) MacCurdy had stated, "*The degree of civilization* of any epoch, people or groups of peoples, *is measured by ability to utilize energy for human advancement or needs"* (White's italics). And indeed, the role of energy in societal evolution became a major tenet in White's theoretical position.

In "History, Evolutionism and Functionalism" (1945), White distinguishes, as his title suggests, three processes—historical, functional, and evolutional, and he notes that already in his article "Science and Sciencing" (1938) he had "endeavored to provide a philosophic rationalization" of the three (243). In his 1945 article he also tells us, "No one is more important than the others." But he quickly qualifies this judgment by adding that "the interpretation supplied by the evolutionist is more basic, more fundamental than the interpretation of the historian or the functionalist" (244). In this same article, he again tells us that the "Boas school has waged war on evolutionism for decades" (246).

In *The Science of Culture* (1949), White writes, "Some, like Boas, are simply not able to grasp the concept of a special science devoted to a distinct and independent class of super-psychological determinants of behavior" (103); and on the next page he explains, "To Boas the 'working of culture' and the effect of the individual upon culture, meant 'the life of the individual as controlled by culture and the effect of the individual upon culture'." Then, abandoning the prosaic language of science, White asserts, "Technology is the hero of our piece." Elaborating on this theme in a summarizing statement near the end of his book, he argues, "Culture thus becomes primarily a mechanism for harnessing energy" (390).

In *The Ethnography and Ethnology of Franz Boas* (1963), White comments that Boas' "historical reconstructions . . . range from the probable through the possible to the preposterous" (62); and three pages later he finds them "worthless for the most part and fantastic in some respects" (65). He also comments that Boas' "psychological explanations are little, if any, better than his historical reconstructions" (63). His conclusion: Boas' "anti-evolutionism did cultural anthropology great harm from which it is recently recovering" (65)—no doubt, to his mind, a consequence of his own endlessly repeated polemics. On the following page, White maintains, "In complete honesty and sincerity I can say that I harbor no hostile attitude towards Boas the man or Boas the scientist." Paraphrasing Shakespeare, I would say, and I am sure many other anthropologists would agree with me, the gentleman doth protest too much.

While these random statements culled from White's writings over more than two decades are no substitute for a verbatim record, they do much to confirm my memory of what he said at the AAA meeting in December 1939, and recently, a well-known anthropologist who was close to White and had been at this 1939 meeting, told me that White, in his attack, had accused Boas of "paying lip service to theory, while actually destroying theory in American anthropology."

As could be expected, Boas' friends (and many had also been his students) quickly rose to his defense, and not a few who supported White's theoretical position also took exception to the distorted image of Boas he had evoked. The eighty-year-old dean of American anthropology alone seemed unmoved. When the session ended he left the room surrounded by those closest to him, his silence louder than any biting retort.

But the White of this Chicago meeting was not the only White—or the earliest White—in the field of anthropology. After receiving his M.A. from Columbia University in 1924, White continued his studies at the University of Chicago, receiving his Ph.D. in 1927. Information regarding his relations to Boas while he was in New York are contradictory. One anthropologist who was then working with Boas claims that White had not taken any courses in Columbia's Department of Anthropology, nor had he met Boas at this time. Another anthropologist, who knew White since the early 30s, insisted that White had "not only met Boas at Columbia, but he actually studied with him." The former also claims that White was first introduced to Elsie Clews Parsons in Chicago in 1926 and that she then suggested he might do fieldwork in the Southwest.

In 1928, and with the support of The Southwest Society, the organization through which Dr. Parsons funneled her help to many anthropologists, White went to Acoma, and not too long afterward to other Keres pueblos (see White, 1962: Introduction). His monograph *The Acoma Indians* was published in 1932 along with Parsons' *Isleta, New Mexico* and Bunzel's papers on Zuni in the 47th Annual Report of the Bureau of Ethnology, and his monograph *The Pueblo of San Felipe* carries the same date. Relevant to an understanding of White's anthropological development is his early and broad acquaintance with the writings of Adolph F. Bandelier, who described, in unusual detail, investigations he had conducted in the 1880s in various and largely Keres societies. White's Acoma and San Felipe studies contain numerous references to Bandelier, and the first word in his "Historical Sketch of San Felipe" is "Bandelier."

White's familiarity with the writings of Bandelier surely sharpened his insights and alerted him to important and un-Apollonian aspects of the Pueblos he was studying. In his Acoma monograph he disposes of the idea—held, he asserts, by the Whites—that the Pueblo is a " 'democratic' community" (1932a: 53). In discussing Acoma's structure of authority, he stresses the strength of priestly control, the presence of a ditch boss who regulates when and by whom water for irrigation may be tapped, and the use of whipping in Kachina initiations and on other occasions, some of them clearly disciplinary. "San Felipe," he writes, "like other pueblos, is a highly organized, social unit. . . . Power is concentrated within a small group of officers and societies who rule the Pueblo. Their power is both political and religious." And he concludes, "Disobedience is sacrilege and heresy as well as treason."

There is little resemblance here to the picture of Pueblo society Benedict painted two years later in *Patterns of Culture.* And there is no reference in this or in White's Acoma study to Lewis H. Morgan—a circumstance that should cause no surprise in view of the dates of their publication. To be sure, already in 1930 White was an assistant professor in the joint Department of Anthropology and Sociology at the University of Buffalo, just a short distance from the University of Rochester, a major repository of data relating both to Bandelier and Morgan. But it seems highly probable that White's Acoma and San Felipe manuscripts were well advanced, perhaps even completed, before his interest in Bandelier led him to Morgan. In 1935, in *The Pueblo of Santo Domingo,* he does refer to Morgan, and in 1940, his outstanding *Pioneers in American Ethnology: The Bandelier-Morgan Letters, 1873-1883,* appeared—that is, in the year following his attack on Boas in Chicago.

A reading of this fascinating compilation more than suggests that White, like Bandelier, was increasingly influenced by Morgan, but seemingly less by Morgan's view of pre-conquest Mexico as a "gens" society than by his unilinear scheme of development. In *The Pueblo of Sia, New Mexico* (1962), and contrary to his early understanding of Keres society and his comments that "some of my Sia informants said that after Mrs. [Matilda Cox] Stevenson left the pueblo, punitive action was taken against those who, either through fear or friendliness, had befriended her" and that "there are even dark hints that some of them may have been put to death," White could conclude, "The world of Sia . . . was a cozy and intimate world . . . one knew everything, the mythology provided answers to all important questions . . . and one knew how to behave on every occasion" (320).

I reviewed this study (1964), but while I then drew attention to White's unexplained turnabout in his evaluation of Pueblo society, I did not sense what I believe today may well be the fact—that much as Bandelier, more than half a century earlier and under pressure from the *living* Morgan, had withdrawn from views of Mexican society he had arrived at after years of careful study, so White, inspired by the *dead* Morgan, had withdrawn from views of Pueblo society he had arrived at after years of careful study.

Bandelier apparently needed no whipping-boy. White apparently did. For more than three decades Boas remained the villain of his piece.

But however deplorable his methods of fighting and the inadequacies of his concept of the "evolution of culture," White has been a major force in shaping the thinking of the post-Boas generation of anthropologists.

11. SECOND FLOWERING

For me 1939 was a watershed year. Since my return to New York four years earlier I had been, from the standpoint of anthropology, an inquiring consumer. Now, after my summer with the Blood, I again became an eager producer. But, as could be expected, the two roles soon interlocked, as indeed they had done in the 1920s. Again I was attending classes and organizing field notes for publication. But, as could also be expected, I entered upon a new and stimulating life when I married Karl August Wittfogel in March 1940.

Before we had met I knew nothing of Karl Wittfogel except what Ruth Benedict had said about him at that weekly luncheon a year or so earlier. But I soon learned much more—that his first years were spent in a small village on the edge of the Lüneburger Heide; that his father was the schoolmaster in the one-room and only village school; that his mother, the daughter of a schoolteacher in a nearby village, presided with understanding and ingenuity over the family's domestic affairs and the raising of her precocious young son (he is said to have read at the age of four and, at the age of six, to have tutored children considerably older); that when he was nine, the family moved to Lüneburg, the ancient city where Johann Sebastian Bach had sung in the church choir; that he then entered the "gymnasium" and, after graduation, studied at various universities, as was not at all unusual in Germany; that he received his Ph.D. from the University of Frankfurt, his thesis having dealt with Chinese economics and society; that he became associated with the Frankfurt Institute for Social Research under the leadership of the historically minded Carl Grünberg and, after Grünberg's death, under the leadership of the philosophically minded Max Horkheimer; that in the early 20s he, like so many talented German artists and intellectuals, joined the Communist Party; that he gained fame as a speaker and writer and an indomitable fighter against Hitler; that he spent months in jails and camps—ultimately in the infamous Moor Camp; that there he became seriously incapacitated by rheumatism, the result of the harsh conditions under which its inmates lived; that he was unexpectedly released, because "Planeten Fischer," the high Nazi official in charge, had found, after studying the prisoner's horoscope, that his "stars were good"; that he traveled to England, America and China—this last to continue his long-time study of Chinese society; that when the Sino-Japanese war broke out he returned to America; that he was appointed Director of the Chinese History Project financed by the Rockefeller Foundation and sponsored jointly by the Institute of Pacific Relations and the Frankfurt Institute, now located at Columbia University; and that he had broken with the Communists immediately after Stalin and Hitler made their Pact in September 1939. When a member of the Frankfurt Institute, who was a friend of the Goldfrank family and had on occasion taken me out, learned that Karl Wittfogel and I intended to marry, he exclaimed, with unflattering amazement, "But he is a genius." And just a few days after our wedding, a scholar-official (to use a Confucian euphemism) who had met Karl in China and seen him frequently during the years he spent there, said to me, "Do you think you will be able to handle that dynamo?"

Genius and dynamo notwithstanding, we have been married for over thirty years, during many of which we worked in close collaboration. Not, however, immediately. Besides my husband, the Chinese History Project boasted three full-time members—two Chinese and one American, each of whom was familiar with important aspects of Chinese history and society. In such a specialized community, there seemed no place for an anthropologist whose field experience was limited to investigations among the Pueblo Indians of our Southwest and the Blood Indians of Alberta, Canada. My most immediate chore was to find a larger apartment (now there would be three of us) and one that was near Columbia.

The Project had been assigned a long but not very wide space between the windows and stacks on the fourth floor of Low Library, one desk ranged behind another like soldiers on a narrow trail; but to any who thought this arrangement somewhat bizarre, Project members would comment with alacrity and a certain pride, "Nicholas Murray Butler works under us." And this was indeed the fact, since the President's suite was located on the second floor of this handsome building, designed by the famous architect Stanford White.

I soon found an apartment, and we moved in June. We were barely settled when we went off to Provincetown, carrying the Project with us—three China specialists and a Russian-born stenographer, along with their books, manuscripts, and office necessaries. They were housed in a pleasant cottage not far from ours, and each afternoon I drove them to the beach for relaxation and consultation. However, the Pact had exposed ideological differences between us in New York, and environmental change failed to resolve them.

There was one time, however, when my advice was eagerly solicited. Toward the end of our stay, the younger of our two Chinese associates asked to speak to me privately—he had an important decision to make. As we sat in our spacious but shabby living room he told me that, for some time, he had been attracted to a young woman student, the daughter of a German mother and Chinese father, and that he wanted to ask her to marry him. But there were two inhibiting circumstances—first, she was older than he, and this was contrary to what the Chinese traditionally considered proper; second, and much more disturbing, her European heritage was blatantly revealed by her brown hair, which marked her off as an outsider among the "black-haired people"—the millenia-old designation employed originally by an imperialist China to distinguish the core group from the ethnically different peoples who had fallen under their sway.

Regarding the first, I quickly told my visitor that I was older than Karl, and, although this also was somewhat unusual in our cultural milieu, it was creating no problem for either of us. Regarding the second, I assured him that chemistry was his ally. All his prospective bride had to do was to dye her hair black and keep it dyed black.

I do not know whether my comments were decisive. Whatever the fact, he married her and, shortly after the Communists seized power, they returned to the Chinese mainland. But the total experience of the summer of 1940 discouraged us from spending other so-called vacations nursemaiding our Project "family."

ON PUBLICATIONS

I had a great deal to learn from Karl Wittfogel—and not just about China, although that country had been his major research interest. Since the 1920s the fundamental question for him had been the effect of water control on societal structure. Long before we met, his investigations had convinced him that the introduction and management of large-scale waterworks for purposes of irrigation or flood control demanded large-scale cooperation, which in turn necessitated the establishment of directing centers of authority—tribal, regional or national—and the institutionalization of communal discipline (see particularly Wittfogel, 1931, 1935, and 1938). In his terms, the pueblos of our Southwest constituted "miniature irrigation societies," and my data as well as those of other students of these communities clearly placed them in this category.

It was not long after Elsie Clews Parsons died in December 1941 that Erminie Voegelin, the editor of the *Journal of American Folklore*, asked me to contribute a paper to a volume in her honor. As her publications indicate, folklore had long been of prime interest to Dr. Parsons. She had served as president of the American Folklore Society and, for many years, as the editor of its journal.

I was pleased that Erminie had asked me to participate in this memorial. But since, in writing on the Pueblos as I was planning to do, I would be drawing on Karl Wittfogel's ideas on irrigation societies (which were then little known to American anthropologists), I suggested that, in view of his scholarly reputation, it would be fairer to him and far more satisfying to me if he were the senior and I the junior author of a joint endeavor. Erminie quickly agreed.

Our paper, "Some Aspects of Pueblo Mythology and Society" (1943), combined, as the title indicates, two areas of investigation, both of which had occupied Dr. Parsons for years. Moreover, she had found Wittfogel's conclusions on the relation of irrigation and social structure highly stimulating. And in our paper these conclusions provided the framework for information gleaned from the accounts of the con-quistadores and from studies of different Pueblos—Zuni, Hopi, Acoma, and Laguna, and those that flanked the Rio Grande. An introductory section, "Mythology and Reality," warned against expecting relevant myths or individual studies to give a complete picture of the reality under investigation. But myths could, we maintained, furnish important leads, and individual studies could illuminate myths. Our paper examined both in relation to types of water-supply (essentially, springs in the West, rivers in the East), the position of women (matrilineality in the West, an increasing tendency toward patrilineality or bilaterality in the East), leadership and discipline (less centralized in the West than in the East). And it served two purposes. As foreseen, it injected Wittfogel's views on irrigation societies into the mainstream of anthropological thinking but, unlike Li An-che, it did not specifically challenge Benedict's views on Pueblo society, which had been widely accepted since the appearance of *Patterns of Culture*.

My summer with the Blood had reawakened my interest in the Teton Dakota, about whom a good deal had been said and written in the 30s. In 1932, Ella Deloria, the daughter of a chiefly Teton family, published her *Dakota Texts*, which she dedicated to Franz Boas— "without him," she wrote, "this book could not be." In 1937 Deloria's notes on the Teton Dakota, which were being kept in Ruth Benedict's files at Columbia, were a major source for Jeannette Mirsky in her paper, "The Dakota," published in Mead's *Cooperation and Competition among Primitive Peoples*. In 1936, the anthropologist H. Scudder Mekeel published his field study, *The Economy of a Modern Teton Dakota Community*; and in 1939, the psychoanalyst Erik H. Erikson published his "Observations on Sioux Education." And Benedict's course on Plains social organization, which I attended in the late 30s, was based in largest part on Deloria's notes—and not only for the Teton Dakota.

The Deloria-Benedict-Mirsky presentations all stressed the

egalitarian character of Teton society—the unimportance of wealth for status recognition, the broad application of Teton kinship terminology to non-kin, the strong institutional restraints on in-group violence, shaming as a dependable means for resolving internal rivalry, the waging of war as a game. My study of the Blood suggested a very different image, and since they and the Teton shared many not-insignificant features—both had been organized in loose bands, both had hunted the buffalo, both had acquired horses and guns, both had found virtue in giveaways, both had institutionalized the favorite child, both had gone on the warpath, both had recognized the taking of enemy scalps and later the stealing of horses as honored ways of enhancing prestige—I wanted to understand why, given these shared features, Blood personality and society, as I had come to know them, differed so markedly from Teton personality and society as reported by Deloria and subscribed to in the classroom and outside it by Benedict.

My search for an answer led me again to early sources—among others to government reports and personal reminiscences, such as Maximilian's *Travels in the Interior of North America*, which was based on his experiences in 1832, and to George Catlin's extraordinary *Illustrations of the Manners, Customs and Conditions of the North American Indians* and, ultimately, to five winter counts, three from the Oglala, the richest of the seven Fire Councils of the so-called Dakota Confederacy and the one that had first moved out on the Plains well-provided with horses and guns that facilitated their access to the benefits of a developing fur trade. (References for these and other documents, quoted or cited in my writings and discussed in the following pages, may be found in the bibliography.)

The three Oglala counts reported the highest incidence of in-group violence. One of them, begun in 1764 and ending in 1884, reported killings during a "civil war" in 1829, during hunting expeditions and during a "serious drunken brawl," killings of kin, and two deaths in the same year involving sorcery. Also reported were killings of horses—"many," "twenty," and, in one instance, specifically "because of jealousy."

None of these early sources could be considered definitive in and of itself, but together they provided me with convincing evidence that, in the early to mid-nineteenth century, Teton social organization and character were quite similar to Blood social organization and character and that, for this period, the Deloria image of Teton society did not fit the Teton reality.

The question then became, "Did it fit the later Teton reality?" Again a variety of sources—the reports of Indian agents, U.S. military personnel, missionaries, travelers, and now also anthropologists—provided valuable clues. The discovery of gold in California enormously increased the flow of Whites into Indian territory. Indian life, and particularly Indian hunting life—and all that this meant in terms of food, shelter, clothing, and trade—was seriously disrupted. To define the respective rights and responsibilities of the U.S. government and the Indians, representatives from eight Plains tribes and Washington met at Ft. Laramie, in what is now Wyoming, and signed a treaty on September 17, 1851, in which it was agreed that these Indian nations, as they were referred to, would "abstain in future from all hostilities whatever against each other," and "against the people of the United States" whether "lawfully residing in or passing through Indian territories." The treaty also established the right of the U.S. government to build roads and posts in Indian territories and, in return, the U.S. government bound itself to protect the tribes from depredations committed by the American people. The Indian nations, on their part, bound themselves to make restitution for any wrongs committed "by any band or individual of their people on the people of the United States."

The accord concluded at this meeting was only temporary. As Whites pressed into their territory, the tribes pressed on each other, and intertribal warfare was a not-infrequent result. The Indians' greatest hostility—directed against the Whites, both settlers and military—culminated in the annihilation of Custer's troops at Little Big Horn in 1876.

But despite breaches in its wake, the Treaty of Ft. Laramie had initiated a new phase in Teton society—and one that began to approximate Deloria's image. Many of the old aggressive modes of behavior still found expression, as did such prized virtues as bravery and generosity. On the former rested the Teton chance for survival, on the latter their hope for support. But as the need for tribal solidarity became more insistent, institutions became less individualistically oriented, and leadership became less diffused. It was during these years that the great chiefs Crazy Horse, Red Cloud, and Sitting Bull became prominent. And from 1855 to 1877, not one of the five Dakota winter counts mentioned an act of in-group violence.

A year after Little Big Horn, the Rev. Thos. W. Williamson (1877) wrote, "The most numerous and until recently the most powerful tribe of Indians within our borders are now completely crushed. We have taken from most of them everything except life. They are now poor miserable beggars unable to avenge their wrongs and they know it" (294). Their horses and guns were surrendered; the buffalo were no more; the old ways of validating prestige were gone; and agriculture, which demanded a steady effort even for a modest return, was considered women's work by these "warriors without weapons," as Gordon MacGregor (1946) titled them.

And then upon the heels of "peace" and after thirty years of emphasis on tribal cooperation and familial solidarity, the record shows a resurgence of in-group violence—most conspicuously, but by no means solely, between chiefs and among their close supporters. In 1881, Crow Dog, a leading sub-chief, killed Spotted Tail, who was then in charge of the police. In 1884, Young Spotted Tail, assisted by Thunder Hawk, murdered White Thunder, who had succeeded to the chieftaincy. But reservation law quickly curbed the destructive trend. In 1885, the breaking up of Teton village life restored order but not hope. As I saw it, the tribal solidarity demonstrated by the Teton in the 60s and 70s grew from political necessity. Their tribal solidarity after 1885—and here I based myself largely on Mekeel and Erikson—derived from economic scarcity. Now the man with money was the traitor and the Church, which previously had had little success among the affluent and hostile Teton, became their greatest comfort. Such teachings of Christianity as the "golden rule" and the blessings of giving seemed to echo Dakota giveaways, laws of kinship, and attitudes toward hospitality. Also Deloria told me that the sons of chiefs now entered the ministry, and that their tribal status lent prestige to their new calling. Already in 1879 the Rosebud Mission boasted six hundred members and an average attendance of seventy.

Clearly, it was in the years after 1885 that the image of the Teton Dakota social character invoked by Deloria accorded best with the reality. And equally clearly, differences in the histories of these Indians and the Blood, and most especially differences in the scale and intensity of the relations of the latter to the Canadian government and the former to the "people of the United States," to quote the Ft. Laramie Treaty, explains the increasingly marked differences in Teton and Blood social character after 1850.

Before sending my final draft off, I showed it to Ruth Benedict. She was quite obviously not pleased with it. For the pre-1850 period I had found that, among the Teton and particularly among the Oglala, wealth was important for status recognition; that warfare was no "game"; that in-group violence was well documented. But while I knew she still rejected the idea of "vested interests" in tribal societies as "a far cry" and "misleading," she did not at this time comment on these points. She did question my conclusion that the broad extension of Teton Dakota kinship terms Deloria had been underlining, was a late development. She asked me: "Have you consulted Morgan's *Systems of Consanguinity?*" I had not, and I said so. But since the Anthropology Library was in the same building as her office, I corrected this omission immediately. On the basis of terms from eleven bands of Eastern and Western Dakota collected before 1866, Morgan had written, "Their system of consanguinity is one and the same among them all in every feature which is material, and in nearly every minute particular" (1871: 174). No mention here of any broad extension of Dakota kinship terms to other Indian tribes—not even by the Oglala. I copied out this passage, not at all unhappy that it bulwarked my position, and I hurried back to Ruth's office. She gave my memo a quick glance and said, "He didn't ask the right questions." When I rose to go she added, "You certainly know how to quote." My article, "Historic Change and Social Character" included Morgan's statement on the Dakota system of consanguinity.

Although my knowledge of Chinese history was a good deal less than elementary, there were aspects of the work being done by the Chinese History Project that were not far removed from recognized concerns of anthropology. This was particularly so in the study of the Liao dynasty (A.D. 907-1125) being made by my husband and his Chinese associate Feng Ch'ia-sheng. In Chinese terms the official History is a short one, but it provides detailed information on the functioning of a society born of conquest—in this case, the victory of the Ch'i-tan, a stock-breeding, hunting, and fishing people, over the sophisticated, agrarian inhabitants of Northeast China.

As Wittfogel later pointed out (Wittfogel and Feng, 1949), under Liao rule, Ch'i-tan society adjusted to Chinese life in many ways. But the conquerors firmly held on to the reins of power. They filled the key administrative posts, controlled the army, continued to rely on the horse wealth that had dominated their tribal days, and ignored such basic Chinese institutions as the examination system. In short, until the dynasty collapsed, Ch'i-tan society exhibited a dual structure, economically, sociologically, and in religious ideas and practices. Symbiosis, yes—fusion, no. Wittfogel also later pointed out—and here he collided head-on with long-held Chinese opinion—that the Chinese had not absorbed their conquerors during the Liao period of Chinese history, nor did they do so during the years when they were under rule of the Golden Chin, Mongols, and Manchus. When the Liao volume was published it was hailed as the most important American study of a Chinese dynasty to date.

Comparison between the Ch'i-tan, particularly in their pre-Liao period, and the Indians of the American Plains became an engrossing topic of conversation at our table. And soon after I completed my paper on the Teton Dakota, I began to read the Liao material systematically. The further I read, the more I found data of anthropological interest—kinship, of course, but much else. In 1943 the director of the Project suggested that I join his outfit in an official capacity. My title: staff anthropologist. Nepotism, if you will, but nepotism unaccompanied by any material acknowledgment. The

Chinese welcomed my presence more, or so it sometimes seemed to me, for my command of English than for my scientific expertise. And while I now spent many hours with them in their Columbia retreat, I did not punch a time-clock and still had time to work on problems more directly related to my anthropological past. In 1945 my monograph on the Blood (1945c) was published, and that same year two of my papers appeared in the *American Anthropologist* (1945a, 1945b).

While working on my Teton Dakota paper, I again consulted Kroeber's *Cultural and Natural Areas of Native North America* (1939) and happened upon his statement, "Both Gladys Reichard and W. W. Hill tell me that maize is a Navaho[30] staple food and that most Navaho farm." And he added, "If so the body of ethnologic literature on the Navaho stresses so important a fact surprisingly lightly" (Kroeber, 144: n. 14). Hill had written, "In connection with moving sheep to the mountains for summer pasturage and the winter move of the household to the foothills for fuel, there has grown up a current belief that the Navaho are nomadic. This is emphatically not the case. While they may be only partly sedentary, they are not in any sense a nomadic people. Whatever their older practices, the Navaho have been since historic times primarily sedentary agriculturists" (1938: 18).

Navajo legend (their First Man was created from white corn, their First Woman from yellow corn), as well as archaeology and written reports, all lead to the conclusion that Navajo agriculture had a long history antedating the arrival of the Spanish conquistadores in New Mexico. Navajo legend also reflects an early knowledge of irrigation agriculture, "The descendants of First Man and First Woman," who got their seeds from the Kisani (the Pueblos), "built a dam and dug a wide ditch." And in 1630 Benavides, in his *Memorial*, noted that "these Navaho are great planters." A century or so later, Rabal, the governor of New Mexico, submitted to his Spanish sovereign the reports of twelve field-observers. In summarizing them Hill wrote, "All deponents mentioned farming and types of crops raised ... less prevalently recurring references include those to horses, sheep, goats, and cattle." (These animals were brought to the New World by the conquistadores, and Navajo legend mentions them rarely.) Except in a few mountainous regions where the moisture level might rise to 20 inches, cultivation in this semi-arid Navajo country had to depend on irrigation of some sort to be successful. Although the Rabal Report already mentioned their irrigation from running water, the Navajo, in largest part, resorted to flood-water farming (often erroneously referred to as "dry farming").

In 1849, three years after the Navajo came under U.S. jurisdiction, the superintendent of Indian Affairs, upon entering the "Cañon de Cheilles," wrote that the Navajo "have extensive fields of corn and wheat . . . and immense flocks of sheep." Manifestly, agriculture was still basic in the Navajo economy, but sheep-breeding had increased notably. However, it was only after 1868, when the Navajo returned to their reservation from their four-year involuntary stay at Ft. Sumner, that sheep became economically important. During these years Navajo farming had fared badly and this, coupled with the unfavorable weather conditions in the years following, motivated the U.S. government to issue 14,000 sheep and 1,000 goats to these hard-pressed people. By 1942, after the government had introduced a program for herd reduction because of extreme land erosion, "the tribe still had 750,000 sheep units . . . 583,569 of which were within the boundaries of the Reservation." But agriculture remained significant. In 1916, a government Geological Survey estimated that 20,000 acres on the Navajo reservation were cultivated by flood-water farming. In 1941, after considerable government outlay, 16,000 of the 40,000 acres devoted to agriculture were irrigated from a permanent water supply.

Given their mixed economy and the different weighting of their agriculture and stock-breeding in different sections of their reservation, the Navajo, it seemed to me, offered an unusual opportunity to investigate the patterns of community organization and leadership that had emerged among them under the stress of their semi-arid environment.

Cooperation beyond the limits of the family was clearly documented for both herding and agriculture. Hill noted that hunting parties usually numbered from four to ten men, but that "planting, especially corn planting, was usually accomplished by communal effort." Kimball and Provinse stated that cooperative community labor arose primarily from problems relating to intensive agriculture, and specifically, besides range use, to problems relating to "water, subjugation and development of farmland, irrigation systems." Kluckhohn and Leighton wrote, "Two or more families or one or more independent biological families, may habitually pool their resources on some occasions—say, planting and harvesting or giving a major ceremonial." Malcolm Collier, who reported on Navajo local organization, presented highly suggestive information on Klagetoh, a farming village before the "long walk" to Ft. Sumner, and on the first permanent settlement at Navajo Mt., established some fifty years earlier, which for thirty years had served only as winter quarters for a single family. In Klagetoh, twelve complexes composed of a varying number of hogan-groups "represent the basic cooperative units," and at times members of one work-group might cooperate on special tasks with members of another work-group. At Navajo Mt., where agriculture was a late development and so negligible that the U.S. Geological Survey made in 1916 did not mention it, "the basic cooperative unit was the smaller hogan-group."

And Collier added: "There is never any cooperation activity between two hogan-groups for herding, but there is a great deal of help in agricultural pursuits." (In 1932 the U.S. government had built a dam in this vicinity.) In concluding this section of my paper, I wrote, "History and geography make it more than probable that the basic units of Navajo cooperation, which operate today, in herding and ceremonial, and formerly also in defense, have developed out of the specific requirements of agriculture in a semi-arid environment."

Concerning Navajo leadership, Hill noted the presence of a local headman, the peace *natani,* who "acted as general economic director . . . planned in advance the work of the community, set the time for planting and superintended planting, cultivation, and harvesting [and] instructed in the proper techniques of agriculture and pastoralism." In fact, "any communal work was under his supervision." The Franciscan Fathers' *Ethnologic Dictionary of the Navaho Language* notes, "The people of Klagetoh have been conscious for many years of the existence of leaders in the country around them. They themselves have been under one leader for 30 years." In constrast, at Navajo Mt., where agriculture had a short history, Collier found that "leadership was fairly amorphous."

Thus, as I saw it, Navajo leadership, like Navajo community cooperation, had developed out of the requirements of agriculture in a semi-arid environment. However, I pointed out that, despite the adoption by the Navajo of many Pueblo technical and ceremonial features, their political organization, reflecting special aspects of their history and the limitations of their water supply, was no mechanical replica of Pueblo organization. Nevertheless, the Navajo experience provided valuable insights into the ways in which contact with an irrigation agriculture could influence a previously hunting and gathering people.

My paper aroused considerable comment. One well-known anthropologist, connected with a large university in the Midwest, wrote me, "The work you have been doing these last few years is contributing a lot to what we around here call social anthropology." Another, equally well-known and from a large Eastern university, wrote me, "You and Sol Kimball are the only people I know of who have dealt with the Navajo as human beings living on a segment of the earth." And a third, also from the Midwest, who knew Pueblo society, wrote me, "Your paper sets forth very well the importance of agriculture among the Navajo." But he added, "If we had more facts about the social organization of the Navajo of 1800 . . . we could make out a stronger case for your thesis than is now possible." And on this point we were in full agreement. The only published criticism I know of is Malcolm Collier's "brief communication"(1946), in which she questioned my interpretation of the data she had presented on Klagetoh and Navajo Mt. In my response (1946a), I presented additional data on these communities which clarified and, I believe, strengthened my position.

My article "Socialization, Personality and the Structure of Pueblo Society (with Particular Reference to Hopi and Zuni)" (1945b) was a further effort to deal with themes presented in the 1943 Wittfogel and Goldfrank paper. Basic among them had been the conclusion that irrigation agriculture, even on the miniature scale engaged in by the Pueblos of New Mexico and Arizona, had necessitated the cooperation of more than a single individual or a single family, and that damming, ditching, terracing, etc., although variously combined and differing in intensity from pueblo to pueblo, had involved the rise of a directing leadership—in their case, a part-time priestly officialdom that functioned in both the ceremonial and economic realms.

In the 30s and early 40s, the relation of infant training to adult personality was being increasingly stressed by psychologists, psychoanalysts, pediatricians, and anthropologists, and much was being written about the deleterious effects in our society of strict feeding schedules, premature toilet training, and insufficient body contact between mother and child in the first weeks after birth. Aware of the differences in the structure of pueblo society and ours, Dorothy Eggan (1943) had concluded that, despite optimal conditions in infancy, the Hopi exhibited an extreme degree of anxiety. This led me to postulate, as a working hypothesis, four categories of societies: those in which infant and later disciplines are weak; those in which infant and later disciplines are severe; those in which infant disciplines are severe and later disciplines are weak; and those in which infant disciplines are weak and later disciplines are severe.

In my inquiry the period of infancy comprised the first two years of life, for, whatever the individual variations, in most societies by the end of this time nursing was completed, children walked (whether they had been permitted freedom of movement from birth or been strapped to a cradleboard) and were able to make their wants known through the spoken word. The "later" years comprised those between infancy and the time when an individual could be said to have assumed his role as an adult. While recognizing that permissiveness and pressure were present in all stages of development, it was clear from the data at hand that Pueblo society fitted my fourth category, and, in the remainder of my paper, I attempted to demonstrate the validity of this judgment.

I concentrated on Hopi and Zuni, pueblos that had been comparatively free from White contact and open enough for trained social scientists, over more than half a century, to have assembled a sizable body of information on their beliefs and life-ways. But while I concentrated on Hopi and Zuni, my own experiences as well as the experiences of many others indicated that, despite their divergencies, the various pueblos were basically similar in structure and utilized similar devices for fitting their young into their society.

On one aspect of Pueblo behavior there was complete unanimity among the observers: parents were permissive in dealing with their offspring during the first years of life. Mischa Titiev, who had made four visits to the Hopi, noted that "Hopi mothers are notoriously over-indulgent to their children." Wayne Dennis, a psychologist, noted that "the Hopi infant is seldom weaned under one year of age and frequently is not weaned before two years." Regarding the establishment of toilet habits, he noted, "No training in this respect is imposed upon the Hopi child until he can walk and can understand simple commands, when he is told to go outside the door. Nor is he exhorted to keep himself clean." In his autobiography, Sun Chief, a native of the Hopi village of Oraibi, gives many details of his early experiences, some of them obviously relying on hearsay, but hearsay confirmed by his later observation of others. He tells us that he got "the breast" whenever he cried, that he was passed "from lap to lap on the cradle," that he was often sung to and rocked to sleep, that he was permitted to suck his thumb and masturbate. In fact, "every male child was tickled in his private parts by adults who wished to win smiles or sometimes to stop crying." His toilet training followed the pattern described by Dennis.

The evidence from Zuni was similar. Clearly Pueblo infancy was characterized by great indulgence—indulgence of the kind that, according to the arguments presented by pediatrician C. Anderson Aldrich in his article "What we Know," would prevent individuals from becoming "confused, resistant, and subject to emotional storms." To be sure, resistance and emotional storms rarely found expression in Pueblo society, but, as Dorothy Eggan pointed out, Hopi parental permissiveness in the infant years did not result in secure, unconfused adults. Dr. Elsie Crews Parsons commented, "Apprehensiveness is a notable Pueblo trait."

If parental discipline in the Pueblos was not severe, what caused this general apprehensiveness? Manifestly, extra-familial influence. And descriptions of Pueblo society underline the continuing pressures imposed by the supernaturals, their temporary impersonators, or their more permanent surrogates, the priestly officialdom.

But even in the period of infancy some training devices hint at later developments. Frank H. Cushing, speaking in 1897 on "Primitive Motherhood" at the first meeting of the National Congress of Mothers in Washington, reported that in Zuni as soon as an infant could "creep about and babble" the mother would hold it in her arms and whisper "a prayer to the beloved gods" over each "pinch" of food before placing it in the infant's mouth. Not a great physical deprivation in view of the Zunis' indulgent feeding habits, but an indication that from the first moment of comprehension, a child is made to realize that it can expect "abundant good fortune" only when something is given up. In this same speech Cushing also reported that the Zuni child was bound on a cradleboard, as the Zunis themselves said, to "learn to lie straight" and "walk straight in the pathway of life, in order that it may learn the hardest lesson one has ever to learn in this life—namely, that it cannot have its own way, cannot have things as *it* would have them, but must e'en be content to take them as they come or are vouchsafed." However mitigating their permissive parental attitudes may have been, the Zunis started early, and with good reason in view of their agricultural needs, to inculcate "a yielding spirit" and train consciously for "sobriety and inoffensiveness"—traits that, according to Benedict, were valued above all others.

Then there was the omnipresent fear of witchcraft. Infants must not be left alone in a room, and an ear of corn and an ash smudge gave added protection. In the early months of life such expressions of anxiety could have had little meaning, but even before the age of two these precautions—and spoken warnings—must have aroused some feelings of insecurity. Moreover, as children grew older, they would learn that even those nearest them, even their parents, might be witches, and that they themselves, and without their knowledge, could be possessed. They would learn that, once possessed, they could not expel the "bad spirit," nor could their relatives or friends do so. Only trained practitioners, medicine men, could exorcise the evil power, and there were times, most frequently times of drought or disaster, when even their power was not considered strong enough to deal with the task at hand. Then the accused was tried and tortured by a body of his peers and priests and in most cases executed, since the need for trial was virtually cause for conviction. "White law" discouraged this legal practice, but witchcraft continued to be the main focus of anxiety in the Pueblos.

In all societies much about life is learned by imitation, but one observer wrote in 1899, "after a somewhat extended personal contact" with the Pueblos, that among them imitation was "except in the earlier years of the child . . . brought about by external constraint." And in this respect story-telling was an extremely useful tool.

From what we know many, if not all, societies have their harrowing tales. In the Pueblos, one of the most harrowing, and one often told, concerns the two Giant Kachinas. A Hopi tale tells of a Kiva leader, an important ceremonialist, who complains that the children "are getting out of control" and that the Giant Kachinas should "snatch and eat them." The male Giant picks up two of them while they are playing on Oraibi Mesa and carries them off in his basket to the female who is to cook them "to a turn." Good fortune, in the shape of the War Twins, also supernaturals, saves the children from this horrible fate.

But in the Pueblos story-telling isn't enough to ensure proper behavior. Every year at Hopi and Zuni, impersonators of the Giant Kachinas, along with their equally well disguised and equally gruesome assistants (in Hopi, one carries a saw, one a knife, one a lariat, one a snare), make the rounds of the village. Brandishing their weapons threateningly, they stop at those houses where they have been advised, usually by worried parents, that a child has been misbehaving. The whole family assembles to witness the confrontation, and at times the impersonators, Titiev writes, force the naked, frightened child "to run a mock race with one of the Kachinas, the little fellow dashing madly to win in the hope that it will save his life." In Zuni, Matilda C. Stevenson writes, "Two gods lecture a boy of 4 years, while two younger children of the family are held close in the arms of their parents. . . . The boy receiving the lecture clings to his mother, and his knees shake as he replies to the questions of the gods. The fear of the child is great as the gods wave their stone knives above him and declare that if he is naughty they will cut off his head." Cushing comments that if parental admonishment has no effect on a recalcitrant child "the masked demons they have heard of in stories . . . are summoned and resistance is at an end."

Cushing apparently believed this was indeed the fact, but the Pueblo priesthoods did not. To these mentors of social behavior the children are still "unfinished." Formal, painful, and terrifying ceremonies of initiation have to be undergone before a male can participate successfully in his society. The first of these ceremonies occurs when he begins to help his father or his mother's brother in the fields, the second when it is felt that he can do a man's work, sacred or secular. Parsons was surely correct when she commented, "Of that docility of the Pueblo child, so striking to the least observant, the discipline of fear, I have often surmised, was an important factor, fear not so much of the elder *per se*—the elder punishes very infrequently—as fear of the unknown or the supernatural inspired by their parents."

In Hopi both boys and girls are initiated, but the treatment accorded girls is comparatively mild. In Zuni, except on rare occasions, only boys are initiated. Julian Steward notes that in Hopi, when the Chief of the Kachina Society asks the whippers why they have come, these punishing agents answer, "They [the children] do not obey their mothers and fathers." Although insisting that he can handle this situation without supernatural help, the Chief admits that the children "do not mind us"; and he adds: "We will let you try to make them obey. We will let you force them to keep these things a secret." At the close of the ceremony the Chief takes the whips away from the gods. Turning to the novices he says, "This is the way we initiate to the kachinas. You children must not tell how this is done to other children who have not been initiated. If you do tell, these kachinas will come around to you and whip you until they cut your flesh." Voth, writing in 1901, describes the "pandemonium" that reigned in the Kiva during this "exciting" and "disgusting" half hour. And Sun Chief, a "little victim" of these proceedings, substantiates both accounts in all essential details.

In Hopi, where the first rites are extremely severe, the children learn at the conclusion that the kachinas who have whipped them were not gods, as they had been taught to believe, but impersonators, sometimes near relatives. Dorothy Eggan commented that because of this deception all informants questioned by her were emphatic in stressing their "intense disappointment in and resentment toward their elders which survived in consciousness a long time." At Zuni, according to Mrs. Stevenson, the Kachina Chief, at the first of these rites, warns that if the novices "divulge the initiatory secrets, especially those associated with the masks, their heads will be cut off."

If the whippings at Zuni were less severe than at Hopi, the threatened punishment was more severe. This, together with the fact that at Zuni the whippers remove their masks and reveal their true identity only during the second initiation rite several years later, cannot have failed to increase the tensions of the Zuni boys during the intervening years. Indeed, projective tests given in the early 40s to children of both groups indicated, as Dr. Dorothea Leighton, who was involved in evaluating them on the basis of what she knew then, wrote me, that there was a considerably greater constriction of personality among the Zuni children than among the Hopi children. And the responses of the Hopi children and Midwestern White children to these same tests were equally revealing of differences in their respective societal structures and training. To give two examples: in the emotional response test on FEAR only one percent of the fears of the White children were attributable to the supernatural, whereas this category accounted for 25.4 percent of the Hopi children's fears. In the emotional response test on the WORST THING, the White children gave discipline a 2.5 percent rating, the Hopi children 17.8 percent.

After noting that Pueblo society is culturally peripheral to the full-fledged waterwork complexes of Aztec Mexico and Inca Peru and that, like them, it is theocratic and depends for survival on water control, I pointed out in this 1945b paper that the low economic potential of Hopi and Zuni made it possible for them to maintain a more egalitarian (sometimes and inaccurately referred to as "democratic") social organization. But more direct access to the benefits of their labors notwithstanding, it was "the 'deeply disciplined' man both at Hopi and Zuni, who is so desired and so necessary to the proper functioning of the community." And I concluded, "Emotional restraint, reserve, avoidance, or the need to reject, is the price he pays for his society's social ideal."

This article, even more forcibly than our joint effort (Wittfogel and Goldfrank, 1943), called into question the image of Pueblo society and personality that Benedict had been so insistently presenting since 1928. Without mentioning her name or views, Clyde Kluckhohn, to whom I had sent a pre-publication typescript, wrote me, "Today I have finally had a chance to read your paper. I like it immensely—it is really a beautiful job both for its rich factual content and for its theory. I have no criticisms to make (unusual for me, isn't it?). . . . I'll get the article to Dot tomorrow. Thanks for letting me see it for I am really very excited by it."[31] After my paper appeared I heard no less approvingly, if less exuberantly, from such psychologically sensitive anthropologists as Weston LaBarre, David Bidney, and David Aberle. Benedict, who in 1945 was still in Washington, D.C., refrained from commenting on it to me then or later, except to say that the Pueblos "bored" her.

But despite her lack of interest, the impact of this paper was surely heightened because it controverted major tenets in her position. It spelled out the harsh coercive mechanisms employed in Pueblo society, not by near ones, to be sure, but by external agents, the priesthoods; and it underlined the fact that in this waterwork society cooperation could be left neither to chance nor to individual vagaries.

The first paper to deal in print, and more than passingly, with our divergent views was by John W. Bennett (1946). After commenting that controversies regarding factual data were not unusual among anthropologists who had worked in the same area, Bennett noted that "in most cases they have no great significance for wider philosophical and theoretical issues in social science." But he believed that "the two principal interpretations of the basic dynamics of Pueblo society," appearing in publications in recent years, were of a somewhat different order. Although they had not taken "explicit formal theoretical positions," they did contain "implicit viewpoints within the matrix of methodological and empirical research on Pueblo communities." And although their proponents had relied on "the same raw data" and had at times cooperated in research and participated in "an interchange of concepts and conclusions," he maintained, "Yet the difference is there." He then asked whether this difference was "a result of choice of problems, choice of fact, or different values held by the respective workers." And this is the question he proceeded to answer in the following pages.

"In the background of the controversy," Bennett noted, "lie the criticisms of Benedict's and others' interpretation of Pueblo culture as 'Apollonian,' which often were not explicit denials of the truth of her characterization, but rather pointed out that there was another side to the story and that her method contained unexpressed value-orientations." Here he quoted Li An-Che (1937). Then he described "by paraphrasing, the two viewpoints"—the Apollonian and the anti-Apollonian—for the first drawing in largest part on the writings of Ruth Benedict and Laura Thompson, for the second on Dorothy Eggan's and mine.

Regarding the first viewpoint, Bennett wrote, "Pueblo culture and society are integrated to an unusual degree, all sectors being bound together by a consistent, harmonious set of values, which pervade and homogenize the categories of the world view, ritual, art, social organization, economic activity, and social control. Man is believed to have the ability to act freely and voluntarily in ordering his own affairs and fitting them into an harmonious pre-literate homogeneous, 'sacred' society and culture." And he added, "Associated with this integrated configuration is an ideal personality type which features the virtues of gentleness, non-aggression, cooperation, modesty, tranquillity, and so on" (362f.). (This he later referred to as the "organic" theory.) Regarding the second viewpoint, he wrote, "Pueblo society and culture are marked by considerable *covert* tension, suspicion, anxiety, hostility, fear, and ambition. Children, despite a relatively permissive, gentle, and frictionless early training, are later coerced subtly and (from our viewpoint) brutally into behaving according to Pueblo norms. The ideal of free democratic election and expression are conspicuously lacking in Pueblo society, with authority in the hands of the group and chiefs, the latter formerly holding the power of life and death over his 'subjects.' The individual is suppressed and repressed. Witchcraft is covert, but highly developed" (363). (This he later referred to as "the repressed" theory.)

After asserting that "like the first this [second] view is qualified in analyses in many ways, and as I have noted, is not necessarily in conflict at all points with the first," Bennett stated, "What is apparent, however, is a tendency among the workers of one side to avoid the conclusions of the other, to 'grind their own axes,' so to speak" (363f.). He then volunteered his own conclusion: "I believe, therefore, that the differences in interpretation, plus the relative avoidance by each of the views of the other, are evidence of a genuine difference in outlook and are not simply the result of conscious, objective choice of problem" (364). As he saw it, "the organic theory of Pueblo culture" has "an implicit value orientation toward solidified, homogeneous group life," while "the 'repressed' theory has a fairly clear bias in the direction of egalitarian democracy and non-neurotic, 'free' behavior."

"The 'organic' approach," Bennett tells us, "can be charged with the following":

> (a) the sin of omission of certain important sets of data; namely, those having to do with severity and authoritarianism of Pueblo socialization processes. The "organic" point of view tends to avoid the apparent fact that the unique Pueblo homogeneity arises in a severe conflict process which is drastically suppressed, and from this standpoint, I think we must award a laurel to the "repressed" school for facing the reality of the situation and seeing the process as well as the end product.
> (b) A tendency to distort or misrepresent some facets of the Pueblo configuration (370) [to support this point, Bennett cited a highly critical passage from Titiev's review of The Hopi Way].
> (c) A tendency to make the interpretation in the long run an entirely personal, subjective affair.(371)

No accusations of this order are charged against the "repressed" approach. "Inspecting the value question more closely," Bennett then wrote:

> I think the issue can be resolved into one of means and ends. To Thompson's way of looking at things, the end is the most important and signficant factor; the "end" in this case being the unique and rather remarkable Pueblo world view. To her this phenomenon has a rare beauty and aesthetic appeal, and one receives the impression that the means of achieving this ideal really do not matter—at least she does not appear to be particularly concerned with them. . . . But to Goldfrank it is precisely the means that count—and that is her bias. She probably grants the organic homogeneous, logico-aesthetic world view, and concerns herself almost entirely with the means for achieving this. These, to her, are important factors; these are what the social scientist should study objectively. . . . One suspects a kind of critical realism here, which contrasts sharply with the impressionistic, evocative approach of the extreme configurationist school. . . . Thompson and Goldfrank, then, clearly disagree over the respective value of means and ends, and this question goes beyond any issue of scientific methodology (372 f.).

And apparently to further clarify this point, he commented, "Obviously Thompson is more subjective and possibly less aware of the influences upon her work, but at the same time we can show that the value orientation is just as marked in Goldfrank's work, only it is a different sort of value and one which happens to appeal strongly to the more literal-minded scientist" (373).

Then Bennett lapsed into conjecture. "It is possible," he wrote, "that a 'repressed' approach could conceal and distort to the same degree as do some specimens of the current 'organic' approach (373)." *Could* conceal and distort! Of course, in our complex world one may believe that anything is possible, but at this point it seems legitimate to ask why Bennett found more comfort in closing his case on a hypothesis than in resting it on the factual record he himself had been presenting. A question of values? Perhaps.

This 1946 winter issue of the *Southwestern Journal of Anthropology* almost certainly appeared later, since it was April 30, 1947 when Dorothy Eggan wrote me, "How do you like being analyzed in public?" And she added, "Since it had to happen to me I'm glad to be in such good company." And since it had to happen to me I was equally glad to be in such good company. Along with her letter, she enclosed a copy of her more-than-two-page single-spaced "acknowledgment to Mr. Bennett," dated five days earlier, in the hope that I "might conceivably answer his 'approach' more fully in print." This I did not do, although I agreed at many points with Eggan's comments.

In 1948 my 1945b paper and Laura Thompson's 1945a paper were included in *Personal Character and Cultural Milieu*, assembled by Douglas G. Haring, professor of anthropology at Syracuse University. The 1956 revised edition also included Bennett's 1946 paper. In introducing my paper Haring wrote, "Numerous anthropologists have studied Pueblo Indian tribes repeatedly and over many years. It is suggested that students begin with Ruth Benedict's *Patterns of Culture*, then read this article by Dr. [!] Goldfrank and the one by Laura Thompson; after doing so, continue with John Bennett's article."

My paper was also included in *The Family: Its Structure and Functions* (Coser, 1964). In the section on "Parental Authority and the Social Structure," it is listed as "The Case of a Primitive Society: The Pueblo Indians," but no changes were made in the body of the text. This paper was also included in the *Selected Papers of the American Anthropologist* 1921-1945.

In 1929 Ruth Bunzel published her excellent book *The Pueblo Potter: The Study of Creative Imagination and Primitive Art,* and she revealed her sensitive appreciation of the spoken word in her "Zuni Ritual Poetry" (1932b). This long paper followed her "Introduction to

Zuni Ceremonialism" (1932a), some of whose shortcomings—and among them some we considered basic—were pointed out in Wittfogel and Goldfrank (1943). The following year she published her *Zuni Texts* (1933) in English along with Zuni transcriptions. For the most part, they had been collected in 1926 during the first of two trips to study the Zuni language. In 1927, her recordings "were completely revised and annotated," and additional material was added "notably" (as she writes in her foreword—and I certainly concur in her use of this word here) "the autobiography" dictated by Lina Zuni, the seventy-year-old, non-English-speaking mother of Flora Zuni, who "had excellent command of English and translated her own texts and interpreted for her father, mother and sisters, and helped with the revision and analysis of all texts."

This so-called "autobiography," which is the only one in the volume, was of particular interest to me, and I quoted it in full in my "Linguistic note to Zuni Ethnology" (1946b). It described the plight of a young boy who, as the Mixed Dance was about to get under way and the fearsome Atocle emerged from the Kiva, had said to one of his frightened companions, "Don't cry. It's not really Atocle. Some Zuni man is just pretending. Atocle is not dangerous." But when this frightened companion told his mother what he had learned, she "got very angry." She asked, "Who said so?" When her son told her, she said, "He has no sense and you have no sense! It is a wonder that Atocle didn't kill you." Then she added, "Some dangerous creature, some angry gods will cut your throat."

Many people were gathered in the plaza and "the angry Katcinas[32] came in." One "was going to cut the boy's throat, just like a sheep. 'He is not valuable,' he said." The boy's father "raised his gun to his shoulder . . . to shoot the katcinas," obviously a protective parental action. "The boy was crying. The katcinas were going to cut his throat in the plaza." Here the "father of the Koyemci," also a powerful Kachina group, intervened. "Don't do that . . . don't cut off his head. Just cleanse him, to frighten our friends. Whip him with yucca" [a tough spiny plant.] "They did not cut off his head. They whipped him. All over his back they whipped him. He had no strength." Then his grandfather, obviously more concerned with upholding tradition than with coming to the aid of his grandson, scolded the Kachinas. "Kill this one who had told our secrets! In order that you may take his head with you to the home of the katcinas you should not let him go. To complete your ceremony you must take his head with you. . . . You will take his head into Katcina Village." And he insisted, "If you want to finish this in the right way you will take his head with you." Again the Koyemci intervened. He "saved the boy from the Katcinas," stressing that "if the little boy had died, the katcinas would have died."

The Kachinas then ran through the whole village and "whipped the people with yucca."

The narrator then launches into a description of how "little boys are initiated"—merging, in his telling, the first and second ceremonies, as in his statement that the whipper "takes off his mask and puts it on the boy" and that the Kachina chief says, "Here you have been initiated. You have seen everything. Don't speak of it. Don't tell the children." And there are other discrepancies in his telling. When the Kachina chief speaks of K'aiyuani, a youth who "had mocked the katcinas," he explains, "He was beheaded. They threw his head up on Corn Mountain. They threw it down again. The katcinas are danger-ous." Two of the most fearsome "kicked his head" and "threw" it "into the Katcina Village." Even "a very little boy, if he sees [recognizes] his own father must not speak of it." And the narrator concludes, "What-ever has happened long ago that we will tell to our children" (88).

Although I believed that even a quick reading of this "auto-biography" clearly supported my thesis that, in "later" years, disci-pline in the pueblos was severe, I also believed, since there are many examples of linguistic usage bulwarking accepted ethnological and historical fact, that a count of key words appearing in it and related to "whipping" would be useful in evaluating the different meanings given this action by different anthropologists familiar with this area.

To pinpoint these different meanings, I noted that the significance of the whipping at Zuni had been variously formulated. Benedict had written that whipping is "to take off the bad happenings; that is, it is a trusted rite of exorcism." Bunzel had written that the reason for initiating children is "to save them; to make them valuable," and she had concluded, "The enormous importance of the rite of flagellation in this ceremony established it as primarily a ritual of exorcism and purification." Parsons, while recognizing the exorcistic function of the rite, had written that "whipping by the Blue Horns or by the disciplinary or bogey kachina of Zuni, or Cochiti, or of Tewa may take on a punitive character." In my 1946b paper I noted that exorcism and punishment are by no means mutually exclusive and that the various observations all fit into the frame of Zuni society and culture. In this connection the results of my word count were illuminating.

It seemed clear from the "autobiography" that a young child's expressed doubts had to be punished and that whipping was the punishment invoked. It also seemed clear that neither his mother nor other villagers intervened effectively in his behalf—his father merely raised his gun to his shoulder. His grandfather demanded that his grandson be killed. This final solution was rejected by the "father of the Koyemci," also a supernatural and the only participant to use the word "cleanse." And this he did only twice. However, when he said, "just cleanse him" the second time, he added, "to frighten our friends." As I saw it, this reason for cleansing raised immediate doubts regarding the primarily exorcistic and purificatory character of the recommended whipping, and indeed, of the ceremony as a whole. According to Professor Morris Swadesh, an outstanding linguist and the editor of *Word*, the journal that published my "Linguistic Note to Zuni Ethnology" (1946b), the term Bunzel translated as "to whip" could mean both "to strike" and "to kill." Equally suggestive was the use of such threatening words as "ferocious," "dangerous," "punish," "kill," and such threatening phrases as "whip severely," "cut his throat," "take his head," and the like, which occurred more than thirty times in the lines cited. In a passage in "The Origin Myth of Zuni" (Parsons, 1923), dealing with the boys' initiation ceremony, comparable words and phrases were used. In a footnote Parsons explained that one of them might mean "to be killed, or whipped, or punished." And in this passage there is no mention of cleansing. Certainly arithmetic supported my thesis that in the "later" years, discipline in the Pueblos is severe, and that the punitive character of whipping is not only *present,* as Parsons claimed, but *basic* in the minds of the community for achieving the society's personality ideal—the cooperative and conforming man.

My interest in Southwest mythology had first found expression in "Isleta Variants: A Study in Flexibility" (1926). It was born of a bit of good fortune—some might see it as a bit of bad fortune—namely, Dr. Parsons' dependence in largest part on the same informant I had worked with previously. But good fortune or bad, ten of the tales he told her he had also given me, and although their identity was clear, they were by no means identical. "In reviewing the analogues," I wrote in 1926, "it is apparent that incidents may be included in one set which do not appear in the other. They may be incidental to the plot, or they may be instrumental in changing it entirely by setting up a new motivation. They may appear at any point in the tale and often are incorporated into a new introduction, which will call for a different development and conclusion. Characters may be changed and the new ones may or may not function as did the previous set" (70). I then concluded that these modifications were not due to lapses in memory but were, in fact, indicative of "values in the materials of story-telling of which the teller is consciously aware, and which have molded new plot complexes from old and familiar themes."

Recordings by different anthropologists of the same myths and tales provided by different informants is by no means unusual, but recordings by different anthropologists of the same myths and tales provided by the same informant is unusual. To my knowledge at the time of writing, there was nothing in print to indicate that in the Pueblo of Isleta two or more researchers had been confronted by such a combination of circumstances. Correspondence I have cited earlier in this book indicates that both Dr. Parsons and Ruth Benedict liked this paper. Nevertheless, and for reasons given in her letter to me and in her Introduction to *Isleta, New Mexico* (1932) Parsons ultimately rejected the idea that the sometimes very different recordings provided us by this same informant on the same ceremonial and non-ceremonial aspects of Isleta life be dealt with jointly.

Mythology was a useful tool in the 1943 Wittfogel and Goldfrank paper, and mythology strengthened my thesis that the Navajos' recourse to irrigation agriculture was no post-Columbian innovation but something they had learned long years before from their Pueblo neighbors—and enemies (in 1936 Sapir had written that "the Navaho word 'corn' . . . can be analyzed with great probability into an older 'food of the enemy,' 'Pueblo food' "). Mythology incorporated in Bunzel's "autobiography" underlined one important way in which the Pueblos trained their young to fit into their society. In 1945, William Morgan had commented on the influence of the "historic route of occasions." In 1942 Kluckhohn had commented that changed conditions might make "a particular type of obsessive behavior or special sort of phantasy generally congenial," and that this, in turn, might result in "the private ritual" being "socialized by the group." In 1944 in his impressive monograph *Old Oraibi*, Titiev had commented on "the speed with which recent events can be woven into the Hopi mythology."

In Wittfogel and Goldfrank (1943) we had stressed the fragmented character of the Hopi water supply and its implications for the relatively fragmented character of Hopi social structure. In 'The Impact of Situation and Personality on Four Hopi Emergence Myths" (1948), I again stressed these points and noted that "the numerous and different versions of the Hopi emergence myth may well reflect the limitations of the Hopi theocracy, and as a corollary, the strength of the Hopi maternal clan." But it was the long-time feuding in the Hopi village of Oraibi, which in 1906 resulted in what Titiev speaks of as "the expulsion" of the Hostiles, that proved to be an excellent litmus test not only for tracing the relation between myth-telling and "the historic route of occasions," but also for demonstrating the "speed with which recent events can be woven into Hopi mythology" and, perhaps more surprisingly, how quickly a "private ritual" can be socialized.

The four Hopi emergence myths best suited to my purpose had been recorded at different times between 1883 and 1932 by three anthropologists and an army officer from three Hopi Indians, each of whom had lived in Oraibi and had played a prominent part in its factional strife. The Hostiles were traditionalists, who opposed "the Americans." The Friendlies, also traditionalists, were nevertheless ready to cooperate with "the White Men," on certain government-initiated programs, particularly schooling.

The first myth was taken down in 1883 by Cushing while he was in Oraibi to obtain ceremonial objects for the National Museum. Lololoma, a member of the Bear clan, the Village Chief, and the leader of the Friendlies, was his sponsor. The Hostiles vehemently opposed his mission. His recording climaxed a vituperative argument between him and a man he described as "chief priest of the tribe and a wizard." No name is mentioned, but there is good reason to believe this "chief-priest" was the head man of the Spider clan, which belonged to the same phratry as the Bear clan. But while the Spider clan alone controlled several major ceremonies, and several others jointly with the Bear clan, only a member of the Bear clan could become Village Chief. As early as 1741 Escalante had noted, "God . . . allowed a grave discord over the election of a chief at Oraibi. On this account the pueblo was divided into two parties, who took arms against one another." According to Titiev, "the Bears were the owners of the entire Oraibi domain, while the Spider clan was allotted only a small piece of land in spite of its ceremonial importance." It was this last that Titiev believed had been a major reason for the long-time feuding in Oraibi. Although members of other clans had joined the Hostiles, a member of the Spider clan was their leader in Cushing's time and as late as 1901.

The second and third myths were given by Yokioma—a member, according to Titiev, of the Kokop clan. The first of them was recorded by Voth in 1903 or 1904—that is, shortly before the split; the second by Col. Hugh L. Scott in 1911—that is, five years after the split. As just mentioned, a member of the Spider clan was the leader of the Hostiles as late as 1901, but it was Yokioma, no doubt a prominent member of the Hostiles, who became the head chief of Hotevilla, the village established by this faction after their "expulsion" from Oraibi. The fourth myth was given to Titiev in 1932 by Tawaqwaptiwa, the nephew of and successor to Lololoma and, like his uncle, a member of the Bear clan.

All the myths begin with happenings in the lowest of four dark worlds, but the details of the Hopi ascent to the uppermost vary considerably. This is the case even in the first three, which were given by two members of the Hostiles. That it should also be the case in the last, given by the Oraibi Village Chief and the major spokesman for the Friendlies, is not surprising.

In all of them the Spider clan has a role—in the first two, a definitely positive one. In the 1883 version, "Spider spins cotton mantle to give light"; in the 1903 or 1904 version, "Spider Woman assists the Flute priest create moon and sun." Later she makes "horses and burros" for "the White Men," who were "more skillful than others." But in the 1911 version, also given by Yokioma, and when he was Hotevilla's Village Chief, both the Spider clan and the Bear clan, after "four years," were said to have accepted the ways of the Spaniards. Now, however, Yokioma stressed the smaller Ghost-and-Bird clan, a sub-clan of the Ghost clan and presumably his own. (Titiev makes no mention of either in his clan and phratry lists in *Old Oraibi*, but he notes that "nearly half a century has elapsed since anthropologists were first mired in the Hopi clan muddle, yet the situation is still full of perplexities.")

No ambivalence regarding the performance of Spider clan and Spider Woman is evident in the fourth myth, given by the leader of the Friendlies. Its first sentence reads, "So much trouble made in Underworld by Spider and Bow clans, which were 'partners' in mischief-making, that Matcito, the Bear clan chief, orders an Emergence." During the ascent, the daughter of Bear Chief dies, "killed by Spider Woman, ancestress [wuya] of the Spider clan." Nevertheless, Bear Chief magnanimously spares Spider Woman "when she shows him his daughter has happily returned to the Underworld."

These latter themes also appear in the myths given by the Hostile storytellers, but their omissions almost invariably enhanced their historic role while reducing or denigrating the role of the Friendlies. In the first of them, overcrowding is the reason for the ascent from the "lowest world cave" (no word of the mischief-making Spider clan). Here it is said that on the way the "daughter of Chief-priest" is killed (no word to indicate that he was a member of the Bear clan). And here the murderess is a "jealous girl" aided by Corpse Demon (no word to indicate that Spider Woman was the killer). Again "chief sees daughter living in the underworld," and he spares the murderess. But her descendants, it is stated, are witches. After a colon, the paragraph ends with the words: "Warning to Americans"—who we are told, "came out of the cave world first."

In the first of Yokioma's versions, "White Man, the Paiute, the Pueblo etc.," all were living in the lower world "in constant contentions," but "some with not too bad hearts." They assembled the chiefs and planned to leave. Village Chief is mentioned first as among those who come out "before reed is pulled up." During the ascent it is not the daughter but the "small son of the chief" who dies. This time the killer is a "witch," who is also spared "when chief sees his son alive in the underworld." Again no mention here of Spider Woman, but in the very next sentence she is named as the co-creator of sun and moon. Skeleton, discovered by a bird, "invites people to share his poor life at Oraibi." He refuses to be their chief, saying that Bear clan chief "should be chief, as he was in the underworld." Then Skeleton "marks off a piece of land which he allots to the Bear clan." But this, the teller implies, is merely a holding action, only "when White Man, 'your elder brother,' comes back here and cuts off the heads of the bad ones will Skeleton own land again." For a time things go well, but then, as their "old men and ancestors" predicted, some White Men—and "they would not be the White Men like our elder brother—would ask us to have our heads washed [baptized], and if we would not want to do what they asked us they would beat us and trouble us and probably kill us." In this first of his versions, Yokioma included what was surely the position of the Hostiles: "But we should not listen to them, we should continue to live like the Hopi. . . . But those Popwaktu [witches] of the Hopi would help the White Men, and they [obviously the Friendlies] would speak for the White Men, because they would also want to do just the same as those White Men would ask them to do."

In Yokioma's second version many of the same themes appear, but often with striking modifications. Now it is "Head chief's daughter" who dies, and this time the murderess is definitely identified as "witch." Again she is spared, and this time she "promises to help chief [obviously Bear chief]." Indeed, at a later time "the talk of white men is incited by witches." Then this son of the outstandingly brave Ghost-and-Bird clan, so well-schooled in Hopi ways of treating an enemy, asserted, "The way for these White Men to conquer the Hopi is to cut off Youkeoma's head. The traditions say that the head of one of the Oraibi chiefs will be cut off, and then the trouble will cease." But he added, "Youkeoma cannot yield, for then the sea would swallow up the land and all would perish."

And he did not yield, nor, so far as I know, was his head cut off. But to judge from petroglyphs in neighboring areas, the severed head of an enemy, Hopi or other, was a valued sign of success in war. Parsons has stated, "Beheading is a recurrent conclusion in Hopi tales." In fact, its simulation is a horrifyingly realistic feature of certain Hopi ceremonies.

The language of these four emergence myths is far from temperate, and one can only guess whether their narrators were the exception or the rule. When Cushing returned to the Kiva after being ordered to get paper on which to write down what the hostile Hopi had to say and "send it back to Washington," he felt so threatened that he hid a pistol under his blanket—and not without reason. His "hosts" had told him his presence "oppressed them as things which cause the stomach to vomit." Their later statements, which he considered too "insulting . . . to be reproduced," might, he feared, be a prelude to more aggressive action. Only after showing his pistol did he venture to move toward the ladder that led to the Kiva roof and safety.

Col. Scott reported that, after spending ten days with Yokioma recording his second version of the emergence myth, this Hotevilla village chief, seeking a further interview, "wrathfully came into the council room. His anger was like that of a trapped animal, his eyes gleamed with hatred, and he fairly quivered with rage."

Leo Crane, agent on the Hopi reserve from 1911 to 1919, said of the leader of the Friendlies, "As his Indian agent, I tried for eight long years to make a sensible human being of him and failed. . . . After having tried him as Indian judge and then as Indian policeman, in the hope of preserving his dignity and authority as hereditary chief, he was found to be the most negatively contentious savage and unreconstructed rebel in the Oraibi community, so filled with mischief-making to his own benefit that a group of his own people petitioned me to exile him from the mesa settlement in the hope that they might exist in peace."

Certainly the often-repeated reference to the "peaceful" Hopi seems to find little confirmation in the behavior of the leaders of the Oraibi Hostiles or Friendlies or, for that matter, other members of their factions. But as I wrote in my 1948 paper "Hopi emphasis on unity and unanimity . . . was strong enough, at least as far as members of the opposition were concerned, to build up feelings of guilt—no matter how just they considered their cause—and to foster the belief that their leader's success would be crowned, not with glory, but with the loss of his head."

Some say the people of Oraibi are different from their fellows in other Hopi villages. For instance, there is no mention of the Americans in the Hopi tales collected by Parsons in or about 1925. Was this due to the historic route of occasions, to a calmer climate in these years than in the years prior to and following the 1906 split? Was this due to an environment less hostile to the U.S. government? Was this due to personality differences? Mythology, it hardly needs saying, can sharpen our insights. But it is well to remember that alone it cannot answer many of the questions raised in the study of societies, simple or complex.

Differences in the structures of Blackfoot and Pueblo society have been indicated in considerable detail in the preceding pages and there is no need to spell them out again here, as I did briefly in the early paragraphs of "The Different Patterns of Blackfoot and Pueblo Adaptation to White Authority." This paper was read in 1949 at the XXIX meeting of the International Congress of Americanists, and was published in 1952. My major aim in this paper was to demonstrate how these different structures had influenced the response of the Blood of

Alberta, Canada and the Zuni of New Mexico to the induction of young men into the armed forces in World War II and to their return "home" after their discharge.

While both Canada and the United States are democracies, there are many differences in their political and social arrangements. This is also true of their policies toward the Indians, although the Canadian program was modeled on ours. Both aimed at the establishment of White hegemony and White advantage. At times the achievement of these objectives was accompanied by great violence; at times, if much less frequently, it was accepted with relief. And this, as I had noted elsewhere, was the case with the Blood, who welcomed reservation status, since it coincided with the disappearance of the buffalo, the primary base of their subsistence and well-being until the 1870s. It was then that the Canadian government, more than any native chieftain, relative, or friend, became, in Blood parlance, the "generous giver"—the one reliable source of aid in a time of need.

White contact with the pueblos had a much longer history, but whether new patterns were accepted freely or under pressure, their well-disciplined populations, "guided" by their respective priestly officialdoms, found ways of fitting them into the old framework. Certain officials were elected to deal with the "outside" world, first with the Spaniards, later with the Americans. But the reins of power remained in the hands of the traditional—and now largely "invisible"—hierarchy.

In Zuni this hierarchy saw the conscription of their young men for service in World War II as a dire threat to their cherished way of life. As John Adair tells it in "The Navajo and Pueblo Veterans" (1947) young Zuni men were increasingly conscripted, and for an indefinite period. The Zuni Council of Priests, which was expected to act only in a time of crisis, quickly went into action. A letter was sent to the Selective Service Board in Gallup, signed by its members with their "official" thumbprints. In it they asked that twelve Zuni men in religious positions be deferred. The Board acceded. The twelve were classified 4-D (clergy-in-training). But this did not satisfy the Zuni Council of Priests. In fact so many exemptions were asked that the Selective Service Board felt compelled to inform the Council that government policy only permitted the deferment of "high priests serving for life," and it urged the Zuni to provide men taken from older age groups or young ones still without important ritual responsibilities. The response of the Council of Priests should not have been unexpected. Wrote Adair "More young men than ever before were selected for Shalako and other religious positions." In addition, dances and ceremonies that had not been given for forty years were revived.

Despite these attempts to circumvent government policy, 213 Zuni were enlisted. "All," according to Adair, "carried prayer meal, and all, at one time or another, said their Zuni prayers during their term of service." But the army life that most American GIs found unbearably restrictive had a different meaning for the Zuni soldier: "Those men who have been away from the village for several years realized for the first time that life could be relatively free of gossip, that others could be disinterested in one's comings and goings, that, within much greater bounds, one could do as one pleased and never be gossiped about. This was a new type of freedom which they had never known."

Most of the Zuni GIs thought that upon their return their war experiences and newly acquired knowhow would add to their prestige, would even recommend them for positions of authority in their village. But only one thing mattered. These 213 veterans no longer behaved like traditional Zuni. In this context I again cite Adair: "They were rough, loud, intoxicated a good deal of the time. They went against the desires of their parents. Some of them refused to go through the cleansing ritual given outside the village. Others refused to take part in the Kachina dances." He added, "The men wore their uniforms, setting themselves off from the rest of the village . . . and they talked a great deal of English in public places."

Parsons, speaking of pueblo motivations, has written that in the social code or theory of conduct as exemplified by the pueblos, "innovation is discouraged and any show of individualism is condemned" (1939: 107). In the case of the returned Zuni veterans, innovation was not only discouraged, but cut off at the root. "When persuasion did not bring good results, gossip, rumor or action by the Council was tried . . . but in most cases rumor (and there can be little doubt that this was frequently priest-inspired) achieved the desired end." (Adair 1947) And rumor did not hesitate at character assassination, "The G.I. who started a veterans' club at Zuni—that is, established what from the standpoint of the priesthoods was a foreign and perhaps potentially rivalrous power center—was stopped in his tracks when word got about that he intended to pocket, for his own use, all dues paid in by his fellow-members." From data presented by Adair, I felt justified in concluding that "perhaps even more devastating to the GIs peace of mind were insinuations that his restlessness and malaise were due to sorcery." To free themselves from this most dreaded condition, not a few of the returned veterans joined one or another of the very societies they had overtly or covertly repudiated.

In comparison, the story of the veterans of the Blood is a simple one. Blood society, despite some newly instituted centralizing factors, still left room for a disaffected tribesman—who in former times might move easily from one leader to another—to carry his complaints to a higher court of control—the Canadian government. Moreover, since the Blood were located in fine cattle country and were familiar with large-scale wheat-farming and stock breeding, the Canadian government apparently did not press for the enlistment of these "feeders" of the nation. Their agent, in reply to my letter asking for information on this point, added that among the few deferments, there were "certainly none for ceremonial reasons."

These two very different histories of contact with White authority had, I believed, "significant implications for policy-makers and anthropologists"—and not only in relation to American Indian acculturation within our borders. While fully recognizing that the advance of civilization had often meant the harsh treatment of native peoples in many parts of the world and the ruthless destruction of their way of life, the unquestioning adherence to the theory of cultural relativism—so basic to much anthropological thinking—warranted modification in the light of our recent experiences. Should we, as anthropologists, "underwrite two sets of values, one for the so-called 'higher' civilizations, and another for primitive societies?" Should we "if we fight a modern state for democratic ends, accept and at times bolster authoritarian trends when they appear in native communities?" After noting that "such trends may be completely indigenous and, as is frequently the case, the communities may be well-ordered," I pointed out that "cultural integration has its negative as well as its positive aspects" and that "it may, and it frequently does, consolidate the interests of one group at the expense of another." It may, in fact, "hamper constructive efforts at cooperation and understanding whether these efforts emanate from within or without." It seemed obvious to me that the theocratic and integrated organization of the Pueblos had "slowed up the whole acculturative process," and that "it has done so primarily by frustrating those very natives who are most eager to share in American thought and action."

To my surprise no questions were asked and no statements, pro or con, were made from the floor after I finished reading. But whatever the inhibitions of the anthropologists may have been, the next day the *New York Times* commented extensively on this 1949 paper. The experiences of the Zuni veterans may well have embarrassed enthusiastic supporters of an all-encompassing theory of cultural relativism but, for the reporter covering this session, my statement was just a timely and not entirely meaningless bit of news.

Despite its concentration on attitudes and behavior related to a single situation—World War II—this paper juxtaposed conceptualizations of Pueblo and Blood society I had been developing for almost a decade. My writings on the Blood, although differing in approach and at times in emphasis, did not controvert in any basic way what had been published previously on various Blackfoot groups. My writings on the Pueblos, beginning with the article jointly authored by Professor Wittfogel and me in 1943, utilized, as did my writings on the Blood, historically recorded facts, mythology, and personal experiences, my own and others'. But not this alone. Benedict, and Haeberlin and Sapir before her, had, in my opinion, correctly pointed out significant differences between the Pueblos and other Indian tribes north of the Mexican border. But very soon after the appearance of *Patterns of Culture,* as I have indicated, I questioned the Apollonian image of Pueblo society so picturesquely and appealingly presented by Benedict. And I did not hesitate to tell her so. However, my years of absence from the academic scene and my lack of direct contact with Zuni or any other Western Pueblo (which last, as I have also indicated, was Benedict's simplistic and undeviating reposte to my arguments) deterred me from expressing my counter-view in formal meetings of Anthropologists or in print. Then not long after I married Karl Wittfogel, I became convinced that his ideas on waterwork societies (Marx's "Asiatic" societies and Max Weber's Wasserbaubürokraie—neither of which I had ever heard of in my courses in economics or anthropology) were equally relevant for an understanding of the water-deficient societies of the Pueblos, and this despite the obvious disparities in the scale of operations and the scope of control between these miniature waterwork societies and the great nation-states of China, Egypt, and Peru. Indeed, Professor Wittfogel, as early as 1932, had included Hohokam and the cliff-dwellers in our American Southwest in his "Asiatic" typology (Wittfogel, 1972: 66).

The Growing Interest at Columbia in Waterwork Societies: Ralph Linton, W. Duncan Strong, Julian H. Steward, Morton H. Fried, Marvin Harris

The Columbia Department of Anthropology, headed by Linton since 1937, was friendly to both of us. I had been participating in the Kardiner-Linton seminars and Linton had expressed interest in my data on the Blood. His interest in Wittfogel's ideas on development was evident as early as 1938, not long after Wittfogel arrived in New York.

And this was hardly accident. Earlier, Linton had studied the Tanala of Madagascar and had recognized that, with a change from dry-rice farming and its attendant loose social organization to wet-rice farming, the "control of irrigation, and even perhaps its installation, made a strong central power essential" (1936b: 251-91). This observation fitted completely with concepts Wittfogel had been propounding for years, and both scholars welcomed the opportunity to share their separate experiences—Linton's with "primitive" groups and Wittfogel's with China.

In 1943 W. Duncan Strong wrote, "The time is coming when the rich ethnological and archaeological record of the New World can be compared in detail and time perspective with similar records from Europe, Egypt, Mesopotamia, India, China and Siberia" (1943: 34), and he himself made a notable start in this effort when some years later he shared in the organization and co-direction of the comprehensive archaeological-ethnological Viru Valley Project in Peru.

In 1946 Julian Steward joined the Columbia staff, and three years later he published "Cultural Causality and Law: A Trial Formulation of the Development of Early Civilization" (1949: 1-27). In it, he utilized Wittfogel's concepts and data more fully in print than any other anthropologist had done previously. Steward wrote, "Gordon Childe [the well-known British prehistorian concerned increasingly with the Middle East] is exceptional in his effort to treat archaeological materials functionally." In the very next sentence, Steward wrote, "Wittfogel has been outstanding in his use of historical data to make functional-historical analyses of the socio-economic structure of early civilizations." For the Old World, Steward cited data on Mesopotamia, Syria, Assyria, Egypt, and China; for the New World on Mexico, the Maya area, and North Peru. His bibliography included a generous citing of Wittfogel's writings—three published before 1940 and the pre-print of his "General Introduction" to *The History of Chinese Society: Liao*, which had been distributed to interested persons since late 1946.

The same year that Steward published his paper on causality and law, the Braidwoods, who were attached to the Oriental Institute and Department of Anthropology at the University of Chicago and who had worked in Mesopotamia, wrote a letter to the editor of the *American Anthropologist* taking exception to certain aspects of Steward's schematization and stressing that, in Mesopotamia, agricultural villages had arisen on the "hilly flanks of the 'Fertile Crescent'" and that later "an era of expansion into the riverine areas, of the specialized technologies, and of towns . . . marked the real beginning of settlement in the Nile-tube and classic Mesopotamia regions and also the beginnings of significant irrigation." In his "Rejoinder," Steward expressed his gratification that his paper had been stimulating "the kind of constructive criticism" he had hoped for. Not only did he accept the Braidwoods' conclusions, which in large part were based on their own archaeological investigations, he also suggested that "it would not be surprising if future research showed that development [in America] paralleled the Near East rather closely in that peasant villages, without irrigation (perhaps also on the hilly flanks) preceded irrigation communities." (As early as 1931, in *Wirtschaft und Gesellschaft Chinas*—Kroeber had said of it "a very Marxist but a very good book"—Wittfogel had indicated that, in China, irrigation agriculture had its beginnings in areas, and probably hilly areas, where irrigation was beneficial but not necessary, and where the population might have engaged in little or no collective hydraulic activities.)

In 1952 the Wenner-Gren Foundation sponsored a conference on Anthropology Today. The proceedings were published under that title in 1953. In his paper "Evolution and Process," under the subheading "Cultural Taxonomy," Steward wrote, "Illustrative of cultural types are Wittfogel's oriental absolute society . . . which involves regularities between a special kind of socio-political structure and irrigation economy . . ." (321). With reference to his 1949 article, Steward wrote on the next page, "In an elaboration of Wittfogel's irrigation societies, the author has tentatively formulated developmental types which include not only social and political patterns but also technological, intellectual, military and religious features that mark successive eras in the history of these societies."

In this connection it is worth noting that, already in *Wirtschaft und Gesellschaft Chinas* (1931), Wittfogel had indicated the impact of these various features on Oriental societies and especially on China—and that in *The History of Chinese Society: Liao* (1949), he had indicated in his "General Introduction" and in his more detailed chapter introductions, their impact on Chinese conquest dynasties—and, specifically, on Liao. To my knowledge, Steward never cited Wittfogel's 1931 book (and this is understandable, since it is long and written in German), but he never cited the Liao volume, except for the "General Introduction," which, as noted, had been distributed previously—and this is less understandable.

In 1953 Wittfogel's ideas on the origin and operation of waterwork societies underlay and, whether supported, modified, or rejected, clearly dominated the symposium on "The Irrigation Civilizations" organized by Steward and held during the annual meeting of the AAA at Tucson. Wittfogel read a paper on "Developmental Aspects of Hydraulic Society," and Robert M. Adams one on "Developmental Stages in Ancient Mesopotamia." The printed record of this symposium (Steward, 1955b) contained an introduction and final statement by Steward, who was unable to be present. Also included was Angel Palerm's paper on Mesoamerica, a replacement for Pedro Armillas' discussion of this area, which he had presented orally at the symposium and never put on paper.

In his introduction, Steward wrote, "The concept of multilinear evolution was provisionally formulated in 'Culture and Process'" (his actual title was "Evolution and Process"). After noting that he had stated "the germ of this concept" nearly twenty years earlier in "The Social and Economic Basis of Primitive Bands," he added, "This approach received tremendous stimulus when Karl Wittfogel formulated the cross-culturally recurrent characteristics of the type that John Stuart Mill had called the 'Orient[al] State'." In his concluding statement, "Some Implications of the Symposium," Steward indicated that he was "prepared to go a little further" than his associates in revising his "general hypothesis or formulation of irrigation civilizations of 1949." He also indicated that his original hypothesis had encountered unnecessary difficulties because he "had failed to pay sufficient attention to the very important typological and developmental differences between key and core regions and the marginal regions within each of the four areas discussed." In this context he pointed to problems of taxonomy raised by developments in Mesopotamia and Mesoamerica. With respect to the first he cited Adams alone, with respect to the second Adams, Donald Collier, and Palerm. In a subsection he stated that, having taken another look at the data, "the concept of Incipient Farming needs revision in several respects" (59). Then, after commenting that "it now appears the first farmers in the Near East, Mesoamerica and North China lived on what Braidwood has called the 'hilly flanks' of the river basin where rainfall was sufficient for farming," he stressed the differing developments in "marginal" and "key" regions and that the key regions benefited from a highly productive irrigation agriculture which afforded a basis for civilization not found in the marginal lands," and one that lent itself "to the construction of large hydraulic works" (59).

At the end of this short subsection, Steward wrote, "Wittfogel, although not primarily concerned with simple agricultural beginnings, had this in mind in stating 'A comparative study of development has to recognize the possibility of single as well as multiple origin, and the possibility of multiple modes of development following upon both types of origin" (59f.). Here Steward cited Wittfogel's "Die Theorie der Orientalische Gesellschaft" (1938). Again familiarity with Wittfogel's 1931 book and a closer reading of the whole *Liao* volume would have shown him that Wittfogel had dealt in very considerable detail with the different agricultural and social developments in marginal and key (core) regions as well as with those factors that enhanced the latter's power potential.

If steward's additional insights were not as conceptually revolutionary as he believed them to be, his interest in culture change and his related discussions of unilinear and multilinear evolution certainly brought much of the relevant data on the Old World and the New into sharper focus. There is no doubt that after leaving Columbia in 1952 Steward was increasingly influenced by Braidwood and later and

189

seemingly more strongly by Adams, both of whom had worked in Mesopotamia and both of whom were connected with the relatively nearby Oriental Institute at the University of Chicago; and more and more his restless and searching mind needed new facts to feed on. In 1956 he initiated a research program in cultural regularities that involved investigations in Mexico, Peru, Africa, Indonesia, and Japan. He spent six months in Japan as director of the Kyoto American Studies Seminar, his stay having ended shortly before Professor Wittfogel and I visited one of his two projects in the late fall of 1957.

But however much Steward felt the need to revise old theses and find new solutions, he did not forget his debt to Wittfogel. In the spring of 1957 Wittfogel's *Oriental Despotism* appeared. The opening sentence of George P. Murdock's review in the *American Anthropologist* reads, "This is a truly great book, one of the major contributions to the science of man in our time." In a letter to Wittfogel, Steward wrote, "Your monumental book [is] a great credit to you and a thing of value to us all." But Wittfogel was not asked to contribute to *Process and Pattern in Culture: Essays in Honor of Julian H. Steward,* edited by his former student Robert A. Manners and published in 1964. A short paper by Braidwood closed the volume. Peculiarly, neither Wittfogel nor Robert M. Adams is mentioned in the index.

But Steward continued to find value in both of them. In 1965, G. L. Ulmen, who had been Wittfogel's teaching assistant at the University of Washington, Seattle, began, as secretary of a committee composed of professors Donald Treadgold and Hellmut Wilhelm (both connected with the University of Washington), Gerhart Niemeyer (University of Notre Dame), Karl H. Menges (Columbia University), and Herbert Franke (University of Munich), to solicit contributions for, and be the editor of, a Wittfogel *Festschrift.* Steward was among the first to be asked, and on July 28, 1965 he wrote Mr. Ulmen:

> I did not answer your kind invitation of last March to contribute to the *Festschrift* for Karl Wittfogel because I immediately began to write a paper and hoped to send it to you at once.
>
> The paper, which I have entitled "Initiation of a Research Trend: Wittfogel's Irrigation Hypothesis" now needs only a final revision. I shall send it to you in a few weeks.
>
> It is very gratifying that Karl Wittfogel is being honored in this way. He has been a great stimulus to my own thinking, and I have had the good fortune to count Karl and Esther among my close friends. It is a privilege for me to share in the *Festschrift,* especially in the company of the scholars you have mentioned."[33]

Steward's paper arrived shortly afterward, but for several reasons, not the least of them the unsettled affairs of the publishing house involved, the *Festschrift* appeared late in 1978. His paper elaborates but does not alter in any substantial way theses Steward had presented a decade earlier. Again he reasserts the need to reexamine Wittfogel's irrigation hypothesis in the light of the "vast amount" of relevant research data that had accumulated since World War II. And on this point he and Wittfogel were at one. To be sure, Steward still failed to recognize how much of what he was saying had already been suggested, and at times spelled out in considerable detail, by Wittfogel, but his differentiating insights both broadened and deepened understanding of the complex history of social development in arid and semi-arid lands.

At the beginning of this paper Steward wrote, "A scholar's contribution to science should be judged more by the stimulus he gives to research—by the nature of the problem he raises and the interests he creates—than by the enduring qualities of his provisional hypotheses." In writing thus he was certainly thinking of Wittfogel's contributions and, as already noted, he later acknowledged the "stimulus" he had received from "Wittfogel's irrigation hypothesis."

The concluding paragraph reads, "In short, instead of throwing out the baby with the irrigation water, the need is to recognize the particular combinations of factors *including the kinds of irrigation,* which operated in each case. Wittfogel's hypothesis challenges the disbelievers to produce alternative explanations which are more than accounts of the uniqueness of individual cases."

In "Cultural Evolution in South America" (1970), Steward again discussed his deviations from "Wittfogel's irrigation hypothesis," and noted here, as he had done in 1965, that "Wittfogel was not entirely wrong." To demonstrate that Wittfogel was not entirely right, he cited "Adams' detailed comparison of state evolution in Mexico and Mesopotamia" (1966). In 1967 Wittfogel reviewed Adams' book, and unlike Steward, he found it factually distorted and theoretically more than problematic. Steward's comment later in this same 1970 article that "in the Hohokam area of Arizona, it [irrigation] seems to have reached a scale that supported states and in the Tehuacan region of Mexico, Coe and Flannery [in Volume I of *The Prehistory of the Tehuacan Valley*] state that 'population density remained low until the introduction of complex irrigation works about 600 BC'," again indicates his openness to new data and new ideas. In further substantiation of the first point, which he had already made in his paper for the Wittfogel *Festschrift* with references to Richard B. Woodbury, he could have mentioned the writings of Emil W. Haury, the long-time head of the Department of Anthropology at the University of Arizona, who in 1954 at the Annual Meeting of the AAA in Detroit had noted, "The outstanding achievement of the Hohokam with political consequences and implications was the development of their irrigation system." Stressing that "it was only by intervillage cooperation that individual ditches, 20 or more miles in length, up to 60 feet in width and 10 feet in depth, could have been constructed," he added, "The planning, construction and maintenance of these ditches reflected some degree of centralized authority." And he concluded, "At the same time the inference can be drawn that the villages [in the Hohokam complex] were under strong political leadership, for labor recruitment would have been at this level." Then after reproducing our statement from Wittfogel and Goldfrank (1943) concerning the social organization of the miniature waterwork societies of the Pueblos, he commented, "If this is true for the Pueblos it may have been infinitely more so among the Hohokam who had superior technological mastery of irrigation" (Haury, 1956: 8f.). In substantiation of the second point, Steward could also have mentioned the writings of Richard S. MacNeish, General Director of the Tehuacan Valley Project and, for other Mesoamerican areas, the Teotihuacan study of William T. Sanders and Barbara Price, the work of Angel Palerm in and around the Valley of Mexico, and Charles DiPeso's in Casas Grandes.

It would be idle to speculate what direction Steward's thinking would have taken had he lived longer (he died in 1972). But one thing is clear, and quite other than Manners would have us believe about his great teacher. Steward, despite his significant and, I may add, sometimes problematic revisions of Wittfogel's "hypothesis," never himself "threw out the baby with the irrigation water." Rather, as "Cultural Evolution in South America" shows, he was still, at this late date, demonstrating his capacity for critically examining and re-examining "an earlier generalization or formulation"—his own included—and not, as Manners noted in his obituary for Steward (1973), and with particular reference to Wittfogel's hypothesis "his capacity for abandoning" them. Indeed, in the first paragraph of "Cultural Facts and Processes in the Evolution of Pre-farming Societies" Steward wrote, "If any of my comments appear to contradict my earlier statements, it is because I endeavor to sharpen and, if necessary, redesign old tools rather than discard them" (1968: 321).

And this is just what two not unknown professors in Columbia's Department of Anthropology have been and are still doing.

Morton H. Fried, who was close to Steward, wrote in his Introduction to Wittfogel's "Theory of Oriental Society" included in *Readings in Anthropology* (Fried, 1968, 2nd ed.), "It is probably not valid to measure the importance of a theory by the controversy it has generated. Nonetheless we are all familiar with a number of great theories which were born in disputation, survive numerous premature announcements that they had been disproved or discarded, and which continue to inform us and to nurture new arguments. Such has been the case, among others, with the contributions of Darwin, Marx, Freud— and Karl August Wittfogel" (179). In his final paragraph, he notes, "the recent increase in interest in the Wittfogel theory," and after warning that this increase "cannot be taken as acceptance," he concludes, "Its sheer intellectual weight and fascinating juxtaposition of cultural and environmental factors command our attention" (180; for specifics in his and Wittfogel's positions, see Fried, 1967: 208-12).

Marvin Harris, whose initial field work was done in a well-watered area in Brazil and whose contacts with Steward were minor, was invited through the good auspices of Fried to attend a three-day meeting in Urbana in 1955 to discuss the "irrigation hypothesis" and related topics. Here he met Wittfogel for the first time and here for the first time he became seriously interested in the relations between irrigation and societal configurations. In *The Rise of Anthropological Theory* (1968), Harris discusses Wittfogel's hypothesis at considerable length (167ff). He writes, "As early as 1926, Wittfogel had begun to apply a cultural-ecological approach to the explanation of the peculiarities of Chinese and other 'Asiatic' societies" (671). And in his most recent book, *Cannibals and Kings* (1977), he has included a chapter captioned "The Hydraulic Trap." In it he notes, "Among modern scholars, Wittfogel has done the most to clarify the relationship between hydraulic production and the emergence of unchanging agro-managerial despotisms" (158). And quite in line with Steward's intent, he adds, "My own view of that relationship borrows heavily from Wittfogel's but does not correspond precisely with his formulation" (ibid.).

Indeed if more recent evidence of the correctness of Fried's 1968 statement regarding the "increase in interest in the Wittfogel theory" is needed, the 1977 annual meeting of the American Anthropological Association in Houston amply provides it—and this not only within Columbia's Department of Anthropology, but in numerous centers in the U.S.A. and outside it.

At this meeting, two sessions dealt with irrigation; the first, chaired by Rene M. Descartes, considered its relation to the origin of the state; the second, chaired jointly by William P. Mitchell and Barbara J. Price, considered its relation to ecology, systems of production, and ideology. Wittfogel was a discussant in both sessions. In the first, and as the final speaker, he was greeted with applause even before he reached the lectern, and with a standing ovation when he concluded his remarks on "Hydraulic Society and Beyond." His reception in the following meetings left no doubt that Wittfogel's "irrigation hypothesis," as Steward named it, was not only alive—but increasingly significant.

The Growing Support of the American Pueblos as Waterwork Societies: Fred Eggan, Edward P. Dozier, E. Adamson Hoebel, Byron Harvey III

In the '30s, Steward had been largely concerned with North American Indian societies, particularly those of the Greater Southwest. After joining the Bureau of American Ethnology in 1935 and assuming the editorship of the *Handbook of South American Indians* (the first of six volumes was published in 1946) the "civilizations" Meso-America and South America increasingly engaged his interest. After coming to Columbia in 1946, and stimulated by Wittfogel's ideas on social structure and development, he included China, Mesopotamia, and Egypt in his comparative studies. The pueblos, although by no means forgotten, understandably enjoyed less of his analytic attention than they had a decade earlier.

However, other ethnologists of the Southwest, and I have already mentioned some of them, found virtue in ideas expressed in the 1943 Wittfogel and Goldfrank paper. Here I would like to mention particularly Fred Eggan, for years Professor of Anthropology at the Unviversity of Chicago; Edward P. Dozier, for years Professor of Anthropology at the University of Arizona; E. Adamson Hoebel, for years Professor of Anthropology at the University of Minnesota; and Byron Harvey III, long-time student of pueblo mores.

Eggan started working with the Hopi in the early 30s, and in 1950 his impressive *Social Organization of the Western Pueblos* appeared. After stating in his concluding chapter that "we have tried to formulate a historical hypothesis which will fit the whole area rather than explain merely selected portions of it," he noted that "an independent approach to the problem of the social organization in the Pueblos has recently been made by Wittfogel and Goldfrank, who have called attention to the importance of irrigation in the Southwest" (318). Then, after reproducing our argument regarding the effects of the varying intensity of irrigation on social structure and the position of the sexes, he added, "Though I have developed the analysis above on broader grounds, the coincidence of my conclusions with those reached by Wittfogel and Goldfrank . . . is striking" (319).

Dozier, the child of an Indian mother and a non-Indian father, was raised in the Tewa Pueblo of Santa Clara, New Mexico. After stating, as we had done, that the need for communal effort in the Rio Grande pueblos was greater than in Hopi and Zuni, he wrote in "The Rio Grande Pueblos" (1961), "Large-scale cooperation on irrigation projects has important implications for the nature of Rio Grande socio-political and ceremonial organization." He continued, "These implications have been recently elaborated by K. A. Wittfogel for oriental society and for ancient America" (Wittfogel 1957). And he added, "Wittfogel and Goldfrank (1943) have also presented a provocative article in which the importance of irrigation is discussed with respect to the nature of Pueblo societies." Regarding our position on institutionalized discipline in these societies, he wrote, "We feel that, in large part, the difference between Keresan and Tanoan sociopolitical and ceremonial organization may be explained by the Wittfogel-Goldfrank hypothesis" (102 f.). Under his heading *Socialization*, and after again referring to the differences between Keresan and Tanoan socialization practices and the resultant personality structures, he stated that "the overwhelming similarities far outweigh the differences." In the next paragraphs, he recapitulated and accepted —without any ifs or buts—the understanding of these practices and structures as set forth in my "Socialization, Personality, and the Structure of Pueblo Society" (1945b: 118 f.).

Years later, and two years before his untimely death, Dozier's view of Pueblo social structure and personality was unchanged. In *The Pueblo Indians of North America* he wrote, "Following some interesting ideas advanced by Wittfogel and Goldfrank (1943) and Wittfogel (1957), I believe that intensive irrigation practices utilizing water from permanently flowing streams have brought about the centralized orientation of the Eastern or Rio Grande Pueblos" (1970: 132). Then, in line with our joint 1943 paper and Eggan (1950), he concluded, "It seems clear that clan organizations [such as existed in the Western pueblos] were inadequate for the intricate demands of an irrigation society, particularly where technology remained on a simple level." He added, "The development of a sodality-type organization appears to be a method for achieving village centralization and for mobilizing and directing the communities' total or at least minimum man-power resources." And after noting that "such an organization was soon put to the direction of other village-wide operations: religion, hunting, warfare and curing," he maintained that "the initial impetus for the [sodality-type] organization . . . was irrigation" (132 f.).

With respect to Pueblo personality, Dozier wrote, "Anthropologists, historians, and others have long held a view of the Pueblos as docile, nonaggressive people." He then noted, and no one would contradict him, "Ruth Benedict in 'Patterns of Culture' (1934), has given this Pueblo stereotype its widest currency; labelling the Pueblo personality type as 'Apollonian,' she characterizes the Pueblo Indians as controlled and unassertive, eschewing excesses of all kinds." And he added, "Actually this stereotype of the Pueblo Indian is controverted by the historical record of the more detailed ethnographic studies now available" (78). Later, after commenting that "the welfare of a pueblo rests on the proper, timely and calendric observance and performance of religious ritual," and just before citing several passages from *Patterns of Culture* and Zuni attitudes to religious observance, he noted that in these passages Ruth Benedict "had captured the essence of Pueblo ceremonialism" (200 f.). But he then stressed that "Pueblo ceremonies vary from rather sedate and monotonous dancing of men and women in single file to hilarious orgiastic rites." As two examples of "non-Apollonian, Dionysian behavior," he mentioned the initiation rite for membership into the Onayanakia Order of the Great Fire Fraternity" and "the orgiastic rites of the Newekwe, one of the Fraternities of the Zuni Beast God associations" (202). He concluded, "Despite Benedict's insight into the meaning and concepts of Pueblo ceremonialism, she obviously never saw or recognized the obvious Dionysian aspects of religious expression present in other Zuni ceremonial rites" (202). In fact, she "presented an unreal calm and unruffled picture of Pueblo life" (203).

Hoebel, who had worked in the pueblo of Sia in the later 40s, was the final speaker in the day-long symposium on the Southwest held in Tucson in 1953. His topic was "Major Contributions of Southwestern Studies to Anthropological Theory." Regarding *Patterns of Culture* he said, "The peculiar thing is that this great contribution (and probably the most influential work, taken at large, in the last thirty years) bears only a tangential relationship to the facts of Pueblo ethnography. The factual criticisms that have found their way into print . . . only begin to indicate the extent of the artistic and poetic idealization of Pueblo culture that Benedict presented" (1954: 724). And in his "Overview of Pueblo Religion" (1972: 210), Byron Harvey III has written, "People who were in long contact with the Pueblos never made the anthropologist's error of assuming the culture was Apollonian and totally peaceful."

Many well-known anthropologists have commented on the work of Ruth Benedict. Most recognize, as I do, her stimulating impact, but few accept her impressionistic method or her conceptual "wholes." It may not be out of place to state here that what I had hoped for in 1943 had indeed come to pass—that, professional and continuing controversy notwithstanding, "Wittfogel's irrigation hypothesis" is a seminal contribution to present-day anthropological thought.

AND ON OTHER THINGS

Of course, in this decade of the 40s, there were many "other things" besides those previously mentioned, but here I only want to mention four of them—the first because it throws some light on the anthropological climate at the time, the second because it meant much to me personally and professionally, the third and fourth because they fill out the factual record.

At the Annual AAA Meeting, December 27-30, 1941

This concerns actions taken and not taken at the evening session on December 27, just one day short of three weeks after Pearl Harbor and the United States declaration of war against Japan.

Margaret Mead was in the chair. She spoke on "morale-building and cultural integration," Ruth Benedict on "ideologies in the life of cross-cultural data," and Elliot Chapple on "the analysis of industrial morale." Then, as stated in the program, there followed a period of "informal discussion" on "the anthropologist's contribution to the contemporary scene."

It was during this period that Mel Jacobs, a member of the Department of Anthropology at the University of Washington, Seattle, rose to protest the U.S. government's decision to uproot Japanese residents from their homes in presumably sensitive areas—essentially in states bordering on the Pacific ocean—and relocate them in less exposed areas, where their movements were already being severely restricted. While broadening the base of Jacob's original statement—and this may well have been done by other speakers—the minutes of the 1941 meeting (*AA*, 1942: 286 f.) noted, under the heading "Report of Committees," that "the suggestion of a group of anthropologists at the University of Washington for united action against the growth of racial prejudice within our borders was commended by the Council, but no agreement was reached on the desirability of centralizing our efforts along these lines."

Undiscouraged by this face-saving but hardly morale-building action (the core Japanese issue remained unmentioned), I also spoke from the floor and asked those present to go on record for equal treatment of Whites and Negroes who were being conscripted for service in our armed forces.[34] During the Pact, a vocal and sizable sector of our population had insistently stressed that more important than aid to a desperate Britain were the needs of "Negroes in the South." As already noted, my priorities were different. But now, or so it seemed to me, was the given time and the given place to take a significant official step toward achieving the racial equality that so many anthropologists, and by no means they alone, had over the years been hoping for and working for. But I couldn't have been more mistaken. One anthropologist sitting across the aisle from me exclaimed (and not *sotto voce*), "Then we'll have another Civil War." A second, who later became president of the AAA, said to me at the close of the session, privately, "You were right, but your timing was wrong." Margaret Mead called me "out of order." And no Council or Committee commended my suggestion. Unanimously adopted two days later was the following:

> Be it resolved, that the American Anthropological Association places itself and its resources and the specialized skills and knowledge of its members at the disposal of the country for the successful prosecution of the war. (AA, 1942: 289)

Without saying so in words, this resolution clearly warned the anthropological community not to rock the "Ship of State" and, as already foreshadowed in the "informal discussion" on the evening of December 27, not to continue agitating for the long overdue improvements in the condition of minorities within our borders. The Negroes got the message. They still remember, and with anger, how quickly their most ardent supporters deserted them. This was not the first time political passions found expression in an AAA resolution. Nor was it the last.

Summer of 1946: Visit to the Southwest

Two decades had passed since I had been to the Southwest and then, except for a day in Acoma, another going up and coming down Mt. Taylor with Dr. Boas, and a short stay at Frijoles and the Grand Canyon with him and Mama Franz, I had been a working anthropologist, spending my time with cooperative informants or looking for them—a geographically limited and not always successful effort.

In the summer of 1946 the war was over and travel was easier. Again the Southwest beckoned. Professor Wittfogel had read enormously on this fascinating area and patiently listened to my on-the-spot experiences. For him, this would be a first visit; for me, a first after many years. There was much we hoped to accomplish in our mixed roles as tourists and participant-observers. Not surprisingly, irrigation would be the focal point of our travels.

We started out in Albuquerque. Florence Kluckhohn was already there and knew we were coming. Through her we met the archaeologist Paul Reiter, who was connected with the University of New Mexico and had published on his researches in Jemez. At the University we also met W. W. Hill, who had written so revealingly on Navajo agricultural and hunting methods. Unfortunately, Leslie Spier had already gone to California, as was his wont in the summer months, and Florence Hawley was unavailable.

We also spent many hours at the Albuquerque Indian Agency gathering statistics on Southwest weather, soil, and water conditions. An Isleta Indian, a member of the Agency's staff and a liaison between it and his village, eagerly volunteered to take us there and show us just how "his people" grew their crops. He was indefatigable—and this did not displease us. First he led us to the Rio Grande, the primary source of their water supply, then along the "mother ditch" that took off from it, and then along several of the smaller ditches that carried this life-giving element directly to the fields. After hours of trudging, we could well understand that the annual "spring cleaning" of this network required, as Lummis had reported, the calling up and supervision of some 500 Isleta men. But dancing helped, too. Immediately after the Corn Dance, our Isleta companion told us, the rains came.

To our guide, perhaps more important than showing us the fields was showing us his comfortable adobe house, and particularly his bathroom. Proudly he opened the door of this *sanctum sanctorum* and there, alone, stood the bathtub in all its pristine glory. Electric power had brought change; kerosene lamps were things of the past. But water—that scarce commodity in this arid land—was still unavailable except by the bucket route. The privy or the unencumbered out-of-doors still served personal needs. But just looking at this newly acquired and immaculately kept acquisition enhanced prestige, and brought "civilization" a step nearer.

After some days we took the train to Santa Fe. Neither of us had ever been there before and its Spanish flavor, architecturally and linguistically, was much stronger in this one-time capital of the conquistadores than in Albuquerque. We stayed at a small hotel two blocks from the Plaza. But the lounge and dining-room of La Fonda, Santa Fe's finest hotel, became a major extension of our crowded quarters.

As soon as our bags were unpacked we walked to the State Museum, which, like La Fonda, flanked the Plaza. Bertha Dutton, well versed in the history and ethnography of the Southwest, personally conducted us through its halls. We returned there often in the weeks following—its coolness a welcome respite from the July sun.

Our next object of interest was the Laboratory of Anthropology. There we met Albert H. Schroeder and Erik K. Reed, both of whom had contributed notably by trowel and pen to archaeological research in the area. Later in our stay we had dinner, along with Carl Coon, at the Walt Taylors. It was a lively evening, none of us being inhibited or shunning disagreement. A decade later Walt, then the head of the Department of Anthropology at the University of Southern Illinois, asked me to substitute for Charles Lange, who would be on leave, and give a course on Southwest ethnology. I had never taught. Needless to say, I was flattered by the suggestion, but I was also frightened by it. When I learned there was no opening in any department for my husband—who, in fact, had highly satisfying commitments elsewhere—

my answer was a relieved "no."

We soon engineered a hitch to Cochiti. Now, after many years, I would see Isabel again. We had not been in touch for well over a decade, and since our timetable was uncertain, I had not told her that this summer we would be in Santa Fe for some weeks. But I felt sure that whenever we arrived we would be greeted warmly.

Parked, we began inquiring for Isabel Ramirez. No one admitted knowing any such person. Then I asked for her cousin, and here too we drew a blank. In 1946, Cochiti was much as it had been in 1922—the irregularly placed dwellings, the smallish plaza where I had first met Isabel, the two round Kivas where most of the ceremonies closed to "foreigners" were conducted, the Catholic Church where only on Sundays the priest, who was permanently stationed in Peña Blanca, regularly held a Mass for his Cochiti parishioners.

Dismayed by the failure of our mission, we reluctantly got back into our car and returned to Santa Fe. The following morning I spoke with the shopkeeper, who I had learned knew Cochiti well, and, more important, some young people who were studying or working in Santa Fe during the week and on weekends returned to their home village. She arranged for a young woman from Cochiti to accompany us on our next attempt. We chose July 14, the Feast Day of San Buenaventura, Cochiti's patron saint. The Corn Dance would be given (according to Lange, the people of Cochiti referred to it as the *Tablita* Dance, in recognition of the thin painted headboards of wood worn by the women) and, of course, virtually everyone in the village who was not a participant would be a spectator.

Our guide, who was studying to be a nurse, spoke excellent English. On the way she told us what we had not known before—that Pedro Ramirez had died and that Isabel had recently married Tomás Garcia, who, unlike Pedro, was a member of the conservative faction and active in village affairs. When we reached the plaza, the Corn Dance was under way. Our guide, pointing to a leading woman dancer, said, "There's Isabel." I could not trust my ears or my eyes. *My* Isabel, who in 1922 had not dared to watch a public dance, was now, two decades later, participating prominently in one of them.

The moment the dance was over I rushed to greet her. "Remember me?" I said. No word. Isabel just stared, but when I said, "I'm Esther," she opened her arms after a moment of unbelief and embraced me—unusual for a Pueblo Indian, but then Isabel had often been unusual. Karl was duly introduced, and Isabel led us to her house, which had a good view of the plaza. I soon learned that it belonged to the Garcia family and that, after her marriage to Tomas, she had moved in with them.

A number of persons were sitting on the open terrace. Some were family members, some friends. With obvious pride, Isabel introduced me to Tomas. He nodded quite perfunctorily—I am inclined to think he had never heard of me. After all, it was more than two decades since I had been in Cochiti, an inquiring anthropologist to be sure, but one who, by the circumstances of investigation in the pueblo at that time, had been more than content to remain out of sight, if not out of mind.

Fully aware that, when visiting Indian friends, proper behavior entails bringing a gift, I had taken with me from New York a dozen "handkerchiefs"—squares of the size that, in former times, every Pueblo woman had hung on her back to signal her virtue. During an interlude between dances I motioned to Isabel to join me indoors. She shook her head and, to be certain I understood, she added an emphatic "no, no." Clearly, she was under the impression that I wanted to revive our past interviewer-informant relation. To reassure her I said, "Ask Tomas to come inside too."·This she did, manifestly relieved. Inside, I opened my package, and Isabel's eyes shone as she examined each square. Tomas, after one short look, returned to his seat on the terrace. I then explained to Isabel that since, excepting for her and her now grown daughters, I knew no women in the village, she would have to decide who would be the chosen ones. This raised no problem for her. Almost before she was out of the room she was back again, followed by what seemed an unending stream of women. But there were just exactly twelve of them counting Isabel. Somewhat to my embarrassment, although I should not have been surprised, each had brought something for me.

No cheap trinkets these. Isabel offered her gift first—a highly-prized Navajo saddle blanket (as already noted, she still asked me about it in a letter written many years later). Among the remainder there were two pottery bowls—one traditional Cochiti, one Laguna in design (I still have both of them)—and a large black stone set impressively in a silver ring. It was all quite overwhelming, and when we stopped on our way home for an evening snack at La Fonda, the "loungers," with some of whom we had become acquainted, approached us first out of curiosity (convinced that we must either have robbed a museum or gone on a wild shopping spree) and then in wonder at our Christmas in July. It took quite a bit of doing to get the rug and the pots to New York. One footnote, substantiating for Cochiti a comment made by Adair in his paper on returned Zuni veterans, may be added to this chronicle of an eventful day. For the first time, I saw drunken Pueblo Indians participating in a sacred dance for rain.

The ease with which Isabel had been located by our young Cochiti companion raised an interesting question. Was it her progressive past or her conservative present that had caused the reticence we had met with on our previous visit? Whatever the answer, and I shall not presume to give one, the morning following Cochiti's Feast Day I thanked our shopkeeper friend for her help. I told her more of my early experiences in the Southwest and I mentioned the problems Isabel—and Pedro—had then been faced with. Quite spontaneously, she told me of two recent disciplinary actions in Cochiti. One almost seemed an echo of Bunzel's Zuni "Autobiography." A young boy who had been watching a masked performance in the Kiva had pointed to a dancer and exclaimed, "That's my father." It was. The next day he was again in the Kiva, and this time, not as a willing spectator, but as an unwilling participant. The proper functionaries proceeded to whip him severely for his "unsocial" behavior.

In the second case, the sufferer was a young woman whose father had told her, "*They* want to see you." She had, it seems, overreacted in a family situation which she did not approve of. But that was not the reason given for summoning her to the Kiva. She too was whipped severely by the proper functionaries. Manifestly, punishment still followed long-favored patterns.

We did not return to Cochiti until 1959, and then we were instantly recognized and warmly greeted by Isabel and her daughters. Again there had been changes. Tomas had died, but Isabel's status had continued to improve. Her oldest daughter was now the wife of a high official and, together, they had prepared a sumptuous repast for members of the village Council, who were to join them after concluding their official business. We were immediately seated at the groaning board. For politeness sake—but also because the dishes were tasty—we sampled every one, and some more than once. A number of wives had already arrived, but they did not join us, preferring to watch TV.

We left before the men arrived. Earlier, Karl took the picture of Isabel, her two daughters, and me that she and I still treasure. But in 1959, unlike 1946, there was no "Christmas in July." For years Isabel's and my gift-exchanges have been restricted to Christmas in December.

We also spent the better part of a day at Taos and on the return trip to Santa Fe stopped off at San Ildefonso. I had never been in either pueblo, but both were famous—Taos for its multi-storied dwellings, reviving memories of times long past; San Ildefonso as the home-base of Maria, already considered by many not only an outstanding Pueblo potter, but the best.

Entering Taos, it was not difficult to understand its attraction for artists and writers, and not a few lived close by. But I found little aesthetic satisfaction in the modern blankets of all shades, striped and unstriped, in which the Taos men were wrapping themselves to fend off the morning chill. I remembered the handsome blankets the Navajo men had worn over their shoulders or carried over an arm during the dancing at Laguna in September 1921. To be sure, their women folk had woven them from the wool of their valued sheep, primarily for family use, but, when the price was right, also for sale or barter. In Taos, twenty-five years later, the "foreigners," who were numerous and no doubt less inconvenienced by rising costs, were eager buyers of Navajo jewelry and blankets, whereas the "natives" were finding comfort, if not prestige, in cheaper factory-made products. However, it is more than possible that, on ceremonial occasions, they, like the people of Laguna, would emerge in traditional—and their best—dress, and that Navajo blankets would then also emerge from storage in back rooms.

We were soon accosted by a young Indian who volunteered to lead us to a second-story dwelling where Indian goods were being sold. We climbed a ladder to an open terrace (an architectural device that long antedated the advent of the Spaniards) and, crossing it, entered a small windowless room, the only light entering through a low narrow doorway. Ranged against the walls were tables weighed down with pottery and other Taos handiwork—in my view, an undistinguished exhibit. Of course, we bought something, but what it was or how we disposed of it, I can't remember. We certainly did not take it with us when we returned to the East. Our purchase concluded, we climbed down the ladder and resumed our walk. We found the "mother ditch," which wasn't difficult, since it virtually bisected the pueblo. But for lack of time, our inspection of Taos' irrigation system stopped there.

Arriving at San Ildefonso in the late afternoon, we had no difficulty in locating Maria—a woman in her middle years, whatever that may mean (long ago, when I asked my seven-year-old daughter "What is middle age?" she answered without hesitation, "ten"). Maria's manner was assured and, although she remained in the display room, she did not push us into buying—this was quite different from our Taos encounter. All of her pottery—and there were bowls and plates of many sizes and shapes—was fashioned out of the black clay, long a San Ildefonso trademark. Being water-conscious, we selected a large round plate featuring a crawling serpent—symbolic of a flowing river. This we did take with us when we returned to the East.

Leaving Santa Fe, and now for the last time, we went by train and bus to Mesa Verde. It was midsummer and it seemed as if the world was vacationing there. Fathers slung their young children over their shoulders; somewhat older children, unhampered by parental admonition and the overprotectiveness so common in the Eastern suburbs, moved about confidently. In largest part they came from Western states and, whether they were city- or country-bred, it seemed to us that something of the freedom of great open spaces had rubbed off on them.

We did the usual sightseeing. But no one, excepting us, was bent on tracing the irrigation ditch that watered the terraces on which crops had been grown by the Indians a thousand years ago, and that, until quite recently, anthropologists, almost to a man, had maintained was a cowpath. As never before we were convinced that the rocky fortresses of the "peaceful" Pueblo peoples served as defenses against more than the sporadic raids of small nomad bands. Ralph Linton had made this point strongly, and contrary to general anthropological thinking (1944: 28-32).

Again by train and bus we now turned south, our destination Gallup. En route, we skirted the Navajo reservation, and, as I mentioned earlier, I then first realized how quickly summer rains could bring summer flowers in this desert land.

In Gallup we again met Mr. Powers, a government adviser on Indian farming, to whom Florence Kluckhohn had introduced us in Albuquerque. Zuni was in his territory, and when he learned that neither Karl nor I had ever been in Zuni, he had suggested driving us there after our arrival in Gallup, which was a convenient take-off point. All went smoothly on the way out, but I was totally unprepared for my first view of this much-written-about village—a row of bleak brick buildings housing, Mr. Powers told us, public services of various kinds. Beyond them, and happily, the landscape became typically "pueblo." Passing old-style adobe houses, we soon reached the Zuni river, which seemed to me little more than an oversized "mother ditch." We spoke shortly, and informally, with a number of villagers known to Mr. Powers and, with him, visited a household busily engaged in fashioning jewelry, an activity inspired by Navajo silverwork and already a popular and lucrative supplement to family incomes. We did not meet anyone who had worked with Parsons, Benedict, or Bunzel. At long last I was in Zuni. But my understanding of the lifeways would continue to depend, as previously, on data amassed by others.

On the way home we had to contend with a cloudburst. Soon we were in a sea of mud, slithering from one side of our unpaved road to the other, uncomfortably aware that, from the edge of both, there was a sheer drop of some six feet to the valley floor. Mr. Powers, long used to the idiosyncracies of summer storms in the Southwest, was unperturbed. Not I, an inveterate worrier. But when I asked him to stop until the rain stopped, he said softly but firmly that we couldn't, that if we did we would be unable to get going again without outside help—and clearly, no such help was within sight. So we continued slithering and, thanks to our driver's skill, returned without mishap.

We had planned to be in Gallup a few days before its highly publicized midsummer fiesta was scheduled to begin. Dances given by Indian groups were a major attraction. Today some of these groups boycott this annual celebration, claiming that the performances are not authentic. In 1946, although we were aware of certain lacks, we put on our tourist hats and enjoyed ourselves. We had been warned that during these days there would be much drinking by both Whites and Indians, and no doubt this was the case. But I can remember no more excessive behavior than I had often witnessed at college football games.

For both of us this was a memorable summer. In 1935, Professor Wittfogel had gone to China to test concepts he had formulated in 1931 in *Wirtschaft und Gesellschaft Chinas*. Now, in 1946, we had gone to the Southwest to test information I had obtained in the 20s and concepts of pueblo social structure we had formulated since 1943. Our on-the-spot experiences, while alerting us to further differentiations, gave added support to our image of Pueblo culture and personality.

Years as an Officer of the American Ethnological Society

In the fall of 1945 I was nominated secretary-treasurer of the American Ethnological Society, the oldest of the American anthropological societies but, for decades, no longer the first among equals (in the mid-40s, the AES had about 200 members, the AAA about 1,300). Because AES had been incorporated in New York State and the understanding at this time was that the election of officers had to be held within the State's borders, [35] New York City invariably was the locale of the annual meeting. For lack of travel funds, its national membership was served by officers drawn almost entirely from museum and other educational facilities within the city, most frequently from the American Museum of Natural History and Columbia University. It was years before a mailed ballot was ordered and, in the 40s, those attending the annual meeting rarely numbered more than thirty. I was duly elected in January 1946 and re-elected the year following. My duties were not onerous. A high-school student one afternoon a week was all the help I required.

During my term of office my greatest contribution was made, at least to my mind, in the unrelated field of publication. Manuscripts for our monograph series were reviewed by all members of the Board, and initial opinions often differed. I argued particularly strongly for the acceptance of David French's *Factionalism in Isleta Pueblo*, convinced that its data were an important supplement to the Isleta field studies Parsons and I had made in the 20s. Only after the editor, Marian W. Smith, said she was entirely willing and, in fact, glad to permit me, as I had suggested, to prepare his manuscript for the printer, did the Board accept my plea.

This was my first effort of this kind (outside of the Chinese History Project) and I was gratified that, in his introduction and later, French acknowledged my "careful editing" of his paper. In 1952, when

I became editor of the AES Monograph Series, I again found that this often derogated activity could be a first step in initiating enduring friendships with "my" authors and a further release of creative energies, both theirs and mine.

In 1948 I was elected president of the American Ethnological Society; Margaret Mead and Julian H. Steward, vice-presidents; Dorothy L. Keur, secretary-treasurer; Burt W. Aginsky, Gordon Ekholm, and Carl Withers, directors; and Marian W. Smith, editor. Four of us had connections with Columbia University, two with the American Museum of Natural History, one with Hunter College, and one with City College.

During the year, I became convinced that in view of our changed position toward the American Anthropological Association, our modus operandi needed to be re-examined and readjusted. In my report at the close of my term (AA, 1949: 371 f.), I noted that, despite certain revisions, we were still "out of focus" because, "in an expanding anthropology, ethnology is only one field of interest." And although our constitution had been amended at various points to meet this situation, the more our Board had "sought to implement its articles, the more it realized how antiquated and unsatisfactory the whole thing was." We had, of course, given considerable thought to this problem, but the task of revision had barely begun. We did, however, at the suggestion of Dr. Aginsky, inaugurate spring meetings directed specifically toward a broader attendance of students, not merely as passive auditors, but as active participants reading papers they had themselves prepared (over the years these student meetings have continued to be an attractive feature of AES programming). Our Board had also suggested that we meet jointly with the various affiliates of the AAA to encourage exchanges between members of different disciplines, which, due to the increasingly large and diffuse character of the AAA meetings, had become increasingly difficult. We also recommended that the incoming Board "get a sense of our total membership regarding our present status and related problems." This, it seemed to us, was a much needed move in view of the geographical concentration of our Board members in the New York area.

These years in the service of the AES, especially the four from 1952 to 1956, when I was editor, all brought me into close and constructive contact with a stimulating mix of scholars, fields, and viewpoints. No doubt they also account for the continuing, and now largely ignored, requests for my *vita* from organizations—some long-established, some newly spawned. But I like to think that my scientific contributions, if not initially decisive, have been a primary reason for this ongoing interest.

The year 1947 initiated an important change in our life-style. It was then that Professor Wittfogel was asked by Professor George E. Taylor, whom he had met in China, to join the Far Eastern and Russian Institute at the University of Washington, which he, after serving in the later years of the war as Director of OWI, the Pacific Theatre, had been instrumental in establishing and was now heading. Besides Wittfogel, outstanding Asian scholars were attracted to the Institute's program, as were outstanding European scholars who had fled Fascism or Communism and were well-versed in the history and/or language of one or another of the areas involved.

Together these scholars created an exceptional environment—a cooperative unit of some forty members who exchanged ideas not only in unstructured meetings but also in weekly staff symposia, during which each participant expressed his agreement—or disagreement—with the main speaker, who usually presented some aspect of his work-in-progress. It was not long before the Far Eastern and Russian Institute, under Taylor's aegis, became a leading center of Asian and Russian studies in our country.

Having also, since the early 40s, acted as liaison between the Institute of Pacific Relations and Columbia University on matters concerned with the Chinese History Project, Taylor recognized the desirability of keeping the Project going. In the East, Wittfogel's primary concern was the Chinese History Project, whose members had little contact with their Columbia colleagues; in the West, his primary concern was awakening his students to the urgency of understanding societies different from our own and those of Western Europe. A highly important by-product was his easy access to members of the Far Eastern and Russian Institute, and theirs to him. For myself, I can count gains on several levels. I continued working with Chinese History Project data, especially the study on Han officialdom. I took courses given by the Institute and the Department of Anthropology, chaired, at the time of our arrival, by my old friend Erna Gunther.

In 1947, we stayed in Seattle briefly; in 1948 the whole summer. After that year and until the early 60s we usually spent one university quarter in our Western homeland. But once Wittfogel gave his course "From Marx to Mao" and the University's Television Studio made tapes of ten related lectures (which were widely distributed throughout the state) he was asked, because of the unusual student interest, to teach two quarters annually. In these years we often arrived in Seattle on December 31, just in time to join with colleagues in welcoming the New Year.

Thus, for close to two decades, we lived in two worlds. For

Rudyard Kipling, East was East and West was West and never the twain would meet. But our two worlds were mutually supportive, and we reaped personal and professional benefits from both. As for those young Westerners who had studied under Professor Wittfogel, they registered their views in print in the 269-page *Course Critique* published in 1966. They not only included Wittfogel in their "Honor List," but their ratings placed him virtually at the top of the almost 500 members of the teaching staff under review. One student referred to his having attended Wittfogel's course as "an unforgettable experience." Indeed, "his previous experiences, strong convictions, and concern for his class," the *Critique* states, "caused many of his students to comment that he was one of the best professors . . . they had ever had," and that "his approach encompassed history, sociology, politics, and economics in an enlightening and inspiring manner."

I have never been sympathetic to student ratings of teachers—which so often expose the weaknesses of the judges as well as the weaknesses of the judged. But I hope I will be forgiven for finding satisfaction in the fact that the "Associated Students, University of Washington" had responded so positively to Professor Wittfogel.

12. "RICH ETHNOGRAPHIC FARE"

ISLETA PAINTINGS

More than a decade had passed since the day in 1941 when Gladys A. Reichard of Barnard College told me about Dr. Parsons' Isleta paintings manuscript, and that it had been dedicated to me (actually, as noted above, to me and Julian H. Steward) "to whom," she wrote, "I owe the opening of Isleta." As Parsons' literary executor, Gladys was faced with many tasks and worked diligently to get this Isleta manuscript published. But no individual or foundation was ready to meet the great cost involved in reproducing the more than 140 paintings included in it.

In May 1949, Dr. Parsons' children presented her notebooks and unpublished manuscripts to the American Philosophical Society in Philadelphia. The year following, Gladys wrote a short report on "The Elsie Clews Parsons' Collection" (1950). In it she particularly emphasized the significance of the Isleta paintings for Pueblo studies.

It was in the fall of 1952 that I first saw the Isleta paintings—and then not by plan, although I knew I would be in Philadelphia at this time attending the Annual Meeting of the AAA. Only when J. O. Brew, director of the Peabody Museum and organizer and director of the immensely rewarding excavations at Awatovi, was proudly showing all and sundry Watson Smith's fine volume *Awatovi Kiva Decorations*, which was just off the press, did I recall that Philadelphia was now the home of the Isleta paintings. Within minutes I was on my way to the American Philosophical Society.

Dr. William E. Lingelbach, the head of the library, welcomed me cordially (in the 40s he had been instrumental in getting the *Liao* volume published). Upon learning my errand, he suggested that I find a seat in the stacks—which wasn't difficult, since no one else was there. Soon an attendant brought me a bulky package loosely wrapped in a crumpled sheet of brown paper. This I removed, with what some might consider unseemly haste, to uncover the first of the Isleta paintings—a woman seated on a sheep pelt and about to give birth. Facing her and supporting her was the kneeling midwife, and behind her stood the medicine "doctor," poised to strike her on the back with his stone club "to loosen the baby." As in the Mexican codices, there was no attempt at perspective, the composition was simple, the colors subdued. I soon realized that Parsons had ordered the paintings topically under several rubrics—birth, curing, death, the ceremonial cycle, etc. The artist's aim, I learned later, had been to provide more and better illustrations for her 1932 Isleta monograph, and this he certainly succeeded in doing.

None of the paintings were signed, since anonymity was of the essence. All were in watercolor on ordinary white drawing paper, the larger ones 18 X 24 inches or thereabouts. With the passing years the artist's palette became less limited, his composition more complex, but his figures continued to be movingly drawn, their actions simply and convincingly portrayed. Here indeed was Pueblo life writ large. Here was a record as unique for the modern Pueblo scene as the Awotovi Kiva murals were for the Pueblo past.

Working my way through this small mountain of paintings, I could hardly contain my excitement. Lingelbach, historian though he was, seemed clearly surprised when I shared it with him. However, he saw no obstacle to sending the paintings to New York, as I requested, should René d'Harnoncourt, the director of the Museum of Modern Art, be willing to examine them and house them temporarily. René (and for brevity's sake I shall call him that, since later we were on a first-name basis) had a lively interest in things anthropological and, for this reason and the paintings' obvious aesthetic appeal, I hoped he would help in getting them published. He readily agreed to their being sent to him for inspection. I kept Gladys fully informed about these new developments, and she was well pleased to learn that the Isleta paintings might be on the threshold of a new life.

René phoned me when the paintings reached him in April 1953 and asked me to join him while he viewed them. One by one he studied them, completely unconcerned with time. Facing him across his desk, I knew, without his saying a word, that his reaction was quite like mine when I first saw them in the stacks of the American Philosophical Society. Upon reaching the last of them, he said simply, "They must be published"; and being museum-minded, he added, "in folio form." Handsome as I knew this would be, I argued successfully, for a less spectacular presentation—a book that would fit on almost any library shelf and thus be more accessible to students.

As a first step toward our goal, René approached the Bollingen Foundation, which had shown an interest in publication and had underwritten significant volumes, not a few of them dealing with anthropological themes. It was some months later that he again asked me to join him in his office when he showed the paintings to John D. Barrett, the Foundation's director, and Maude Oakes, his associate. To avoid excessive handling, we spread the paintings on the floor, five or six at a time. Our Bollingen guests, like René and myself, were deeply impressed by them. As previously, the cost of publication was a stumbling block. But Mr. Barrett did help us over one hurdle. He volunteered to pay for typing five copies of Parsons' text, which time was not treating kindly.

This was a start, but there was still a long way to go. To enlist substantial aid, the paintings would have to be shown to interested audiences (how many, I could not predict). I could not haul them from pillar to post (they and I would have suffered—and they irreparably—had I attempted to do so). Photographing them was an imperative. After a number of rebuffs, I advanced the necessary funds (years later the American Philosophical Society reimbursed me). René suggested that the photographing be done in the Museum and by the Museum's photographer, and this is how it was done in April 1955, thanks to him and to the unbelievably cooperative Museum staff, and especially Benjamin Karpel, who, from the time of the paintings' arrival some two years earlier, had never put me off when I asked—and by no means infrequently—to have them brought to me in the library reading room for study or viewing by interested anthropologists. But the end of the road was still not in sight.

Just one month after the transparencies were made, I was given the opportunity of showing a selected number of them at a joint meeting of the American Anthropological Association and the American Folklore Society in Bloomington, Indiana. In explanation, I used the captions Parsons had recorded in her manuscript, many of them direct quotes from the artist's letters and paintings. The size of my audience compared well with the attendance at other sessions, but it was no match for the scholarly interest displayed when Alfred Kinsey, author of the already famous *Kinsey Report*, showed slides of pre-Columbian pottery that very realistically portrayed Peruvian sexual practices.

Gladys had not been well in the first months of 1955. Seemingly recovered, she planned another summer with her beloved Navajo. But shortly after her arrival in the Southwest she suffered a fatal heart attack. Her death placed full responsibility for the future of the Isleta paintings on me. It was an ironic twist of fate that Gladys, who had worked so hard to get them published, should be denied the happiness of seeing this accomplished.

In November 1955 I showed slides of the Isleta paintings at a joint meeting of the American Ethnological Society and the New York Academy of Sciences. Also in that month, Joe Brew arranged for me to give an unprogrammed talk at the annual meeting of the AAA in Boston. Both times the viewers were charmed by the paintings, and those who were familiar with Pueblo society immediately recognized their importance. But, like Old Mother Hubbard's, our cupboard remained bare.

Early in December I went to Washington, D.C. While I was there, Matthew W. Stirling and Frank H. H. Roberts, Jr. organized a "show" for me in their quarters in the old red-brick Smithsonian building. Only a handful of the Bureau's staff attended, but that was of little moment. What counted, and counted big, was Stirling's saying, when my "show" was over, that he was interested and would like to see Parsons' full text. On December 16, he acknowledged receipt of the "Parsons material" and, after commenting that it required "a fair amount of editing," he added the magic words, "If it was in shape, I would be happy to publish it as a Bureau Bulletin and to defray all costs of publication other than color plates."

Having seen some of the estimates that Gladys had gotten, I realized how much the Bureau was willing to do. But, in justice to the artist, it seemed important to have some plates in color. However, I agreed with Dr. Stirling that the bulk of the paintings should be reproduced in black and white. Since I was familiar with Isleta and the "Parsons material," I was not surprised when he asked me to put it "in shape." Of course, I said yes, although I knew this would take considerable time and effort, including trips to Washington. But when *Isleta Paintings* finally appeared in print seven long years later, I felt that the greatest gain had been mine. Under both Stirling and Roberts, the staff of the Bureau gave me every support, as did Paul H. Oehser, Chief of the Smithsonian's Editorial and Publication Division, whose office was just down the hall from the BAE. For all of us, *Isleta Paintings* became, in Blackfoot parlance, a "favorite child."

But funds still had to be found for the color plates I thought so necessary. Again I spoke to René. He was delighted with the turn of events and again was ready to help out. In February 1956, he wrote Barrett asking if the Bollingen Foundation would make a grant to the Smithsonian Institution to cover the cost of eight or ten plates. In March, Barrett wrote him that he would be happy to present his request to the Foundation's Board of Trustees at their next meeting in May. To me that seemed a long way off and, believing that two irons in the fire would be better than one, I appealed to the editors of *Life* magazine for help. They used a large format and many of their articles were generously illustrated, some in color. If they gave Isleta paintings a good spread and reproduced some of them in color they might hand over their plates to the Bureau.

When I showed my slides to the young woman who was charged with making the initial decision (she seems to have been an assistant reporter) her response was heartening. Then the unexpected—she asked me to leave my slides with her (some 40 of them) which I most reluctantly did, since I had only one set. But I knew final decisions rested with the higher-ups and, presumably, if pictures were involved, this was normal procedure. Before she was ready to return them at the end of March, she made a much more disturbing request. To do the job right, she claimed, they would need to work from the originals. This meant getting an O.K. from the American Philosophical Society—which, to my surprise, was granted—and making sure that after *Life* was through with them, the Museum of Modern Art would again be willing to house them—which, they assured me, they would do. *Life*'s careful editors had also checked on my *bona fides* with Edward Dozier, then at Northwestern University, who was able to assure them "that pueblo ceremonial life is still very much alive and also extremely integrated and colorful." If the magazine wanted further corroboration on this point, he suggested that they check with John Adair and W. W. Hill, professors at the University of New Mexico—which indeed they did.

Before I went West in the spring of 1956, I was shown a "dummy" of the eleven paintings that had been selected for publication. They were well-arranged on five "*Life*-size" pages. I left New York happy in the thought that we were really moving along. But when I returned in July I found that nothing further had been done, and that, after seven months of endless and time-consuming demands, we were, for all practical purposes, not far from our starting-point. To be sure, there had been no hard—or soft—commitments by me or by *Life*. But this hadn't seemed necessary, since all I wanted was the color plates, and I had reason to believe that, after using them in their spread, they would be willing to give them to the BAE. Over the phone I finally asked my major contact whether *Life* ever intended going beyond the "dummy" stage. As I wrote Dr. Stirling on July 12, she called back to give the answer "almost before I put the phone down." Without preamble, she said, "We have decided to kill it." My reaction was not unexpected. I wrote Stirling, "I blew my top," but, I added, "there wasn't anything she could do from her small spot, even had she wanted to."

I still had one hope. I would appeal to the managing editor, whom I knew. He was genuinely dismayed by my story, but, bureaucracy being what it is in the academic and business worlds, he told me he could not overrule a decision made in another department. A few days later the deputy managing editor wrote me most apologetically. However, he found one plus, "It may be that your inconvenience [!] has served some good purpose in that it will prevent future recurrence of this kind of thing." Perhaps so. Eventually *Life* sent me the transparencies they had made. But my hope regarding their usefulness was soon dashed. The firm that would be doing the color work found they didn't fit the kind of volume the Bureau was contemplating.

Yet there was a happy ending. The Bollingen Foundation made a $3,000 grant for the color plates, payable to the Smithsonian Institution on January 1, 1957. Now we could turn to the remaining and, in my opinion, much more fascinating problems involved in the publication of the "Parsons material."

The first of these problems, I thought, was format. But cost was still the paramount concern. Letters went out to most of the foundations and individuals Gladys and I had approached. The result was the same polite but firm rebuff even when the request was made by Dr. Leonard Carmichael, head of the Smithsonian Institution.

Stirling retired as BAE Chief on December 31, 1957 and Frank H. H. Roberts, Jr. succeeded him. Fortunately Frank was familiar with the paintings (as already noted, he and Stirling had organized the "show" I gave in December 1955). And he was also familiar with negotiations since that unforgettable time. Most important to my mind, he was just as enthusiastic about the paintings and just as determined to get them into print as was Stirling, who had written me two years previously that he would be happy to publish the "Parsons material" as a Bureau Bulletin.

Of course, I knew what a Bureau Bulletin looked like—a normal-sized volume, bound in dull green cloth, the print clear, the margins small. All in all, a completely adequate, if not aesthetically notable, way to present often very complex anthropological data. Whatever my reservations, and I had quite a few, I certainly was not going to rock the boat by voicing them. In fact, as soon as Stirling saw the originals, he himself rejected the Bulletin format and suggested we explore the possibility of putting out a volume like the Smithsonian's Miscellaneous Publications. Together we walked down the hall to sound out Paul Oehser. He proudly showed us John Pope's recently published volume on Chinese art. It was lavishly illustrated, and its generous size immediately recommended it to us.

Paul Oehser was as enthusiastic about the paintings as we were and as eager to get them before the public. But unforeseen complications stymied joint action. In the spring of 1958 responsibility again rested with the Bureau. In October 1959, Frank felt the book was becoming a reality. He wrote me, "Under our present schedule it will probably go to press sometime next spring." In April 1960 he wrote me, "We have decided to use a format similar to that of our old Annual Reports"—which, size-wise, was a great improvement over the Bulletin. But perhaps because, first and foremost, Frank was an archaeologist, he kept on digging in long-forgotten places, and by good luck came up with a geographical report made by Franz Boas and issued by the Bureau in 1893. It had been the beginning—and the end—of a series. Its dimensions, we all agreed, were perfect for our needs, more perfect than the slightly longer and narrower pages of the "old Annual Reports." Not only was the 1893 format the chosen one but the Bureau asked for and was given permission to use non-government printers who "would get better results."

Better or not, the results were eminently satisfactory—this was due in no small part to Mrs. Eloise Edelen, who prepared the final copy for the printers, meticulously read galleys and page proof, and never complained about last-minute changes—most of them mine. Without her and Frank Dobias, the Bureau's authority on matters artistic, and, of course, without Frank Roberts and Paul Oehser, *Isleta Paintings* could not have been the thing of beauty it became.

In a memorandum dated September 1941, Dr. Parsons wrote, "Pictures and Commentary and Introduction in order." After reading her manuscript Dr. Stirling, as already noted, wrote, "If it was in shape I would be happy to publish it." In Parsons' terms, her manuscript was indeed "in order," but in Stirling's it was not—and I agreed with him. Changes could improve readability and design, and it was taken for granted that they would be my responsibility. Additions to the text and footnotes carry my initials. To eliminate repetition and clutter, Parsons' "captions" were included in her explanatory comments. The Isleta glossary she had requested from George L. Traeger of the University of Buffalo was brought into line with his further study of the Tiwa language. Titles of relevant writings published since Parsons' death were inserted in the Bibliography. Her Isleta "Who's Who," which she had planned as a sort of appendix, was temporarily shelved, because I feared that on the basis of internal evidence, any knowledgeable Isletan would be able to determine the identity of the artist, which Parsons had assured him would remain secret. Also ruled out was any reference to his letters, except those included in Parsons' Introduction.

By early 1957 I had written my short Foreword. But what I had done thus far was only a beginning. There followed an extensive correspondence with Mrs. Edelen as proof followed proof. There were frequent discussions with Mr. Dobias regarding types of script, the placement of the paintings and the texts. There were talks with Frank Roberts regarding the appearance of the title page (I had asked that the more abstract Smithsonian seal be used instead of the Bureau's reproduction of an anthropological site, and this Frank agreed to reluctantly, since he had just had the Bureau seal recut. There was my plea for a lively russet instead of the old dull green binding, and this too Frank agreed to. There was Paul Oehser's suggestion that the volume be jacketed, and this again Frank agreed to. In 1960 he asked me if I was willing to be named "editor." My answer is not difficult to guess. *Isleta Paintings* was issued as BAE Bulletin 181. To the Bureau's enduring credit, it is a Bulletin in name only.

THE ARTIST OF "ISLETA PAINTINGS" IN PUEBLO SOCIETY

The reception given *Isleta Paintings* was most gratifying to all of us and, as might be expected, anthropologists familiar with Pueblo society were particularly lavish in their praise. Reviewing it in the *American Anthropologist,* Edward P. Dozier wrote, "*Isleta Paintings* represents the only pictorial ethnographic account of Pueblo ceremonial life executed entirely by a native artist." He continued, "It is unlikely there will ever be another collection quite like it, for Pueblo Indians who are cognizant of esoteric ritual, and who have in addition the talents of artists are rare." In the next sentence he moved from the personal to the social. "Perhaps," he tells us, "most unlikely is the possibility that another native Pueblo artist will have the courage to venture on a project of painting ceremonial activities. Pueblos zealously guard the religious aspect of their culture and the strictures that befall the informer are so stringent that few dare to reveal ceremonial secrets" (1963: 936f.).

Dozier's comments take on unusual significance coming, as they do, from someone who was raised in a Pueblo and who, during his mature life, returned there for weeks at a time with his wife and children.

When *Isleta Paintings* appeared there was much speculation about the artist. Who was he? How had he been able, without being detected and over a period of five years, to paint these many pictures while residing in a village where, except for certain ceremonial secrets, everyone's daily actions were, and probably still are, an open book. In his letter to Parsons dated June 15, 1936, he had written, "It will be all right if you [make them] public some day, but don't you tell who did

this. It [would be] hard for me. I know they will never find out."
During his lifetime "they" never did find out, and Parsons and all of us
who had worked to get his paintings "public" kept the trust. But it was
not long before I learned through the anthropological grapevine that he
had died in 1953 or thereabouts.

Now his name, Joe B. Lente, could be divulged—it would no
longer be "hard" for him, although during his lifetime this had been no
idle fear. An Isleta woman, having seen some of his paintings,
commented, "If they had known he was doing that they would have
killed him." But now Lente was dead, and had been for almost a
decade. As editor of *Isleta Paintings,* I felt it was my duty—both
scientific and artistic—to learn all I could about this highly gifted
Pueblo Indian who had left us such a memorable record of life in his
native village.

The anthropologist who had shown some of Lente's paintings to a
number of Isletans wrote me, "Whatever view informants took of the
artist's personality, his integration into the traditionally socio-
ceremonial organization, or the ethics of his decision to violate the
taboo against recording Pueblo life, they were able to specify only
minor errors in the few examples of his work which they saw." Indeed,
"the very intensity of their reactions seems to guarantee that the
representations were valid." Nor has this judgment ever been
challenged.

Pursuing my goal, I went first to Philadelphia, this time to reread
the Lente-Parsons correspondence in the library of the American
Philosophical Society, and to extract all references to his forebears,
education, places of employment, and religion as well as to his hopes,
his fears, and his work.

The personal data given in Lente's letters to the Bureau and to
Parsons are thin, and I didn't learn much more from other sources. In
his letters he mentions his father, grandfather, two great-uncles, his
mother, and a brother, and that the first two had held high ceremonial
positions. His grandfather had also been a sheriff and one great-uncle
had been a governor of Isleta. His mother, whose age in 1939 he gave as
87 and in 1941 as 98 (an obvious number reversal) owned some land
that he hoped to inherit. Both his mother and father belonged to the
Blue Corn group, as did he.

From time to time Lente farmed on his brother's "place at Isleta."
In his letter dated May 1, 1936, to H. W. Dorsey at the Bureau, he
wrote, "I am an Indian and have no way of making a living, no farm. I
worked at the ATSF Railway Company for about eight years . . . and
left the service on account of my health." A Mr. Young, who lived in
Isleta but has not been further identified, had written the BAE six
months earlier, "This Indian . . . has been educated in our English-

speaking schools," and he enclosed a sample of Lente's paintings with the wish that the Bureau would commission more of them and give him "some monetary consideration for his work."

It was these two letters and two of Lente's paintings (he had submitted six more) that Stirling sent to Parsons on May 15, 1936, thinking she "might be interested." She was. Two days later she wrote Lente offering to pay him $5.00 each "for others equally good." Looking back it seems a strange quirk of memory that Stirling remembered neither the Lente paintings he must have seen in 1935 and 1936 nor his May 1936 letter to Parsons. In fact, he said to me some twenty years later, "If I had written Dr. Parsons about Lente she would have dedicated the manuscript to me instead of Julian Steward." And had Dr. Parsons in taking her unprecedented action also suffered a strange quirk of memory?[36]

Through my anthropological grapevine I also learned that Lente had a sister, that he was a bachelor, that he had worked from time to time as a silversmith in an art shop in Albuquerque, that this art shop had bought some of his paintings, and that, in his later years, he had worked with another anthropologist, this time face to face. In his interviews he had pointed to some incorrect statements in Parsons' *Isleta, New Mexico* (1932), but he never mentioned that, for years, he had sent her paintings, and been paid for them—to be sure, at a very low rate. In his letter of March 29, 1939, he asked for an increase, since they were becoming more complex, both in detail and in the number of persons he was portraying. But he added, "Well, my friend, I will let you set the price of this as you did before." Dr. Parsons ignored this request and Lente did not renew it until February 1, 1941, and apparently with the same result. On March 2, 1941, he wrote, "Thank you very much for my pay $20."

Lente's religious attitude can be described as a straddle. His paintings exhibit many non-Indian features. In the series on death, the cross is conspicuous, but the face of the corpse is painted Indian-style. In the series on Christmas, itself a non-Indian concept, there is dancing in the Church, but the dance patterns are typically Indian, as are the costumes worn by the dancers. The image of the Christ Child, resting on a modern chair framed in leafy branches, is just another stone fetish of the kind the Indians regularly make offerings to in gratitude for past favors and in the hope of more to come.

In Lente's letter of April 14, 1938, he wrote, and this was an often repeated theme, "It is wonderful you are getting the whole secret that no one has ever seen or knows, and that they will never get to see or know until they see your book." And in this same letter he wrote, "I hope to my heavenly father God they [the Isletan priestly hierarchy] will never get me." On November 29, 1939, he wrote, "Merry Xmas to you and happy New Year . . . I will be looking for this mail on the 18 or 19. This will be my Santa Claus money to buy Xmas presents." And in this same letter he wrote, "I hope I won't get burned up for this" [an obvious reference to Hell], and he concluded, "I will go and drink holy water [!] in my clan Water bubbling (Pachiri) blue corn."

It was a sad story I had elected to tell—the story of a talented artist astride two cultures. In neither of them did he find fulfillment. Until his death he remained in the pueblo of his birth, haunted by the knowledge that what he was doing not only transgressed its most valued lifeways but also, if discovered, threatened his very life. The world outside, while offering him a living of sorts—work on a railway, in an art shop, and collaborating with Parsons—gave little hope of a satisfying integration. He remained in his pueblo, a "kindly man" as one anthropologist said, generous in making gifts, particularly to children, and participating, insofar as he was permitted to, in village activities. However inadequate the "monetary consideration" accorded him, his paintings and his letters are witness to his unshakeable integrity. At one point he wrote, "I don't care who it is, he would [not] know how to write about or draw things he didn't see with his own eyes." And then he added, "I cannot draw a picture of war in Poland because I don't know what is going on [there]. If I was there and learned I might, but I cannot do it without seeing. I have to be there a long time before I learn. It's the same here." The more I learned the more certain I was that Lente's story had to be told.

In the spring of 1965, I sent my paper to the *Southwestern Journal of Anthropology,* then to the *American Anthropologist,* and then to *Ethnology.* In each case, the editor found it interesting (which was a comfort), but in each case it was rejected. George P. Murdock, editor of *Ethnology* and my good friend, wrote that the given place for it would be the Smithsonian Miscellaneous Publications. Actually, this had been my original plan, but I jettisoned it in the belief that elsewhere the paper would have a different and, perhaps, more anthropologically oriented audience, and thus would stimulate a further interest in *Isleta Paintings.*

In July I sent my paper to Paul Oehser. I knew that Frank Roberts had retired in 1964 because of illness and that the BAE had been dissolved. But despite these drastic changes, there was still considerable continuity, some of the Bureau's functions having been assumed by the Office of Anthropology—headed by Dick Woodbury, who became a highly valued supporter of *The Artists*—and some by Paul Oehser, who had done so much to make *Isleta Paintings* notable. Except for a change in her letterhead—it was now the Smithsonian Institution—Mrs. Edelen was still smoothing the road to publication.

On October 19, after having submitted my paper to several

readers, Paul wrote me and included their comments. The major problem, surprisingly, was not that I had written too much—but that I had written too little! One reader believed that my paper would fit into the first volume of the newly established *Smithsonian Contributions to Anthropology,* "to be made up of shorter items." A second found it "a fascinating study of a Pueblo Indian in revolt" and one that "constituted valuable documentation for those who are opposed to the still-prevailing view [and this was 1965!] that Pueblo culture is essentially Apollonian." This same reader recommended that I give more background data and ethnographic detail. A third, who also asked for "some introductory material on what Isleta is, what the paintings are, and why the personal life of the artist is of interest," added, "I would urge, beyond this, reprinting many of the letters in full, or as fully as they bear on the subject."

The big questions raised by this last—and most welcome— thought were "how many" and "how." To answer them took months of discussion and experimentation. Finally, in the spring of 1966, a decision was reached. Not parts, not typescripts, not linecuts. Only complete facsimiles of each and every Lente letter. Costly, yes. But in terms of reproduction, it was the method best suited to our purposes (the linecuts were unsatisfactory when Lente's letters were written in pencil, and quite a few of them were). Moreover, having all of them between covers and available in many libraries throughout the country would make it unnecessary for scholars to consult the fragile originals being preserved in Philadelphia. And this, I think, tipped the scales in its favor.

On November 20, I sent my revised manuscript to Paul. Its title now: *About the Artist of "Isleta Paintings" in Pueblo Society* (the *About* was later dropped). At this time, I also suggested that, since Lente was dead, Parsons' "Who's Who in Isleta" could now be safely included in what was no longer being discussed as one paper in a volume "to be made up of shorter items," but as "Whole Volume 5" of the *Smithsonian Contributions to Anthropology.*

In June 1966, Mrs. Edelen retired; Susan Colby was her successor. She was more familiar with *The Artist* than I had expected, and it was not long before she opened a Pandora's box. Parsons had listed the names of all persons mentioned in Lente's letters and paintings. With respect to the first, she had given the dates of relevant letters, with respect to the second the numbers of relevant paintings, and she had also listed relevant page numbers from her 1932 *Isleta, New Mexico.* But she had given no other specifics. And this lack is what led Susan to suggest that Parsons' "Who's Who" would be a much more valuable document if they were added.

Of course, she was right—and, of course, we immediately set to work. Our sleuthing took more time than we had expected and, in addition, it meant retyping Parsons' whole manuscript—a task that fell entirely to Susan, since my typewriter could not cope with the big sheets of paper needed for our new tabulation.

"Troubles" aplenty—but at the bottom of our Pandora's box there was more than "Hope." Parsons' "Who's Who," I knew, had gained much from our efforts. My recognition of Susan's initiative and efficiency was deleted before *The Artist* went to press. No longer was it permissible to thank Smithsonian staff members in print, however deserving they might be.

The Artist of "Isleta Paintings" in Pueblo Society was published in 1967. The following year, it was reviewed by Alfonso Ortiz, then professor of anthropology at Princeton University (Ortiz, 1968: 838f.). Like Ed Dozier, he had been raised in an Indian pueblo—in his case San Juan. Understandably he deplored the thinness of my data, noting that "very little information is given of Lente's early life and even less of the dozen or so years by which he survived Parsons" (838). He was certainly correct. However, at our first meeting some months later, he regretted having asked his "few questions." He should have known, he told me, that in large part my omissions were due not to a lack of inquisitiveness but to the Pueblo mores and attitudes with which he was so familiar. And in his introduction to *New Perspectives on the Pueblos* (1972, XVII), he spells this out in print. But his "few questions" notwithstanding, Ortiz, in his review, recognized that "in Lente we had not only a talented artist but a resourceful and perceptive observer," whose paintings and letters, taken together, "provide rich ethnographic fare" (1968: 839). Here, too, he was certainly correct.

Both editions of *Isleta Paintings* (the second was issued by the Smithsonian Institution Press in 1970) are exhausted, as is *The Artist of "Isleta Paintings" in Pueblo Society*. Frustrating though my field work in Isleta had been, it prepared me to embark on one of the most creative experiences in my anthropological career. The years after these two volumes were published continued to be satisfying, but for me no project would ever again bring with it so much scientific, aesthetic, and personal fulfillment.

13. THAT LONG IS MY AUNT'S BACKBONE

It was in Laguna that, with the support of my "ceremonial father," Franz Boas, I took my first anthropological steps. I find it fitting to end my tale as my Laguna friends, Ko·'tᴵe, Solomon Day, and his wife, Katie, had done so often in 1920 and 1921. While the meaning of this story coda "is still a mystery"—as a linguist who is no stranger to

Pueblo Indian languages wrote me recently—for me, a Keres Indian by adoption (Laguna, like Cochiti, is a Keres-speaking pueblo), it not only marks the end of my tale. It also serves as a useful reminder that there is continuity in an undirected life—even mine. So now I close, as they did, with the words, "That long is my aunt's backbone."

NOTES
Part One

1. All outstanding professors, some members of the Barnard faculty, some "borrowed" from Columbia or willing to open their classes across Broadway to Barnard juniors and seniors.

2. See bibliographer's note in AAA Memoir 61 (1943), 93. See also "Patriotism" in *Race and Democratic Society,* edited by his son, Ernst. New York: J. J. Augustin, 1945: 159-69. Read, according to the editor, on March 7, 1917.

3. "Freedom of Thought," published posthumously and for the first time in *Race and Democratic Society*, pp. 178-84.

4. To mention a few titles: in 1914, "Amerika's Sympathien"; in 1915, "Kinship of Language a Vital Factor in the War," "Will Socialism Help to Overcome Race Antagonisms"; in 1916, "Our National Ideals," "Why German Americans Blame America"; in 1917, "Preserving our Ideals," "Professor Boas Dissents, Blames the President for the Break with Germany"; in 1918, "The Mental Attitude of the Educated Classes"; in 1919, "As an American of German Birth, I Protest." (Given, along with others, in his Bibliography, *AAA Memoirs,* 61).

5. Bureau of American Ethnology, 23rd Annual Report for 1901-1902 (Washington, D.C.: Government Printing Office, 1904) pp. xxxiv f.

6. See her letter of April 24, 1920, below, p. 41.

7. Of interest in this connection is footnote 8, p. 41, in the Ph.D. thesis of Jay Miller, assistant professor at the University of Washington, Seattle. This thesis is entitled "The Anthropology of Keres Identity," and dated January 1972. The note reads, "This is the final vindication of the original contribution of Esther Goldfrank. When she first proposed tri-partite organization of Cochiti, she was criticized for it. Elsie Clews Parsons . . . who sponsored Goldfrank's work, thought she had exaggerated what was only a tendency at Cochiti. Lange . . . duplicated Goldfrank's finding.

8. Margaret Lewis, a Cherokee married to a Zuni. See Parsons, 1939, and Pandey, 1972.

9. In her letter Dr. Parsons called him by his Spanish name. As she did in her *Isleta, New Mexico* (1932), I employ here and elsewhere the pseudonym she chose for him.

10. I have not reproduced the page of ethnological comment that Dr. Parsons included in this letter.

11. All citations from Benedict's journal are taken from Mead, 1959a. No changes have been made either in punctuation or capitalization.

12. The several pseudonyms Benedict used—Ruth Stanhope and Edgar Stanhope (the Stan was the first part of her husband's first name) and somewhat later, Anne Singleton—suggest her search for another identity, and her refusal after her marriage to include her maiden name, "Fulton," added importance to the masculine implications of "Benedict." In fact, as early as 1912 she wrote in her diary, "To me it seems a terrible thing to be a woman (Mead, 1959a: 120). Edward Sapir's reaction to her pleasure in the "charm of concealment" was expressed very definitely in his letter to her on March 23, 1926. "Pen names," he wrote her, "are an abomination. You know how I feel about even toying with the idea of dissociation of personality I hate it. Lie outright if you have to, but for God's sake

222

don't stylize the lie into a petty institution" (Mead, 1959a: 182f.). And in his letter to her on February 7, 1925, while he was trying to get some of her writings published, he wrote: "By the way, what shall I use instead of 'R.F.B.' to which you object?" Enough here to more than suggest a deeply felt sexual ambivalence.

13. *Go* is a Japanese name for a game similar to Chinese checkers. *Bang* means "board." Apparently it became customary in the West to call the game *go-bang* (See Encyclopedia Britannica, 11th ed., 1911, p. 159 c). It is difficult not to believe that the name of this game and its frequent repetition in her 1923 diary served as an outlet (mask, if you will) for her very ambivalent attitude toward married life.

14. In this connection the following story is of interest. I heard it third hand from a colleague at the AAA meetings in Seattle in November 1968. Benedict, so the story goes, was so irked because her husband always beat her at chess that she went to a nearby library (probably in Bedford Hills or its environs) and asked for all the books they had on this game. These she studied assiduously and shortly was rewarded by being able to beat him regularly.

15. Victor Barnouw made this point in his unusually insightful discussion of Benedict's work and personality, "Ruth Benedict: Apollonian and Dionysian," in the University of Toronto Quarterly (XVIII, No. 3, April 1949). Benedict (1922) does quote from Haeberlin's MS on Puget Sound, but only for a single detail (cf. Mead, 1959a: 18, 529, n. 1).

16. See their letters to me from Portland, Oregon, August 7, 1922, below pp. 90 f.

17. I use no pseudonyms for my Laguna acquaintances or informants, since the names they are known by are given in publications by Dr. Boas, Dr. Parsons, and me in the 1920s.

18. Lévi-Strauss (1970) obviously felt differently on this matter.

19. It is interesting to remember the Indians' impressive use of the fungus that is now the basis of penicillin.

20. These letters have been edited slightly, mainly for punctuation and capitalization.

21. Taken by me of Carl Leon after his participation in the Comanche dance (see below, p.   ).

22. I did, and Carl made me Laguna-style moccasins of deerskin. I wore them so much that they soon needed cleaning and, because of the soles, not even Leathercraft would undertake the task. In desperation I wrote Carl and he sent me a packet of the hardened gray clay the Indians use for this purpose. It was most effective. The moccasins were his part in the traditional Indian gift exchange. My contribution had been a small check.

23. In his last letter in his own hand (see below), he wrote "1963."

24. See his letter of March 10, 1923, and my note.

25. I have described this day's activities in "Notes on Two Pueblo Feasts" (1923), which was used for comparison and time depth by Vogt (1955: 820-39).

26. In looking over my snapshots, it seems clear that the rowboat was used in years when the river was high. (I think a small fee was charged for the ride.) When the river was low, as it no doubt was in the fall of 1925 when Benedict was there, crossing by horse and cart was the norm. In fact, I heard from an informant in July 1922 that "the Indians are not rowing the boat any more because they can ford." And six years later I was told, "We have a new bridge, so all cars can cross now."

27. I use no pseudonym in referring to John Dixon, since, in *Keresan Texts,* Dr. Boas refers to him as one of his major informants. However, for other Cochiti Indians I do use pseudonyms, since my data are sometimes personal.

28. Boas (1928: 290) writes "I did not learn anything about a naihiya"—and he refers his readers to my *Social and Ceremonial Organization.* . . . Professor Jay ·Miller (1972) suggests that in earlier times the nahia ranked above both the cacique and the war chief and was, in fact, the official who coordinated the activities of a number of Keres pueblos.

29. In *Tales of the Cochiti Indians,* Benedict dates their collection in 1924, but her letters show that while she might have visited Cochiti briefly in that year, her major work there was done in 1925. Her letter of September 1, 1925 indicates that she had no contacts in the previous year of the kind she describes in her Preface, p. ix.

30. This may be as good a place as any to correct a misprint in both the first and second editions of *Isleta Paintings.* On p. 206 of the first edition and p. 111 of the second, the sentence beginning "Lummis, who died in 1891" should read "Lummis, who did in 1891." Lummis did not die until after the turn of the century. Just the difference of one letter, but here a most significant one.

31. Dr. M. Estellie Smith has in recent years been making an intensive investigation of government and governing in Isleta. I have given her a copy of my notes, which constitute one base line for evaluating the numerous changes in more than 40 years.

Part Two

1. In 1971 when I lunched with Jeannette she claimed that she had been staff anthropologist as early as 1935, and she couldn't remember ever seeing Opler at any of the seminars. Obviously, memory has played one of us false.

2. Her important book *To the North: The Story of Arctic Exploration from Earliest Times to the Present* was published in 1934 with an introduction by Vilhjalmur Stefansson.

3. In 1926, Benedict wrote Mead, "You'd like him [Malinowski] a lot. He has the quick imagination and the by-play of mind that makes him a seven day's joy. . . ." (Mead, 1959a: 305)

4. For a much modified view, see Kardiner and Preble, 1965.

5. Benedict speaks of "Thursday" lunches. The day may well have been changed since the early 20s. (See Mead, 1959a: 57)

6. See note under Boas in Bibliography.

7. This was one volume in the Fund for the Republic series on Communism in American Life, under the general editorship of Professor Clinton Rossiter of Cornell University.

8. Dr. Boas was invited to deliver this keynote speech by Jerome Davis, who was then running for president of the A.F.T. (Iverson, 1959: 115)

9. It is of interest that twenty years earlier and also in a politically charged atmosphere, Dr. Boas found intellectual freedom a highly congenial issue on which to base his attack on U.S. policy. (See Boas, 1945: 192f., 196f.)

10. Hearings on the Institute of Pacific Relations before the Subcommittee to Investigate the Administration of the Internal Security Act and other Internal Security Laws of the Committee on the Judiciary of the United States Senate, August 7, 1951 (1: p. 312). For clarification regarding the locale of this study group, see report of the above Subcommittee, December 31, 1957. (Sect. 7: p. 106, n. 9)

11. Snow, 1940: 277f. For the Communist attitude toward England after the signing of the Stalin-Hitler Pact, see Howe and Coser, 1962: 389f.; for the

Communist attitude toward civil liberties, ibid., p. 400.

12. For one documented example, see Boas' international broadcast made over NBC on September 7, 1941. (Boas, 1945: 1)

13. Kroeber (1943a: 5) gives December 21 as the date of Boas' death.

14. Virtually all the data included in this chapter have been taken from my field notes, some of which were incorporated in a number of articles and, most extensively, in *Changing Configurations in the Social Organization of a Blackfoot Tribe during the Reserve Period (The Blood of Alberta, Canada)*, American Ethnological Society, Monograph VIII. (Goldfrank, 1945c)

15. Ultimately, the six-year-old, though still unappeased, consented to the old man's taking his original position, while he hugged my side, his left arm possessively entwined with my right.

16. In 1931 polygamy was legally outlawed, but we knew of one old man who still boasted two wives. In a family picture taken during our stay and reflecting marital priorities, the first wife is standing to the left of her husband, the second to the left of the first wife.

17. These cards are still in my possession, and any interested scholar may consult them. In the spring of 1972, Margaret Mead sent me some notes made by Ruth Benedict along with a paper on adoption written by Marjorie shortly after her return to New York but never published. I submitted it to the *Plains Anthropologist* with an introductory statement by me. It appeared in the spring of 1974. Marjorie, it seems, dropped out of anthropology in the early 1940s.

18. Recently Harry told me that his notebooks had been removed inadvertently from his office desk while he was away for some time, and he has not been able to locate them.

19. See letter, p. 143.

20. In 1939 I had neither the desire nor the time to engage in a detailed study of Blood societies, dance associations, bundles, or esoteric features of the Sun Dance and related ceremonials. Fortunately, I had at my disposal the numerous monographs published some thirty years earlier by Clark Wissler, long-time Head Curator of Anthropology at the American Museum of Natural History in New York City. Although his main efforts were directed toward the study of the Southern Piegan on the Blackfoot Reservation in the U.S., the similarities were many and striking between their customs and what I learned from my informants and saw directly. Supplementary information relating to the Blood was given me informally by Harry Biele and Marjorie Lismer. In addition I read extensively in the *Sessional Papers of the Dominion of Canada* and in journals of early explorers and traders. (See Goldfrank, 1945c for specific titles.)

21. I kept no diary of our daily activities, so I am unable to document precisely on just which days the ceremonies we witnessed occurred. Wissler has commented on the differences in accounts of the order and details of Sun Dance ceremonials, not only on the U.S. Blackfoot reservation but also among the Blood. (Cf. Wissler, 1918: 230n, 231n.)

22. For an excellent account given by a Blood woman on "The Horns," with additional comments, see Wissler, 1913: 410-18.

23. Wissler, 1912: 415, describes this part of the transfer in Latin.

24. This year and it seems for many years, "The Torture Ceremony," as Wissler refers to it (1918: 262-67), was prohibited in both the U.S. and Canada. It involved the insertion of skewers (after the required incisions had been made by medicine men) in the breasts of young males about to participate and obviously bent on proving their courage and endurance.

The skewers were attached to ropes fastened to the top of the tipi's center pole. A further deep incision was made in the back of each entrant, and a wooden stick was inserted on which a buffalo skull or heavy ball was hung, inevitably increasing the agony of the experience. Through violent gyrations either on the ground or suspended several feet above it and with the ropes pulled taut, the young men struggled until the skewers were freed. Not all succeeded in completing this bloody test; some fainted, some withdrew. But those who achieved their sacrificial aim offered their mutilated flesh to the Sun. At times, the group resorted to "capture" in order to assure an adequate number of "volunteers." In his account of "The Torture Ceremony," Wissler includes a report made by John McLean, who witnessed it among the Blood in 1888. Cf. also McCracken, 1959: 104-10, for a discussion of this ceremony and reproductions of Catlin's pictures of its gruesome reality.

25. Some months before her father's death and due to his illness, the family had gone to live on her maternal grandfather's farm. (Mead, 1959a: 97)

26. This passage is introduced by the statement, "The second running-away I remember added a codicil to my rule of life, and it was a codicil I phrased explicitly before I phrased the main proposition." (Mead, 1959a: 102)

27. In a pencilled memo quite similar to this one and included in the papers Mead sent me in 1972, Ruth had listed a chapter to be written by "Esther Wittfogel."

28. In his Introduction to the second edition, Devereux goes to considerable lengths to clarify his use of this term (which he found had often been misunderstood by his readers) and to emphasize its differences from cross-cultural psychiatry and psychotherapy (cf. Devereux, 1969: xxiv f.). Devereux noted that "in 1968, this book continues to be what it was in 1951: the only complete published account of any psychotherapy." (1969: xxvi ff.)

29. In August 1964, at the International Congress of Anthropological and Ethnographic Sciences, held in Moscow, White sat on the dais in the Great Hall of the University during the two-day symposium on Lewis H. Morgan. Helen Constas, who was scheduled to read her paper "Lewis H. Morgan in the Light of Anthropological Theory" at the first session of this symposium, was told by the chairman, the Soviet professor D. A. Olderogge, just minutes before the symposium started, that she would not be permitted to read her short final section on "Morgan and Marx." When she reached it, she was summarily stopped by the Chairman on the grounds that she had used up her allotted time. No such stricture was invoked against White when the paper he had presented earlier had run more than 20 minutes beyond his allotted time. (See Constas, in press.)

30. In my article I also used this spelling, but in these *Notes* I have substituted a "j" for the "h" in line with current usage. In citations from this article the original spelling is retained.

31. In 1953, speaking at the day-long symposium on the Southwest held during the Annual Meeting of the AAA in Tucson, Kluckhohn called this paper "notable." (AA, 1954: 690)

32. Bunzel's spelling; I retain it when quoting from her.

33. I wish to thank Mr. Ulmen for permitting me to cite Steward's letter to him in full and to quote from his paper. The *Festschrift,* under the title *Society and History,* and a companion volume by Mr. Ulmen, *The Science of Society: Toward an Understanding of the Life and Work of Karl August Wittfogel,* both being published by Mouton & Co., the Hague, are expected to appear in 1978.

34. Cf. Cohn and Platzner, 1978, pp. 114 ff.

35. Some years later this restriction was officially lifted.

36. Not until after *Isleta Paintings* was published did I learn that Stirling, and not Julian Steward, had written Parsons about Lente.

BIBLIOGRAPHY

Adair, John
1947   "The Navaho and Pueblo Veteran." *The American Indian,* IV, i, 5-11. Association for American Indian Affairs.

Adams, E. B., and Fray Angelico Chavez
1956   *The Missions of New Mexico, 1776.* See Lange, 1959, p. 11.

American Anthropological Association
1920   Report of December 1919 meeting. *American Anthropologist,* NS, 1920, 22, 1:93ff.
1921   Report of December 1920 meeting. *American Anthropologist,* NS, 1921, 23, 1:102ff.
1923   Report of December 1922 meeting. *American Anthropologist,* NS 1923, 25, 1:117ff.
1940   Report of December 1939 meeting. *American Anthropologist,* NS, 1940, 42, 2:311ff.
1942   Report of December 1941 meeting. *American Anthropologist,* NS, 1942, 44, 2:281ff.
1977   Program, AAA meeting. Houston, Texas.

Associated Students, University of Washington
1966   Course Critique, University of Washington, Seattle.

Bandelier, Adolph F.
1880   Journal for October 24, 1880. See Lange, 1959, p. 14.

Barnouw, Victor
1949   "Ruth Benedict: Apollonian and Dionysian," *University of Toronto Quarterly,* XVIII, 3 (April).

Bell, Daniel
1952   "Marxian Socialism in the United States," *Socialism and American Life,* I, Donald Drew Egbert and Stow Persons, eds. Princeton: Princeton University Press.

Benavides, Fray Alonso de
1916   *The Memorial of Fray Alonso de Benavides, 1630.* Trans. Mrs. Edward E. Ayer. Chicago.

Benedict, Ruth
1922   "The Vision in Plains Culture," *American Anthropologist,* XXIV, 1:1-23.
1923   "The Concept of the Guardian Spirit in North America." *Memoir of the AAA,* 29:1-97.
1930   "Psychological Types in the Cultures of the Southwest." *Proceedings of the 23rd International Congress of Americanists,* New York, pp. 572-81.
1931   *Tales of the Cochiti Indians.* Bureau of American Ethnology, Bulletin 98. Washington, D.C.: Smithsonian Institution.
1934   *Patterns of Culture.* Boston and New York: Houghton Mifflin.
1935   *Zuni Mythology,* I and II. Contributions to Anthropology, 21. New York: Columbia University Press.

Bennett, J. W.
1946   "The Interpretation of Pueblo Culture: A Question of Values." *Southwestern Journal of Anthropology* 2, 4:361-74.

Blos, P.
1941   *The Adolescent Personality: A Study of Individual Behavior.* Foreword by Caroline Zachry. New York: Appleton-Century.

Boas, Franz
       Complete references for articles and speeches of Franz Boas, mentioned only by title in text, can be found in the bibliography included in *Franz Boas 1858-1942. AAA Memoir*, 61, pt. 2:67-109.
1911   *Introduction to the Handbook of American Indian Languages.* Bureau of American Ethnology, Bulletin 40, pt. 1. Washington, D.C.: Smithsonian Institution.
1919   "Scientists as Spies." Letter to the Editor, *The Nation*, 109, 2842:797.
1928   *Keresan Texts*, VIII, pt. I. New York: The American Ethnological Society.
1938   "An Anthropologist's Credo." *The Nation*, 147:201-04.
1939   "Intellectual Freedom." *The New Masses*, 30:8-17.
1940   "Racial Purity." *Asia Magazine*, 5:40, 231-34.
1941   "Greetings to the Soviet Union," *Embassy of the Soviet Socialist Republics Information Bulletin*, Special Supplement, November 7, p. 16.
1943   "What Are We Going to Do With Germany?" *PM*, January 4.
1945   *Race and Democratic Society.* Ed. Ernst Boas. New York: J. J. Augustin.

Braidwood, Linda, and Robert J. Braidwood
1949   "On the Treatment of the Pre-historic Near Eastern Materials in Steward's 'Cultural Causality and Law'." *American Anthropologist*, 51, 4, pt. 1:665-69.

Bunzel, Ruth L.
1929   *The Pueblo Potter: A Study of Creative Imagination in Primitive Art.* New York: Columbia University Press, pp. 1-134.
1932a "Introduction to Zuni Ceremonialism." 47th Annual Report of the Bureau of American Ethnology. Washington, D.C.: Smithsonian Institution, pp. 467-544.
1932b "Zuni Ritual Poetry." 47th Annual Report of the Bureau of American Ethnology. Washington, D.C.: Smithsonian Institution. 611-835.
1933   *Zuni Texts*, XV. New York: American Ethnological Society.
1959   See Margaret Mead, 1959b, pp. 33-35.

Catlin, G.
1841   *Illustrations of the Manners, Customs and Conditions of North American Indians.* London: Henry G. Bohn. (See McCracken.)

Cohn, Michael, and Michael K. H. Platzer
1978   *Black Men of the Sea*, New York: Dodd, Mead.

Collier, Malcolm
1946   "Leadership at Navajo Mountain and Klagetoh." *American Anthropologist*, 48, 137f

Committee for the Study of Adolescents
1938   Revision. No author. Rockefeller Foundation.

Constas, Helen
1978   "Lewis H. Morgan: In the Light of Anthropological Theory." In *Society and History: Essays in Honor of Karl August Wittfogel.* Ed. G. L. Ulmen. The Hague, Paris and New York: Mouton.

Coser, Rose Laub
1964   Ed. *The Family: Its Structure and Functions.* New York: St. Martin's Press.

Cushing, Frank H.
1882-   "My Adventures in Zuni, I." *Century Magazine*, NS, 3 and 4.
1883a

1882-   "My Adventures in Zuni, III." *Century Magazine*, NS, 3 and 4.
1883b

Deloria, Ella
1932   *Dakota Texts*, XIV. New York: G. E. Stechert.

Devereux, George
1951   *Reality and Dream.* New York: International Universities Press. 2nd ed. 1969. New York: Doubleday.

Dozier, Edward P.
1961   "The Rio Grande Pueblos." *Perspectives in American Indian Culture Change.* Ed. E.H. Spicer. Chicago: University Press.
1963   Review of Elsie Clews Parsons, *Isleta Paintings. American Anthropologist*, 65, 4:936ff.
1970   *The Pueblo Indians of North America.* New York: Holt, Rinehart and Winston.

Dumarest, Noel
1919   "Notes on Cochiti, New Mexico." Ed. Elsie Clews Parsons. *AAA Memoir*, VI, 3.

Eggan, Dorothy
1943   "The General Problem of Hopi Adjustment." *American Anthropologist*, 45, 3, pt. 1.

Eggan, Fred
1950   *Social Organization of the Western Pueblos.* Chicago: University of Chicago Press.

Engels, Frederick
1951   "Origin of the Family, Private Property, and the State." (1884) In *Karl Marx and Frederick Engels*, 2 vols. Moscow: Foreign Languages Publication House. 155ff.

Erikson, Erik H.
1939   "Observations on Sioux Education." *Journal of Psychology*, 7:101-56.
1950   *Childhood and Society.* New York: W. W. Norton.

Fort Laramie Treaty
1851   United States Government Report. Department of Indian Affairs.

Fox, Robin
1967   *The Keresan Bridge: A Problem in Pueblo Ethnology.* London School of Economics, Monographs on Social Anthropology, 35. New York: Humanities Press.

French, David H.
1948   *Factionalism in Isleta Pueblo.* American Ethnological Society, Monograph XIV. New York: J. J. Augustin.

Fried, Morton H.
1967   *The Evolution of Political Society, An Essay in Political Anthropology.* New York: Random House.
1968   Ed. *Readings in Anthropology.* 2nd ed. Vol. 2. *Readings in Cultural Anthropology,* New York: Thomas Y. Crowell.

Goldfrank, Esther S.
1923   "Notes on Two Pueblo Feasts." *American Anthropologist,* 25, 2:188-96.
1926   "Isleta Variants: A Study in Flexibility." *Journal of American Folklore,* 39:71-8.
1927   "The Social and Ceremonial Organization of Cochiti." *AAA Memoir,* 33.
1937   *Culture Takes a Holiday.* Profile of Ellery Sedgwick. Unpublished.
1943a   "Historic Change and Social Character: A Study of the Teton Dakota." *American Anthropologist,* 45, 1:67-83.
1943b   "Some Aspects of Pueblo Mythology and Society," Wittfogel and Goldfrank, below.
1943c   Review of Leslie A. White, "The Pueblo of Santa Ana." *Journal of American Folklore,* 56, 221:234f.
1943d   "Administrative Programs and Changes in Blood Society in the Reserve Period." *Applied Anthropology,* 2, 2:18-24.
1945a   "Irrigation Agriculture and Navaho Community Leadership: Case Material on Environment and Culture." *American Anthropologist,* 47, 2:262-77.
1945b   "Socialization, Personality, and the Structure of Pueblo Society." *American Anthropologist,* 47, 4:516-37.
1945c   *Changing Configurations in the Social Organization of a Blackfoot Tribe During the Reserve Period.* American Ethnological Society, Monograph VIII. New York: J. J. Augustin.
1946a   "More about Irrigation Agriculture and Navaho Community Leadership." *American Anthropologist,* 48, 3:473-82.
1946b   "Linguistic Note to Zuni Ethnology." *Word,* 2, 3:191-96.
1948   "The Impact of Situation and Personality on Four Hopi Emergence Myths." *Southwestern Journal of Anthropology,* 4, 3:241-62.
1949   Presidential Report at Annual Meeting of the American Ethnological Society, December 30, 1948. *American Anthropologist,* 51, 2:371ff.
1951a   "Observations on Sexuality among the Blood Indians of Alberta, Canada." *Psychoanalysis and the Social Sciences,* III. Ed. Géza Roheim. New York: International Universities Press, 71-98.
1951b   " 'Old Man' and the Father Image in Blood (Blackfoot) Society." Ed. George B. Wilbur and Warner Muensterberger. In *Psychoanalysis and Culture.* New York: International Universities Press, 132-41.

1952   "The Different Patterns of Blackfoot and Pueblo Adaptation to White Authority." In *Acculturation in the Americas*, 29th International Congress of Americanists. Ed. Sol Tax. Chicago: University of Chicago Press. 74-79.

1954a   Discussant of Ruth Underhill's Paper "Intercultural Relations in the Greater Southwest." *American Anthropologist*, 56, 3:658-62.

1954b   "Notes on Deer-Hunting Practices at Laguna Pueblo, New Mexico." *Texas Journal of Science*, 6, 4:407-21.

1955   "Native Paintings of Isleta Pueblo, New Mexico." *Transactions of the New York Academy of Sciences*, Ser. II, 18, 2:178-80.

1962   Ed. *Isleta Paintings*. Introduction and Commentary by Elsie Clews Parsons, Bureau of American Ethnology, Bulletin 181. Washington, D.C.: Smithsonian Institution, Smithsonian Press. 2nd ed. 1970.

1964   Review of Leslie A. White, "The Pueblo of Sia." *American Anthropologist*, 66, 3, pt. 1, 68ff.

1967   *The Artist of "Isleta Paintings" in Pueblo Society*. Smithsonian Contributions to Anthropology, 5. Washington, D.C.: Smithsonian Institution.

1974   Introduction to Marjorie Lismer: "Adoption Practices of the Blood Indians of Alberta, Canada." *Plains Anthropologist*, 1, 2:19-63.

Goldschmidt, Walter
1959   Ed. *The Anthropology of Franz Boas*. AAA Memoir, 89.

Haeberlin, Herman K.
1916   "The Idea of Fertilization in the Culture of the Pueblo Indians." *AAA Memoir*, III, 1.

Hanks, L. M.
1954   "Psychological Exploration in the Blackfoot Language." *International Journal of American Linguistics*, 20:195-205.

Hanks, L. M., and Jane Richardson
1942   "Water-Discipline and Water Imagery among the Blackfoot." *American Anthropologist*, NS, 44:331-33.

1945   *Observations on Northern Blackfoot Kinship*. American Ethnological Society, Monograph IX. 1-31.

1950   *Tribes under Trust*. Toronto.

Haring, Douglas G.
1956   Ed. *Personal Character and Cultural Milieu*, 3rd ed. Syracuse: Syracuse University Press.

Harris, Marvin
1968   *The Rise of Anthropological Theory: A History of Theories of Culture*. New York: Thomas Y. Crowell.

1977   *Cannibals and Kings*. New York: Random House.

Harvey, Byron, III
1972   "An Overview of Pueblo Religion." In *New Perspectives on the Pueblos*. Ed. Alfonso Ortiz. New Mexico: School of American Research Books. 197-213.

Haury, Emil W.
1956   "Speculations on Prehistoric Settlement Patterns in the Southwest." In *Prehistoric Settlement Patterns in the New World.* Ed. G. Willey. Viking Fund Publications in Anthropology, No. 23:3-10.

1976   *The Hohokam.* Tucson: University of Arizona Press.

Henry, Alexander, and David Thompson
1897   *Journals,* II. Ed. E. Couse. New York.

Herskovits, Melville J.
1943   "Franz Boas as Physical Anthropologist." In *Franz Boas, 1858-1942. AAA Memoir,* 61. Ed. Ralph Linton.
1953   *Franz Boas: The Science of Man in the Making.* New York: Scribners.

Hoebel, E. Adamson
1954   "Southwestern Studies in Anthropological Theory." *American Anthropologist,* 56, 3:720-27.

Howe, Irving, and Lewis Coser
1962   *The American Communist Party.* New York: Frederick A. Praeger.

Iversen, Robert W.
1959   *The Communists and the Schools.* Gen. ed. Clinton Rossiter. New York: Harcourt, Brace and World.

Kardiner, Abram
1939   *The Individual and His Society: The Psychodynamics of Primitive Social Organization.* New York: Columbia University Press.

Kardiner, Abram, and Edward Preble
1965   *They Studied Man.* Cleveland and New York: World.

Kluckhohn, Clyde
1954   "Southwestern Studies of Culture and Personality," *American Anthropologist,* 56:685-708.

Kroeber, Alfred L.
1939   *Cultural and Natural Areas of Native North America.* University of California Publications in American Archaeology and Ethnology. Berkeley: University of California Press.
1943a   "Franz Boas, The Man." *AAA Memoir,* 61.
1943b   "Elsie Clews Parsons." *American Anthropologist,* NS, 45, 2:252-55.

Lange, Charles H.
1959   *Cochiti: A New Mexico Pueblo, Past and Present.* Austin, Texas: University of Texas Press.

Leap, William L.
1969   *Compartmentalization vs Ceremonial Synthesis at Isleta Pueblo, New Mexico.* Unpublished.

232

Leighton, Dorothea, and Clyde Kluckhohn
1947   *Children of the People.* Cambridge, Mass.: Harvard University Press.

Lévi-Strauss, Claude
1970   *The Raw and the Cooked: Introduction to a Science of Mythology.* New York: Harper and Row.

Lewis, Oscar
1941   "Manly Hearted Women among the North Piegan." *American Anthropologist*, 43, 2, pt. 2, 173-88.
1942   *The Effects of White Contact upon Blackfoot Culture, with Special Reference to the Role of the Fur Trade.* American Ethnological Society, Monograph VI.

Li, An-che
1937   "Zuni: Some Observations and Queries." *American Anthropologist*, NS, 39:62-76.

Linton, Ralph
1936   *The Study of Man.* New York: Appleton-Century.
1939   Foreword and "The Tanala of Madagascar," in Kardiner, 1939.
1943   Ed. *Franz Boas 1858-1942. AAA Menoir*, 61.
1944   "Nomad Raids and Fortified Pueblos." *American Antiquity*, 28-32.

Lismer, Marjorie
1939   Census Cards, Blood Indian Reservation, Alberta, Canada, Summer. Unpublished.
1974   *Adoption Practices of the Blood Indians of Alberta, Canada.* Introduction by Esther S. Goldfrank. *Plains Anthropologist*, 19, 63:25-33.

Lowie, Robert H.
1944   "Franz Boas (1858-1942)." *Journal of American Folklore*, 57: 59.

Lummis, Charles
1897   *The Land of Poco Tiempo.* Albuquerque: University of New Mexico Press.

Macgregor, Gordon
1946   *Warriors without Weapons: A Study of the Society and Personality Development of the Pine Ridge Sioux.* With the collaboration of R. B. Hassrick and W. E. Henry. Chicago: University of Chicago Press.

Mandelbaum, David G.
1949   Ed. *Selected Writings of Edward Sapir.* Berkeley and Los Angeles: University of California Press.

Manners, Robert A.
1964   Ed. *Process and Pattern in Culture: Essays in Honor of Julian H. Steward.* Chicago: Aldine.
1973   Obituary of J. H. Steward. *American Anthropologist*, 3:886-98.

Maximilian, Prince of Weid-Neuwid
1843   *Travels in the Interior of North America, in the years 1832-1833 and 1834.*

McCracken, Henry
1959   *George Catlin and the Old Frontier.* New York: Dial.

Mead, Margaret
1959a   *An Anthropologist at Work: Writings of Ruth Benedict.* Boston: Houghton Mifflin.
1959b   "Apprenticeship under Boas." In *The Anthropology of Franz Boas, AAA Memoirs*, 89.

Mekeel, A. Scudder
1936   *The Economy of a Modern Teton Dakota Community.* Yale University Publications in Anthropology. New Haven: Yale University Press.

Mishkin, Bernard
1940   *Rank and Warfare among the Plains Indians.* American Ethnological Society, Monograph III. 1-66.

Miller, Jay
1972   *The Anthropology of Keres Identity.* Rutgers University. Unpublished.

Mirsky, Jeannette
1934   *To the North: The Story of Arctic Exploration from Earliest Times to the Present.* New York: Viking.
1937a   "The Dakota," *In Cooperation and Competition among Primitive Peoples.* Ed. Margaret Mead. New York: McGraw-Hill.
1937b   Report on Fieldston School. Assisted by Esther S. Goldfrank. Unpublished.

Mitchell, William P.
1976   "Irrigation and Community in the Peruvian Highlands." *American Anthropologist*, 78:25-44.

Morgan, Lewis Henry
1871   "Systems of Consanguinity and Affinity." *Smithsonian Contributions to Knowledge*, XVII. 291-382.
1877   *Ancient Society.* New York.
1959   *Indian Journals*, 1859-1862. Ann Arbor: University of Michigan Press.

Murdoch, George P.
1959   Review of Karl A. Wittfogel, *Oriental Despotism: A Comparative Study of Total Power. American Anthropologist*, 59, pt. 3: 545f.

Ortiz, Alfonso
1968   Review of Esther S. Goldfrank, *The Artist of "Isleta Paintings" in Pueblo Society. American Anthropologist*, 70:838-9.
1969   *The Tewa World: Space, Time, Being, and Becoming in a Pueblo Society.* Chicago: University of Chicago Press.

Palerm, Angel
1955   "The Agricultural Basis of Urban Civilization in Meso-America." *Irrigation Civilizations: A Comparative Study.* Ed. J. H. Steward, Social Science Monographs, No. 1. Washington, D.C.: Pan-American Union.

Pandey, Triloki-Nath
1972   "Anthropologists at Zuni." *Proceedings of the American Philosophical Society*, 116, 4.

Parsons, Elsie Clews
1906   *The Family.* New York.
1913   *The Old-Fashioned Woman.* New York.
1915   *Social Freedom.* New York: Knickerbocker Press.
1916a   "Zuni Inoculative Magic." *Science*, NS, XLIV, 1135:469-70.
1916b   "The Zuni Adoshle and Suuke." *American Anthropologist*, XVIII:338-47.
1918   "Notes on Acoma and Laguna." *American Anthropologist*, XX:162-86.
1920a   "Notes on Isleta, Santa Ana, and Acoma." *American Anthropologist*, XXII:156-69.
1920b   "Notes on Ceremonialism at Laguna." *The Anthropological Papers of the American Museum of Natural History*, XIX, pt. IV.
1921   "Further Notes on Isleta." *American Anthropologist*, XXIII:149-69.
1923a   "Laguna Genealogies." *The Anthropological Papers of the American Museum of Natural History*, XIX, pt. V. New York.
1923b   "The Origin Myth of Zuni." *Journal of American Folklore*, XXXVI.
1932   *Isleta, New Mexico.* 47th Annual Report, Bureau of American Ethnology. Washington, D.C.: Smithsonian Institution.
1939   *Pueblo Indian Religion.* 2 vols. Chicago: University of Chicago Press.
1962   *Isleta Paintings.* Ed. Esther S. Goldfrank. Bureau of American Ethnology, Bulletin 181. 2nd ed. 1970. Washington, D.C.: Smithsonian Institution Press.

Price, Barbara J.
1971   "Prehistoric Irrigation Agriculture in Nuclear America." *American Research Review*, VI, 3:3-60.
    See also below: Sanders, William, and Barbara Price

Reichard, Gladys A.
1943   "Elsie Clews Parsons." *Journal of American Folklore*, 36, 219:45-48.
1950   "The Elsie Clews Parsons Collection." *Proceedings of the American Philosophical Society*, 94. 3:308f.

Roheim, Géza
1951   Ed. *Psychoanalysis and the Social Sciences*, 3. New York: International Universities Press.

Rorschach, Hermann
    See Sicha, below.

Sanders, William T., and Barabara Price
1968   *Mesoamerica: The Evolution of a Civilization.* New York: Random House.

Sapir, Edward
1949   "Central and North American Languages." *Selected Writings of Edward Sapir.* Ed. D. G. Mandelbaum. Berkeley and Los Angeles: University of California Press.

Sessional Papers of The Dominion of Canada
1896   10, 14:272ff.

Sicha, Karel and Mary
n.d.   Translation of Hermann Rorschach, *Psychodynamics*.

Simmons, Leo W.
1942   Ed. *Sun Chief, The Autobiography of a Hopi Indian*. New Haven: Yale University Press.

Smith, M. Estellie
n.d.   *Governing in Isleta*. Unpublished.

Smith, Watson
1952   "Kiva Mural Decorations at Awatovi and Kawaika-a." Reports of the Awatovi Expedition, 5. *Papers of the Peabody Museum of American Archaeology and Ethnology, XXXVII*. Cambridge, Mass.: Harvard University Press.

Snow, Edgar
1940   "Interviews with Mao Tse-Tung." *China Weekly Review*, 91:277ff.

Spier, Leslie
1943   "Elsie Clews Parsons." *American Anthropologist*, NS, 45, 2:244ff.

Stevenson, Matilda C.
1889-   *The Sia*. 11th Annual Report of the Bureau of American Ethnology.
1890   Washington, D.C.: Smithsonian Institution.

Steward, Julian H.
1949   "Cultural Causality and Law: A Trial Formulation of the Development of Early Civilization." *American Anthropologist*, 51, 1:1-27.
1953   "Evolution and Process." In *Anthropology Today*. Chicago: University of Chicago Press. 313-26.
1955a   *Theory of Culture Change: The Methodology of Multilinear Evolution*. Chicago: University of Illinois Press.
1955b   Ed. *Irrigation Civilizations: A Comparative Study*. A Symposium on Method and Result in Cross-Cultural Regularities. Social Science Monograph, 1. Washington, D.C.: Pan-American Union.
1968   "Causal Factors and Processes in the Evolution of Pre-Farming Societies." *Man the Hunter*. Ed. R. B. Lee and I. DeVore. 321-34.
1970   "Cultural Evolution in South America." *The Social Anthropology of Latin America: Essays in Honor of Ralph L. Beals*. Ed. Walter Goldschmidt and Harry Hoijer. Los Angeles: University of California Press. 199-222.
1978   "Initiation of a Research Trend: Wittfogel's Irrigation Hypothesis." In *Society and History: Essays in Honor of Karl August Wittfogel*. Ed. G. L. Ulmen. The Hague, Paris, and New York: Mouton.

Stocking, George W., Jr.
1968   *Race, Culture, and Evolution: Essays in the History of Anthropology*. New York: The Free Press.
1974   Ed. *The Shaping of American Anthropology 1883-1911: A Franz Boas Reader*. New York: Basic Books.
1976   Ed. *Selected Papers from the American Anthropologist, 1921-1945*. Washington, D.C.: American Anthropological Association.

Strong, W. Duncan
1943   *Cross Sections of New World History.* Smithsonian Miscellaneous Collection, 104, 2.

Tanner, J. M.
1959   "Boas' Contributions to Knowledge of Human Growth and Form." *Anthropology of Franz Boas.* Ed. W. Goldschmidt. *AAA Memoir*, 89, 61, 5, pt. 2.

Thompson, Laura
1945   "Logico-Aesthetic Integration in Hopi Culture." *American Anthropologist*, 47:540-53.

Thompson, Laura, and Alice Joseph
1944   *The Hopi Way.* Indian Education Series, 1. Chicago.

Titiev, M.
1944   *Old Oraibi, A Study of the Hopi Indians of the Third Mesa.* Papers of the Peabody Museum of American Archaeology and Ethnology, XXII, 1. Cambridge, Mass.: Harvard University Press.

Ulmen, G. L.
1978a   *The Science of Society: Toward an Understanding of the Life and Work of Karl August Wittfogel.* The Hague, Paris, and New York: Mouton.
1978b   Ed. *Society and History: Essays in Honor of Karl August Wittfogel.* The Hague, Paris, and New York: Mouton.

Viking Fund
1950   "Memorial for Ruth Benedict." New York.

Vogt, Evon Z.
1955   "Study of the Southwestern Fiesta System as Exemplified by the Laguna Fiesta." *American Anthropologist*, 57, 4:320-39.

Voth, H. R.
1901   *The Oraibi Powamu Ceremony.* Publication 61, Anthropological Series, III, 2. Chicago: Field Museum of Natural History.
1912   *Brief Miscellaneous Hopi Papers.* Publication 157, Anthropological Series,
1912   XI, 2. Chicago: Field Museum of Natural History.

West, James [Carl Withers]
1945   *Plainville U.S.A.* New York: Columbia University Press.

White, Leslie A.
1932a   *The Acoma Indians.* 47th Annual Report of Bureau of American Ethnology. Washington, D.C.: Smithsonian Institution. 17-192.
1932b   "The Pueblo of San Felipe." *AAA Memoir*, 38.
1935   "The Pueblo of Santo Domingo, New Mexico." *AAA Memoir*, 43.
1938   "Science and Sciencing." *Philosophy of Science*, 5.
1940   *Pioneers in American Ethnology: The Bandelier-Morgan Letters, 1873-1883.* 2 vols. Ann Arbor: University of Michigan Press.

1943   "Energy and the Evolution of Culture." *American Anthropologist*, NS, 45, 1:335-56.

1945   "History, Evolutionism and Functionalism: Three Types of Interpretation of Culture." *Southwestern Journal of Anthropology*, 1, 2:221-48.

1949   *The Science of Culture: A Study of Man and Civilization.* New York: Farrar, Strauss.

1959   *Evolution of Culture: The Development of Civilization to the Fall of Rome.* New York: McGraw-Hill.

1962   *The Pueblo of Sia, New Mexico.* Bureau of American Ethnology, Bulletin 184. Washington, D.C.: Smithsonian Institution.

1963   *The Ethnography and Ethnology of Franz Boas.* Texas Memorial Museum, Bulletin No. 6. Austin: University of Texas Press.

Whitman, William

1947   *The Pueblo Indians of San Ildefonso: A Changing Culture.* Columbia University Contributions to Anthropology, 34. New York: Columbia University Press.

Wissler, Clark

1911   "The Social Life of the Blackfoot Indians." *Anthropological Papers of the American Museum of Natural History*, VII, pt. 1.

1912   "Ceremonial Bundles of the Blackfoot Indians." *Anthropological Papers of the American Museum of Natural History*, VII, pt. 2.

1913   "Societies and Dance Associations of the Blackfoot Indians." *Anthropological Papers of the American Museum of Natural History*, XI, pt. 4.

1918   "The Sun Dance of the Blackfoot Indians." *Anthropological Papers of the American Museum of Natural History*, XVI, pt. 3.

1947   Review of Esther S. Goldfrank, *Changing Configuration of the Social Organization of the Blackfoot Tribe during the Reserve Period.* Journal of American Folklore, 60, 237:308-9.

Wittfogel, Karl A.

1931   *Wirtschaft und Gesellschaft Chinas.* Leipzig.

1935   *The Foundations and Stages of Chinese Economic History.* Zeitschrift for Socialforschung, IV:26-60.

1938   *Die Theorie der orientalischen Gesellschaft.* Reprinted in English translation in *Readings in Anthropology.* Vol. II. *Readings in Cultural Anthropology.* 1st ed. 1959; 2nd ed. 1968. New York: Thomas Y. Crowell.

1957   *Oriental Despotism.* New Haven: Yale University Press.

1960   TV Guide to "From Marx to Mao." Seattle: University of Washington Press.

1967   Review of Robert McAdams, *The Evolution of Urban Society: Early Mesapotamia and Prehispanic Mexico.* American Anthropologist, 69, 1:90ff.

1972   "The Hydraulic Approach to Pre-Spanish America." *Chronology and Irrigation.* Ed. F. Johnson. *Prehistory of the Tehuacan Valley.* Gen. ed. R. S. MacNeish. Austin: University of Texas Press.

Wittfogel, Karl A., and Esther S. Goldfrank

1943   "Some Aspects of Pueblo Mythology and Society." *Journal of American Folklore*, 56, 219:17-30.

Wittfogel, Karl A., and Feng Chia-sheng
1949   *History of Chinese Society: Liao.* Philadelphia: Transactions, American Philosophical Society, XXXVI.

Zachry, Caroline, and Margaret Lightly
1940   Ed. *Study of Adolescents: Emotion and Conduct in Adolescence.*

Morgan, Lewis H., 151, 154, 161-162, 226n29
Morgan, William, 178
Mozart, Wolfgang Amadeus, 3
Murdock, George P., 190, 218
Mussey, Raymond, 1
Muzzey, David, 1

Nash, Philleo, 149
Nelson, Nils, 17, 38, 113
Niemeyer, Gerhart, 190
Nietzsche, Friederich, 38

Oakes, Maud, 210
Oehser, Paul H., 211, 213-215, 218-219
Olderogge, D. A., 226n29
Opler, Morris, 100, 224n1
Ortiz, Alfonso, 220

Pagenstecher, Rudolph, 12
Palerm, Angel, 188-189, 192
Papa Franz (see also Boas, Franz), 91
Parsons, Elsie Clews, 4, 16-17, 21-35 *passim*,
   38-39, 41, 43-49, 52-55, 57-59, 61, 71-72,
   75, 79-80, 84, 94-97, 113, 153, 157-158,
   167, 169, 176-178, 181-182, 204-205,
   208-211, 213-220, 222n7,9,10, 223n17,
   226n36
Peabody, George Foster, 6
Pearl, Raymond, 5
Pitkin, Walter, 43
Platzer, Michael K. H., 226n34
Pope, John, 213
Posnansky, Gitel (also Steed), 128, 134
Powell, Major J. W., 16, 89
Powers, Mr., 204
Price, Barbara J., 192-193
Provinse, John, 164

Rabal, 163
Radin, Paul, 5, 8, 18
Ransome, Marius, 7
Red Cloud, 160
Redl, Dr. Fritz, 100, 105
Reed, Erik K., 199
Reichard, Gladys, 15, 17-19, 23-24, 34, 91, 93,
   97, 113, 163, 208-209, 211, 213
Reiter, Paul, 198
Richardson, Jane, 128, 144, 147-148

Rivet, Paul, 7, 121-122
Robbins, Jeannette, 91
Roberts Jr., Frank H. H., 211, 213-215, 218
Robinson, James Harvey, 1
Rorschach, Hermann, 125-126
Rossiter, Clinton, 224n7

Sanders, William T., 192
Sapir, Edward, 17-20, 127, 178, 186, 222n12
Schiff, Esther (see Goldfrank, Esther Schiff)
Schroeder, Albert H., 199
Scott, Colonel Hugh L., 179, 182
Seager, H. R., 1
Sebeok, Thomas, 62
Sedgwick, Ellery, 108-110
Seligman, E. R. A., 1
Shakespeare, William, 1, 152
Shapiro, Harry, 122
Shotwell, James T., 1
Simango, C. K., 6
Simmons, Lee W., 39
Sitting Bull, 160
Smith, M. Estellie, 224n31
Smith, Marian W., 205-206
Smith, Watson, 209
Snow, Edgar, 118
Spicer, Edward H., 39
Spier, Leslie, 16-18, 23-24, 34, 37-38, 113, 198
Spotted Tail, 161
Stalin, Josef V., 114, 116-118, 124, 141, 156,
   224n11
Steed (see Goldfield, Robert)
Stefansson, Vilhjalmur, 224n2
Steinen, Carl von den, 12
Stern, Bernhard J., 114
Stevenson, Matilda Cox, 39, 154, 169-170
Steward, Julian H., 34, 39, 58, 169, 186-194,
   206, 208, 217, 226n33,36
Stirling, Matthew W., 34, 211-214, 217,
   226n36
Stocking Jr., George W., 7, 15, 121
Stone, Harlan F., 16
Strong, W. Duncan, 33, 58, 99, 111, 113,
   186-187
Sun Chief, 167, 170
Swadesh, Morris, 177
Swanton, John R., 7, 13